The OUTSPORTS Revolution

JIM BUZINSKI *AND* CYD ZEIGLER JR.

alyson books
NEW YORK

This book is dedicated to Dan and Bill,
the two most important people in our lives.
—Cyd and Jim, May 2007

Manufactured in the United States of America.

This trade paperback original is published by Alyson Books
245 West 17th Street, New York, New York 10011
Distribution in the United Kingdom by Turnaround Publisher Services Ltd.
Unit 3, Olympia Trading Estate, Coburg Road, Wood Green
London N22 6TZ England

First Edition: July 2007

07 08 09 10 11 a 10 9 8 7 6 5 4 3 2 1

ISBN: 1-59350-005-X
ISBN-13: 978-1-59350-005-4

Library of Congress Cataloging-in-Publication Data are on file.

Cover design by Victor Mingovits
Cover photo credits (left to right, top to bottom):
Cyd Zeigler Jr.
Ross Forman
Brent Mullins
Jim Buzinski
Brent Mullins
Cyd Zeigler Jr.
Chuck Martin
Interior design by Elliott Beard

ACKNOWLEDGMENTS

Producing Outsports is a collaborative effort, utilizing the talents and insights of many people. Compiling this book was no different. The list of those who have contributed is too lengthy to single out everyone, but we recognize that the web site and this book would not be successful without everyone who has contributed.

Two guiding lights in Outsports' journey have been Patricia Nell Warren and Dave Kopay. Patricia's novel *The Front Runner* has inspired millions of gay people, and her insight and advice have helped many gay athletes. Dave is a pioneer. The first major pro athlete to come out, he is still a relevant voice for generations of gay jocks. His courage has been inspiring.

Outsports is truly a community, with readers contributing story ideas and photos and making our discussion board the go-to destination for gay sports fans. Special thanks go to the moderators of the board, Jim Allen and Dee White. Their tireless efforts and occasional cracking of the whip have kept the discussions focused and free from diversionary personal attacks common to many message boards. Also a big thank you to our web developer Rory Ray, who keeps the site going.

We would be remiss in not acknowledging our "Outsporters," members who have made the site infinitely richer. It's impossible to name them all here, or even all of those who have made a huge impact. However, there are a few who have been with us from the beginning: Joe in Philly, GeorgeTwinsFan, Canmark, Larry Felzer (aka Scottie), Munson Man, Mariner Duck Guy, and Chip. We hope these few will accept our thanks on behalf of every member who has contributed so deeply to Outsports.

Our list of writers and photographers is also too lengthy to enumerate, but we need to single out photographer Brent Mullins, whose thousands of images have brought to life the beauty of athletics.

And finally, the biggest thanks go to the athletes, coaches, administrators, and fans who have come out to their teams, families, and communities, showing the guts, grace, and perseverance that are the hallmarks of what it means to be an athlete. Without you, the Outsports Revolution would not be underway.

CONTENTS

PART II

ELITE ATHLETES AND BIG-TIME SPORTS

PART III

GETTING IN THE GAME

FOREWORD

The worst thing somebody could call you when I was growing up during the 1970s, in my working-class Long Island town, was "faggot." It was a powerful insult that sparked countless shoving matches and fistfights on the ball fields and basketball courts where my friends and I spent most of our free time. When somebody called you a faggot, he was accusing you of enjoying the acts the nuns told us violated every law laid down by God, nature, and man. He was questioning your masculinity. He was saying you were weak and strange.

That attitude was deeply ingrained in my young mind by the time I moved to Colorado to attend college. As had I, many of my friends had attended Catholic schools and grown up in suburbia, and we shared similar views about sexuality. We cracked gay jokes. We called each other homos when we were clowning around. We called each other faggot when we were angry. We had gone to college to broaden our worldview, but we still looked at the world with the same prejudices we'd grown up with.

One of my college buddies was a guy named Bob. Bob told great stories, and he was a good guitar player who knew tons of cool old folk songs. He was also a master mechanic who kept our crappy cars on the road long after they should have been junked. He ran the campus bar and took great pleasure in introducing people he thought should be friends.

But there were times when Bob would become withdrawn. He'd disappear for days at a time and wouldn't return our phone calls. I'd see him walking in the student union with his head hung low, his shoulders slumped, looking whipped and defeated. He'd drink beer and whiskey like a one-man fraternity, often passing out at his kitchen table.

A few years after I met Bob, he invited a few friends to his house, promising us he had some exciting news. He looked serene, dignified, even as he struggled to spit out the words. Finally, it all came out: Bob told us he was gay. Finally, we knew why he sometimes seemed so miserable and so lonely.

Once Bob started talking, he couldn't stop. He told us he feared we'd ridicule him. He was afraid he'd anger his religious mother. He thought his family would reject him. But he couldn't hide the truth any longer. He was no longer willing to feign interest in women or drown his own sexual appetites with cheap liquor. He was no longer willing to hide his identity, especially from himself.

These were not easy words for us to hear, and not everybody immediately embraced the new Bob. But we didn't reject or ridicule him either. For many of us, this was the first realization that gay people weren't weird perverts who deserved ridicule. They were our brothers, our sisters, and our friends. Bob's coming out changed all of us. We were forced to look at our old prejudices. And Bob was free to be the person he'd tried to hide for so long. In fact, he blossomed during the following spring months. He stopped being so moody and he stopped binge-drinking. He lost weight and looked happier and healthier than I'd ever seen him.

So much has changed since the night Bob came out 25 years ago. The generations that followed mine are far more open-minded—far more intelligent—when it comes to sexuality and gender. I look at my beautiful 5-year-old son, and I'm glad he's growing up in a more sensible world. I'm glad he won't feel the pressure Bob felt to conform and bury his identity. And I'm glad he won't grow up in the world that filled me with fear and prejudice.

I'm not naïve. I understand the world is still full of homophobes. But Americans have become far more tolerant over the course of my lifetime, and those changes are now apparent in our culture every day. Homosexuality was once the love that dare not speak its name. Now gay storylines and gay stars are staples of hit movies, TV, and music.

And as Cyd Zeigler and Jim Buzinski document every day on their trailblazing web site Outsports.com, these changes are even coming to the world of sports. Outsports has become a must-read for many journalists, and Cyd and Jim have become an important source for those of us looking for cutting-edge story ideas from the intersection of sports, culture, art, and politics.

My colleagues and I at the *Daily News* recently went through a file of our old stories, and I was amazed by how many originated with an item from Outsports. Thanks to Outsports, we learned that former NFL commissioner Paul Tagliabue was a key supporter of PFLAG. Thanks to Outsports, we knew that the NFL had once refused to sell personalized jerseys that say "GAY," just like it wouldn't sell jerseys that say "BIG-BUTT," "DAHMER," "FLATULENCE," or "ORGY." And thanks to Outsports, we reported that many pro teams—once so reluctant to do anything that might upset suburban fans or corporate sponsors—are now eager to sell blocks of tickets to gay and lesbian groups. They'll even put the names up on the scoreboard, just as with Boy Scout troops, electrician union locals, and church organizations.

True, sports are in many ways still a haven for knuckle-dragging bigots. Athletes, coaches, and sports executives who wouldn't dare mock someone's skin color or religion routinely rank on gays and lesbians; Reggie White, Ozzie Guillen, Matt Millen, and Jeremy Shockey are just a few of the Neanderthals who have embarrassed themselves and their teams with ugly anti-gay remarks.

It's also true that the locker rooms that have long welcomed religious fundamentalists are still hostile turf for gays; it's not surprising that no NFL, NBA, NHL, or Major League Baseball player has ever identified himself as homosexual during his playing days—even though plenty have come out after they retired.

But as Cyd and Jim report every day, the Outsports Revolution is here to stay. Gay players and fans are now a part of life in women's sports; Sheryl Swoopes, the greatest player in WNBA history, announced she was gay at the height of her career. And the NHL and the Toronto Maple Leafs gave a film production company the green light to use their jerseys and logos in a gay-themed film.

Even attitudes in locker rooms are changing. I once asked Yankee pitcher Mike Mussina how he would feel if he learned one of his teammates was gay. "I'm going to make the assumption that I already have, that there already is a player like that out there," Mussina responded. "I don't have any problems with it. It's part of society."

Jackie Robinson changed American history when he broke baseball's color line in 1947, but my guess is that things will be different for the big leagues' first openly gay athlete. He won't be an established player who rocks the world with an "I am gay" press conference. He'll be a gifted athlete who realizes he's gay at an early age. He'll be emotionally tough; he won't hide who he is as he climbs through the minor league ranks. His sexuality will most definitely be an issue when he makes the Show, because he'll be the first openly gay player in the Major Leagues. But after a while that will be old news, and then he'll be judged like every other ballplayer—by his ability to hit, field, or pitch.

I wish Bob and I had grown up in a world like that. I'm glad my son will grow up in that world, thanks to Outsports.com.

Michael O'Keeffe
Sports Reporter, New York Daily News

INTRODUCTION

THE REVOLUTION BEGINS

It was on a gorgeous August afternoon in 1999 that Outsports first took shape. We were in the middle of a weeklong trip to Cape Cod, sitting in a small café on Main Street in Chatham. We started talking about sports and how there was really no media outlet catering to gay sports fans or athletes, no place for them to get together and talk sports the way they wanted to talk sports. There was a void, and we decided we were the best two people to fill it.

When Outsports first hit the web that November, it was just a couple of thoughts about the National Football League (NFL), why Doug Flutie was a chump, why Drew Bledsoe was the hottest quarterback in the league, and why the Tennessee Titans might hold the best chance to knock off the St. Louis Rams. The response was overwhelming and immediate. Within days, without any advertising, we were getting requests from readers who stumbled across us through Yahoo! They wanted college basketball columns. They wanted National Hockey League (NHL) picks. They wanted a place to post their e-mail and information about themselves so they could meet one another. But most important, in those first few weeks of Outsports's existence, we got e-mails like this from a reader at the University of Kansas: "One of the best things that's happened to me since coming out has been discovering that I'm not the only queer out there who LOVES sports. Your site is awesome. I'm more of a casual watcher of football, but found your site to be informative, fun, and just gay enough to make me feel at home."

Though we didn't know it at first, it didn't take long to realize what we had created: something that would change how society views gays and lesbians as athletes.

Since that e-mail, we have gotten thousands more. Some of them have been from athletes trying desperately to figure out how to be a gay athlete when the support structure, though constantly growing, still has so few resources. Others have been from those who wish we'd go away, like this gem we received from someone named M. Conway in autumn 2006 in response to an ongoing series we have featuring one of our writers visiting college football tailgate parties:

> Male homosexuals cannot have a place in sports. You are the absolute sissies of the world . . . and THIS is why America is great, that our most macho professions, like NFL player and NBA [National Basketball Association] player have NEVER had an open and out player. Can you imagine how sissified the NFL would be if gays were allowed to be open on the field? . . . I find it horrendous that these liberal students on college campuses accept you sissies at tailgate football games (you know damn well NO actual college players would let you near them). Why do you continue to try and push the envelope and seek acceptance from manly, all-American men with whom the very idea of accepting gay "men" would hinder their play? The day an open male homosexual plays in pro football, baseball, or basketball . . . is the day American sports, as we know it, will degrade. Take me back to 1986 baby, when the homophobic hard partying Mets won the World Series, the blue collar Boston Celtics won the championship, the Chicago Bears did their football dance yet had no queers around . . . and you sissies were cruising in back alleys like the scum you are and were far away from being open. America was better then, and you know it. Bye sissies!

The paradox of these two e-mails accurately reflects the state of gays in sports. Whereas ten years ago there was little support or awareness of gay athletes and the unique issues they face, there has been in the past two years a flood of media coverage and an outpouring of support. The National Football League is including sexual orientation in its rookie symposium. The National Collegiate Athletic Association (NCAA) is attacking the issue of homophobia in recruiting. And more and more higher-profile athletes are coming out of the closet to open arms. Still, people such as M. Conway continue to try to keep the closet door locked, boarded, and permanently shut for gay athletes.

Luckily, the gay-sports revolution that has taken place since Outsports first started publishing has put Conway and others like him in the minority. This book tracks some of the developments of that revolution—much of it propelled by Outsports: the events leading up to it, the incredible progress made during it, and the work that still needs to be done to help open more closet doors in sports. It is not an exaggeration to say that Outsports has driven coverage of gays and lesbians in sports. We have made dozens of appearances on sports talk radio to discuss the issue, debated the subject on CNN and ESPN, and been the source for dozens of articles in the mainstream media. The list includes the BBC, *New York Times, Los Angeles Times, Boston Globe, Sports Illustrated (SI), Playboy, Chicago Tribune, New York Daily News,* and *ESPN the Magazine,* among others.

This book is also meant to be a bridge for those who may not consider themselves sports fans or athletes but are tired of buying into the stereotype, propped up so mightily by much of both straight and gay cultures, that gays—especially men—don't like sports. Whether it's not knowing how to host a Super Bowl party or figuring out how to handle a boyfriend who likes basketball, sports can be an intimidating force in the life of gay people who long ago decided it wasn't for them. Our aim is to make sports just a little less daunting and a lot more fun for them.

Most important, we're hoping this book opens some eyes. There has been great progress since 1999, but much more still needs to be done. With more understanding will come more willingness for change in the sports world. Much of what is in these pages would have been a surprise to even us a few years ago, and we continue to be amazed by the stories and ideas we are lucky to publish. Our hope is that what lies in these pages will continue to develop that much-needed understanding and help strengthen the Outsports Revolution.

Cyd and Jim

PART I

THE PLACE OF GAY SPORTS IN SOCIETY

"WHY SHOULD I GIVE A DAMN ABOUT SPORTS?"

Why sports? Why not the opera? Or theater? Or movies? What's so terrific about sports that anyone should care about them? Although those other diversions are certainly wonderful in their own right, sports is the ultimate theater, the ultimate reality show, the ultimate cliffhanger with an ending no one can predict.

There is a myth out there that gay men do not care about sports (many lesbians, on the other hand, are allegedly born with the sports gene instilled in them). Although there are some truths in every stereotype, gay men can be just as fanatical about sports as their straight brethren. The success of Outsports attests to that. This chapter, however, is designed for those men and women who wonder what all the fuss is about.

Sports Theater at Its Best

Picture it. January 2006. The Indianapolis Colts are playing the Pittsburgh Steelers in the NFL playoffs. In Los Angeles, three gay men are watching at the home of David Kopay, the former NFL player who made history in the 1970s by coming out of the closet. His 1977 coming-out autobiography, *The David Kopay Story*, has inspired gay men and lesbians for more than thirty years with its unflinching and honest account of the shackles of living a lie. But on this day, Kopay is just another fan. In one chair sits Kopay, Outsports contributor Jim Allen is in another, and Jim Buzinski is in a third. All three are passionately rooting for the Colts. Buzinski has been a Colts fan, off and on, since he was a kid growing up in northeastern Pennsylvania in the 1960s. Allen is a fan because he thinks the Colts have some of the hottest guys in professional football. Kopay is a fan because Colts quarterback Peyton Manning is the son of one of his former teammates, Archie Manning, and he fondly remembers Archie and his wife taking him in for Thanksgiving dinner in New Orleans in the 1970s.

Shockingly, the favored Colts are losing to the Steelers, 21–3, entering the fourth quarter. But then the Colts strike. Peyton Manning throws a touchdown pass to tight end Dallas Clark. It's 21–10. He then throws an interception, which a referee's review surprisingly overturns, keeping the Colts alive. A few plays later, the Colts score another touchdown, and suddenly the score is Pittsburgh 21, Indianapolis 18. The three fans in Kopay's house are on the edge of their chairs, hoping they are watching a miracle occur.

The miracle apparently ends when the Steelers stop the Colts and get the ball deep in Indianapolis territory with less than two minutes remaining. All Pittsburgh has to do is run a few plays, and the game is over. The three begin looking at menus to order food, resigned to the fact that all is lost. But then something happens that literally causes millions of Americans to leap from their chairs screaming. Sure-handed Pittsburgh running back Jerome Bettis gets the ball and heads toward the end zone. He is met at the line of scrimmage by a Colts linebacker whose helmet hits the ball, causing it to pop up into the air. Fumble!

There's nothing like the feeling of being part of a team.

Photo by Brent Mullins

A Colts defensive player scoops up the loose ball and begins running toward the Pittsburgh end zone. You've never seen three grown men bolt from their chairs in such unison, yelling as if they'd just won the lottery, as you would have at Kopay's house. In New York City, three thousand miles away, Buzinski's brother Paul, a huge Steelers fan, is screaming but for another reason: he is watching his beloved team's season slip away. In Pittsburgh, one Steelers fan literally has a heart attack as the Indianapolis defender is running the ball back. As the ball carrier tries to make a move around midfield, Pittsburgh quarterback Ben Roethlisberger reaches out in desperation, and his arm trips up the Indianapolis defender, who falls to the ground. "Do you believe this?!" CBS announcer Dick Enberg screams.

The Colts, with new life, begin their drive for what will either be the game-winning touchdown or a field goal that will send the game into overtime. The fans in Kopay's house have forgotten all about ordering food and instead have found religion, praying that the Colts can somehow pull it out. On the last play of the game, Colts kicker Mike Vanderjagt, the most accurate kicker in the history of the NFL, lines up to attempt a forty-six-yard field goal that will tie the game. CBS flashes a statistic that shows Vanderjagt has not missed a field goal at home all season. His kick never has a chance, veering wide right, heading toward Muncie. Pittsburgh hangs on, Colts fans are crushed, Steelers backers are elated, and the fan with a heart attack awakens to hear that his beloved Steelers will live to play another day.

Had this been a movie, someone would have known the ending—the screenwriter, the producers, the director, the actors, the grips, and anyone else associated with production. Even many moviegoers would have somehow found out what had happened. There would be suspense certainly, but very much of an artificial type.

In contrast, no one knew what was going to happen in Indianapolis, not the coaches, players, league commissioner, or the guy selling the overpriced beer. The true suspense riveted football fans across the nation. The Bettis fumble would go down in NFL lore as one of the most stunning turn of events in league history. And it was all unscripted.

That's one of the beauties of sport—its total unpredictability, its ability to see the story line change in such a way that even a fiction writer wouldn't dare suggest. It's just like life itself—it unfolds one minute, one play, one drama at a time. It's why most Hollywood sports movies can never live up to the real thing. For anyone who is tired of so much in the world being scripted, sports offers the ultimate "Can you believe this?" experience.

The Wonderful Power of Community

Studies have shown that for rabid sports fans, the thrill of watching their favorite team in action can rival a sexual experience. No joke. For many, it's even better than sex. As the *New York Times* reports: "Some researchers have found that fervent fans become so tied to their teams that they experience hormonal surges and other physiological changes while watching games, much as the athletes do. The self-esteem of some male and female fans also rises and falls with a game's outcome, with losses affecting their optimism about everything from getting a date to winning at darts, one study showed."

Any true sports fan will know that this research rings true. For better or worse, a lot of sports fans live and die with their teams. In places like Pittsburgh, where the Steelers are a civic religion, the whole city can go into mourning after a tough loss or into euphoria after an exciting win. It's even more extreme in soccer, where the psyche of entire nations is affected by how their national heroes perform. Wars have broken out over contentious soccer matches, and, sadly, people have died.

No one would suggest that this is entirely healthy, and in fact there's a reason the word *fan* is derived from *fanatic*. Some people take it way too seriously, as if their essence is somehow tied to their team winning or losing. The same *New York Times* article discusses a study in Georgia that showed that "testosterone levels in male fans rise markedly after a victory and drop just as sharply after a defeat." One researcher told the paper that "the results suggest fans empathize with the competitors to such a degree that they mentally project themselves into the game and experience the same hormonal surges athletes do. The contest, however, must be an important one, like a playoff game. We really are tribal creatures," he said.

The word *tribe* is an interesting one and reflects the communal nature of sports. It allows fans to feel they are part of something, part of a larger team. This is well reflected on any university campus, where students, faculty, and alumni identify with their school's sports teams. Customs, traditions, chants, and cheers are passed down from one generation of students to the next. An eighteen-year-old student and seventy-year-old Florida State alum would appear to have very little in common, but when they hear the Seminole fight song, they become brothers in tomahawk-chopping arms.

In many ways, people carry their school and team identity throughout their lives. For many gay people, who often feel shunned by the larger

Love of your alma mater, like that of these these Boston College fans, transcends differences.

Photo by Todd Heustess

world, this identity can be a bridge in finding common ground with others. On the Outsports Discussion Board, when alums from the same school find each other, it's akin to discovering a new family member. As with any group identity, everyone feels his customs and traditions are clearly superior to any other. Texas fans say that no one tailgates like they do, but try telling that to people who went to Penn State, Michigan, Georgia, Nebraska, or any of a hundred other universities.

The tribal nature certainly also extends to professional sports. In Boston, they refer to fans of the local baseball team as part of Red Sox Nation. Until 2004, Red Sox fans wore their eighty-six years of World Series futility as a perverse badge of honor. And when the Sox finally won the World Series in October 2004, whole generations celebrated, and some elderly fans even joked that God might as well take them now since life on earth could not possibly get any better. Boston fans were in love that year with long-haired outfielder Johnny Damon, who had he decided to run for mayor would have won in a landslide. However, two years later, when Damon decided to sign a free-agent contract with the hated New York Yankees, he quickly became the "enemy."

When it comes to the National Football League, entire social calendars are built around the release of the NFL schedule. Woe unto any unsuspecting bride in Green Bay, Wisconsin, who decides to get married the weekend of a Packers home game. Season tickets in Green Bay and in many other NFL cities are handed down from generation to generation as priceless heirlooms. They even factor into divorce settlements, with access to tickets worth more to some people than a set of expensive china.

If done in the spirit of fun and entertainment and with a degree of moderation, being a sports fan is a wonderful way to expand one's social outlet. Many gay people have parties to watch the Academy Awards, complete with pools to predict everything from Best Picture to Best Costume Design. It's really no different from having a Super Bowl party or playing fantasy football—except in the case of sports, the winners are determined on the field and not through some highly politicized ballot procedure. If one can get into three hours of lame jokes and dance numbers, it's just as easy to get into three hours of *Monday Night Football*.

Eye Candy

Outsports has debunked the myth that gays do not like sports. It is probably true that a higher percentage of gays, especially men, are not as outwardly interested in sports as the rest of society. But for those who are sports fans, the passion is no less intense than among straight sports fans. One could argue that, in one way, being a gay male sports fan is more rewarding than being a straight male fan. It comes down to what might be called the "eye-candy factor."

Face it: men are visual creatures. There's no mystery why *Sports Illustrated*'s most popular issue each year is the one chock-full of female swimsuit models. There's no mystery why most sports teams have cheerleaders, virtually all female. There is no mystery why tennis star Anna Kournikova is more recognized for her pinups than for her play. It's all about the eye candy.

For gay guys, watching sports played by men puts the eye candy on display front and center. Fans needn't wait for the camera to give a passing sideline shot of a hot female cheerleader—the visuals appear on every play, from that stud receiver making a catch to that lanky pitcher throwing a strike to that amazingly muscular gymnast swinging pommel horse. Gay fans needn't wait for *Sports Illustrated* to give one issue a year of babes, babes, and more babes; they get that fifty-two weeks a year in the magazine photos that are still predominantly of men. Of course, straight guys and lesbians can get their fix watching women's sports, but the reality, for better or worse, is that men's sports still get the lion's share of coverage. That's a good thing if you're a gay male sports fan.

Each year, Outsports holds a contest called "King of the Hardwood," run by a devoted member who goes by the name MarinerDuckGuy. The contest is a derivative of the NCAA men's basketball tournament, but instead of a bracket featuring sixty-four teams, King of the Hardwood features what our readers consider the hottest sixty-four athletes in the world. Because most of these athletes have gotten tremendous exposure, they are household names. People have seen them in competition, in training, and giving interviews; it makes for a very well-informed voting public. At least among straight men, who do not watch women's sports at a high rate, people would be hard-pressed to come up with sixty-four female athletes. This is again because of the relative lack of exposure of most female athletes.

For two years running, football player and skier Jeremy Bloom won the contest. He was gracious enough to give Outsports an interview, in which he said he would rather be praised for his personality than his looks. But it was not his personality that won him the most votes. Bloom excels at posing shirtless for magazines and on his web site. He has a built-in fan base that has seen him baring his chest and rippling abdominal muscles for years. There is little doubt that Bloom is better known for his smooth pecs than his smooth moves on the football field or the slopes.

This admiration of athletic bodies is not a recent phenomenon. Go back and read accounts of the first Olympics in the time of ancient Greece. Athletes then performed in the nude, and champions were just as highly praised and rewarded as they are now. People of the time took note of the athletes' physiques, from the burly or sinewy wrestlers to the lean, streamlined runners. Being of sound body as well as sound mind was very much a Greek ideal.

Today, of course, with the rise of ESPN and the Internet, fans are awash in sports and athletic imagery. This has made it much easier for the uninitiated to become a sports fan. People see a hot jock, which can create a desire to see that person perform, whether it be on the field, on the court, on the links, in the pool, or on the track. This is something very positive, and something seen regularly on Outsports: people will hear others talk about an athlete and then check out that person for themselves. This is not something sexual. (Well, maybe it is in part.) But it's also admiring someone who has pushed his or her body to its highest level, which is a beautiful thing in many ways. It's the same as watching the astounding athleticism on display at a ballet.

Participation Has Its Rewards

In addition to being wonderful entertainment for fans, sports are also a phenomenal participatory tool, one that is becoming more and more prevalent in the gay and lesbian community. Joining a team, a league, or a group is a terrific way to socialize, bond, and meet new people. Sports also have the added benefit of helping people get and stay in shape.

It's rewarding to be part of a team. You share with your teammates common goals and rituals, and you build new traditions together. For many gay men especially, this team aspect was something that was either denied to them or rejected by them while growing up. Rediscovering it can be powerful as an adult. Take gay flag football, for example. It's a sport that is growing within the gay community, thanks to terrific organi-

Sports build camaraderie, even among opponents.
Photo by Jim Buzinski

zations in cities from California to New York. Cities have formed leagues with dozens of teams, and each year a national tournament (called the Gay Bowl) is held. Participating in the Gay Bowl is, for many players, the highlight of their year. The competition is fierce, but what many find most rewarding is the camaraderie, not only among their own teammates but also with players from other cities.

Playing in a tournament game is a great example of the nature of building a community. With any team, leaders have to be chosen, and goals and strategies have to be devised. Then the players must execute those strategies with the hope of reaching their goal, which is to score the most points and win the game. It's wonderful to see people pull together for a couple of hours around a common goal and to see the joy and sense of satisfaction when the goal is achieved. It teaches a great life lesson and one that can be used in other aspects of life. Even losing in these adult-league and tournament games can be encouraging, as often even greater lessons are learned when you come out on the short end of the stick. And as opposed to other areas of life, like vocation and romance, the consequences are relatively inconsequential.

The example of flag football is duplicated over and over in every one of the dozens of sports that are played in the gay community. Whether it is team sports such as football, softball, water polo, or soccer, or individual sports such as swimming, running, bodybuilding, or cycling, the goals remain the same even if the strategies are different. Through participating in leagues and teams, many people come to embrace sports in a way they never thought possible growing up, as sports can be misused by parents, coaches, and administrators. And such problems certainly occur within gay sports organizations. But athletes need not let a few bad experiences sour them on something that can be so rewarding.

Tackling Stereotypes

Gay people openly playing sports is in many ways subversive and turns on its ear notions of masculinity (at least among men playing sports). It's always somewhat of a shock to straight guys who wind up playing with openly gay guys in sports. In flag football, straight guys who play in gay-oriented leagues come in with one set of assumptions and leave with quite another. They realize that once the whistle is blown, gay and straight go out the window, and it's all about who can play ball. For too long, gay men have been stereotyped as weaklings or sissies who throw like girls. Seeing a gay man throw a football forty yards with a perfect spiral goes a long way toward destroying those sometimes hurtful stereotypes.

When gays and lesbians play sports for the love of the game and unapologetically, it can do more to shatter preconceptions than a hundred diversity-training seminars. There's no reason straight people should be allowed to have all the fun. What could be cooler than getting together with a group of friends with a case of beer and some pizzas and watching a football game, or heading down to the local bar after a fun night of softball? These were things that for too long gay people denied themselves, playing into the notion that sports were for others. It's a notion that, no doubt, some gays still hold. But for more and more gay people each day, sports are becoming an integral part of their lives.

So, if you want to strike a blow for equality, learn who Peyton Manning is, when *SportsCenter* is on, and who should be playing when the women's Final Four is held. Or head out to a field or court and learn how to catch a ball or hit a jump shot. At the very least, it'll be the most fun you'll ever have making a social statement.

A BRIEF HISTORY OF GAYS IN SPORTS

I f you can't fix it, you gotta stand it." Those were the words spoken by Heath Ledger's closeted character, Ennis Del Mar, in the award-winning film *Brokeback Mountain*. The words reflected a culture that did not allow two men to love one another and live together. They also could be spoken by closeted athletes everywhere and can accurately sum up the history of gays in sports.

Brokeback Mountain is first set in 1963 when Ennis meets Jack Twist. The two Wyoming ranch hands fall in love, but it's a love that can never be fully realized. Although the story ends in 1983, as far as sports go, the movie could be set in the present and be just as relevant.

When it comes to sports, especially for elite male athletes in big-time leagues who happen to be gay, *Brokeback*'s themes of yearning, fear, and forbidden love resonate strongly. Society has come a long way in the acceptance of gays, but sports still remain the final closet, and in some corners the door is still firmly shut.

It is an amazing statistic: there has never been a male athlete from a major pro team sport (the NFL, NBA, NHL, or Major League Baseball [MLB]) who has come out while playing. The same is true of elite jocks at major college programs. They are out there (no one legitimately disputes this), but they remain closeted.

In 2006, Lauren Keyes, a postgraduate education student at the University of Southern California, studied seven closeted gay male USC students, including three athletes. One athlete, according to the *Daily Trojan* student newspaper, said that he remained closeted "for reasons beyond his control," elaborating that, although he is not ashamed to be gay, there were people who "would or could destroy my athletic career if they knew."

The fear of having their athletic careers destroyed is the biggest motivator in keeping athletes closeted. It has been ever thus. There have been several big-time female athletes who have come out while active, but for the most part sports remain the final closet.

Bill Tilden

In 1949, the National Sports Writers Association named tennis player Bill Tilden the most outstanding athlete of the first half of the century. "Big Bill" owned men's tennis in the 1920s—he won three Wimbledon titles, seven championships at the U.S. Open, seven U.S. clay court titles, and six U.S. doubles championships. He had a perfect body for tennis, described by one writer as "tall, lean, and gangly, with long arms, enormous hands, and exceptionally broad shoulders."

Author Paul Fein, in his book *Tennis Confidential*, summed up Tilden with words that could describe many of today's top athletes: "egotistical, opinionated, temperamental, controversial, witty, scrupulous, arrogant, willful and enigmatic."

Despite his high profile as an athlete, Tilden was gay, a fact known throughout the tennis world in the 1930s. "They may have believed the conventional wisdom that all gay men were effete powderpuffs who couldn't cut it in sports—but they had to sit there and watch Big Bill go into macho overdrive and beat the shorts off every man who ever faced him across the net," wrote Patricia Nell Warren in a 2003 profile of Tilden for Outsports.

> Now and then, to tweak everybody, Tilden would drop the macho stuff and swish just a little. Or he would make provocative comments like: "Tennis is more than just a sport. It's an art, like the ballet. Or like a performance in the theater. When I step on the court I feel like Anna Pavlova. Or like Adelina Patti. Or even like Sarah Bernhardt. I see the footlights in front of me. I hear the whisperings of the audience. I feel an icy shudder. Win or die! Now or never! It's the crisis of my life." Macho fans winced. Baseball great Ty Cobb openly called him a fruit.
>
> But it wasn't his swishing, or even the sodomy laws bolted in place in every state, that finally got him in big legal trouble. It was his fascination with teenage boys. Even in his amateur days, Tilden had raised eyebrows by the way he hovered over a succession of cute young male tennis protégés.

Tilden was twice jailed for "contributing to the delinquency of a minor," in 1946 and 1949. He died in 1953 at age sixty, according to his biographer Frank Deford, "in his cramped walk-up room near Hollywood and Vine, where he lived out his tragedy, a penniless ex-con, scorned, forgotten, alone."

With much of gay life hidden in the United States in the 1950s and 1960s, it is no surprise that this was reflected in sports. There is not a major sports figure from the era who has come out, even years after retiring. The reaction of Los Angeles Dodger pitching great Sandy Koufax to a rumor sheds light on why.

Sandy Koufax and Gay Rumors

Judging by the reaction to a 2003 gossip item about Koufax, one would have thought the *New York Post* had accused him of helping Saddam Hussein build weapons of mass destruction, or of having become a San Francisco Giants fan. The *Post*'s actual crime? Insinuating Koufax is gay.

Koufax, the Hall of Fame pitcher for the Los Angeles Dodgers, temporarily broke his forty-eight-year connection to the team two months after the New York paper ran this note in its Page Six gossip column: "Which Hall of Fame baseball hero cooperated with a best-selling biography only because the author promised to keep it secret that he is gay? The author kept her word, but big mouths at the publishing house can't keep from flapping."

It was easy to put two and two together and come up with Koufax, the subject of Jane Leavy's biography, *Sandy Koufax: A Lefty's Legacy*. At the time, the *Post* and the Dodgers were owned by Rupert Murdoch's News Corporation, and Koufax decided to sever his ties because "it does not make sense for me to promote any" of the company's businesses. The *Post* apologized for "getting the story wrong."

Whether Koufax is or is not gay was never the point in what became a minifuror. What is instructive is that the mere printing of an unnamed gossip item was enough for him to publicly dissociate himself from the Dodgers, an organization he had been associated with for decades, and caused many in the media to accuse the *Post* of irresponsible rumormongering.

Koufax's decision regarding the Dodgers seemed like an overreaction. What's so bad about having been alleged to be gay? He never explained that in his statements to the media about the matter. If he is a heterosexual, one would hope that he would have been comfortable enough to laugh it off ("Me, gay? Yeah, right, just ask my ex-wives and current girlfriend!") If he is in fact a homosexual, then his reaction was that of a sixty-seven-year-old man who has lived in the closet his whole life, which evokes feeling of both pity and sympathy.

The Fatal Power of the Maricon

Although Koufax's reaction to rumors about his sexual orientation decades later sparked verbal outrage, boxer Emile Griffith, a contemporary of Koufax, reacted to similar taunts with deadly force.

On March 24, 1962, at Madison Square Garden in New York and before a national TV audience, Emile Griffith regained the welterweight boxing title with a twelfth-round knockout of Benny "Kid" Paret. Griffith ended the fight by pummeling Paret in the corner with as many as twenty-five uncontested punches in a matter of seconds. "It was like a baseball bat demolishing a pumpkin," Norman Mailer wrote of the fight. "Griffith was uncontrollable. . . . [H]e was off on an orgy." Paret, comatose, was taken out of the ring on a stretcher to a hospital. The twenty-four-year-old died ten days later, leaving a wife and a two-year-old son. The death haunts Griffith to this day.

The subtext that binds the story together (told magnificently in the 2005 documentary *Ring of Fire*) is Griffith's alleged homosexuality, which Paret's taunts of *maricon* before the final two of their three fights were used to exploit and belittle. "He called me a *maricon*. I knew *maricon* meant faggot. I wasn't nobody's faggot," Griffith said of his opponent. For a boxer to be considered gay in 1962 was, as historian Neal Gabler notes, "oxymoronic. . . . This was a society in which Liberace wasn't thought to be homosexual."

There is little doubt that Griffith is gay. He frequented New York City gay bars in the years after his brief 1971 marriage to a woman he met in his native Virgin Islands. He said he went to them with gay and straight friends, but one night in 1992, a very drunk Griffith was set upon by a group of men who viciously beat him so badly he was hospitalized for a month; he has suffered short-term memory loss since, and the attack was labeled a hate crime.

"Some people think I'm gay," Griffith said near the end of *Ring of Fire*. "As long as I know right from wrong, I'm not doing anything wrong. I'm OK." Griffith even said he would be more than happy to serve as grand marshal for New York's Gay Pride Parade.

David Kopay is the pioneer of athletes who came out and made a difference.

Photo by Jim Buzinski

Two of the Seventies' Gay Athletes

In 1969, the Stonewall riots erupted in New York City, ushering in the modern gay-rights movement. At the same time, David Kopay was in the middle of his NFL career, one that spanned nine years and five teams. Nothing on the gridiron, however, brought him as much attention as his 1975 revelation to the *Washington Star*—after he had retired—that he was gay. If the gay sports movement has a godfather, it is Kopay.

His autobiography is still in print and has been cited as a source of inspiration by scores of gays and lesbians, including baseball player Billy Bean, tennis legend Billie Jean King, and football player Esera Tuaolo. Kopay left the closet and has never looked back, becoming a regular on the speaking circuit, on television, and in newspaper editorials debating the likes of one-time antigay activist Anita Bryant. In contrast, his Washington Redskins teammate Jerry Smith ("my first major [gay] experience and the first person I thought I could love," Kopay said of Smith) publicly denied his own homosexuality, even as he lay dying of AIDS in 1987.

Kopay agrees that sports still lag behind the rest of society in their acceptance of gays, but, he contends, "we are making progress." He is blunt when asked how straights could coexist with openly gay teammates in locker rooms: "We've been trained since we're very young to not pay attention to other men. . . . Why is it that every heterosexual man thinks every gay man wants his ass?"

Although Kopay's revelation of his homosexuality caused a stir in the 1970s, news in 1976 that figure skater John Curry was gay caused barely a ripple, though that doesn't mean it was accepted. "While John had never denied being gay, he feared that public prejudice could jeopardize his ice dance project," said Britain's Channel 4 in a profile. "Attending the annual sports writers' dinner after being voted 1976 Sports Personality of the Year, he experienced bigotry on a more immediate level. After-dinner comedian Roger de Courcey's mocking reference to John as a 'fairy' was offensive enough; what was worse, the assembled journalists appeared to endorse it, their laughter humiliating John just as his career peaked. John's dealings with the press grew guarded, and he gained a reputation for aloofness and hostility."

Curry won the gold medal in figure skating at the 1976 Olympics, and he went on to form a critically acclaimed balletic ice-dancing company. "In 1987 John was diagnosed as HIV positive," Channel 4 said. "He developed AIDS in 1990 and returned to Britain to live with his mother. In 1992, facing media inquiries with unflinching honesty, he went public about his condition. In April 1994, weakened by AIDS, he died of a heart attack. He was 44."

Strides in Women's Tennis

The 1980s were marked by two high-profile female tennis players coming out. Tennis legend Martina Navratilova came out as a lesbian after bursting onto the tennis scene in the late 1970s. Navratilova saw some success early in her professional career but became dominant in the 1980s only after falling in love with Nancy Lieberman, the basketball star who developed (in Chris Evert's derisive term) a "kill Chris" strategy, according to a 2005 book, *The Rivals*, which chronicles the rivalry between Navratilova and Evert.

Navratilova was, in many ways, ahead of her time, and she never regretted coming out at a relatively early age. "I have not heard of one person that came out of the closet that wishes they could go back in," she said in a 2005 interview. "And that is the key right there—nobody wants to go back in the closet, and have to pretend, and lie, and try to keep track of who you lied to, who you are not out to, what did you say to that one, what did you say to this person, who is this person [deep sigh]. I know women that were together for 20 years, and they were rearranging the furniture when the parents came to visit, and the parents knew, and they were still pretending that they didn't know!"

Another tennis legend, Billie Jean King, also came out. Or, more correctly, she was outed in 1981 when her longtime lover sued for palimony. King was married at the time, and she spent years dodging questions about her sexuality. "When I was outed, I felt I was then out," King told the *Advocate* in 1998. "It was like, 'That's done.' But I guess the gay community never felt that way, that's for sure. When I said it was a 'mistake,' I meant it was a mistake because of the monogamy issue, not because of the gender. I mean, I was pretty stressed-out—nobody likes to be outed, especially that way. I felt very violated. It's like rape, probably. I would just never out anybody. I think everyone has to find it in their own way and their own time. Any therapist will tell you that when you're ready, you will [come out]. To be outed means you weren't ready."

King has had quite a life: she was the first female athlete to earn one hundred thousand dollars in a year (which got her a congratulatory phone call from President Nixon); won a record twenty Wimbledon titles; is an ardent feminist who had an abortion in 1973 (and whose husband told *Ms.* magazine about it, much to her chagrin); was best buds with Elton John (who wrote the song *Philadelphia Freedom* in her honor); founded the Women's Tennis Association, which pushed for bigger paydays for women players; was married for years before being outed in 1981 in a palimony suit; and was named by *Life* magazine as one of the one hundred most important Americans of the twentieth century. She has also become a forceful advocate for gay rights, and her tennis star has never diminished. In 2006, organizers of the U.S. Open tennis tournament renamed their venue the Billie Jean King National Tennis Center.

Glenn Burke

Like King, baseball player Glenn Burke was a pioneer, but not one who was honored. In 1977, Burke popularized the "high five," what has now become a universal symbol of congratulations. In 1982, Burke revealed to *Sports Illustrated* that he was gay, three years after he retired.

Burke had such amazing talent that one coach called him the "next Willie Mays." But in 1978, in his third season, he was traded from the Los Angeles Dodgers to the Oakland Athletics for a player thought to be washed up. It was a curious trade, and Burke always suspected it was because the Dodgers knew about his sexual orientation. "The Dodgers, one of the most image-conscious organizations in an image-conscious sport, would not have tolerated a gay ballplayer in the '70s," Bob Brigham wrote in a profile of Burke for Outsports. "They might in today—if he could hit

Ian Roberts

Although no American elite male team athlete has come out while active, there was one successful exception overseas. Ian Roberts, an Australian star in the world of rugby, came out in 1995 while at the top of his game. He was generally accepted by those in the sport and the fans, and he was not shy about confronting stereotypes that permeate the issue of gays in sports. "I take offense at the old locker room argument which assumes a man cannot, in any circumstances, control his urges," Roberts said in a 1996 interview. "Any self-respecting human being can respect the rights and ways of another human being. The idea, then, that gays can convert, or want, heterosexual guys, is ludicrous. We want to play the game, not the field."

.500 with 150 home runs. But they would have to come up with a cover story. General Manager Al Campanis once suggested that it would be a good idea if Burke got married."

In his autobiography, *Out at Home*, written with Erik Sherman, Burke says that he felt his close association with Spunky Lasorda, the son of Dodgers manager Tommy Lasorda, was something Spunky's dad could not tolerate, Brigham writes. Although the rest of the world accepts that the Dodger manager's son was gay and died of AIDS, Tommy is still publicly in total denial on both counts.

Burke's ending was not a happy one. Once hailed as a hero by San Francisco's gay community (he was a star in the city's gay softball league), Burke turned to drugs and panhandling. He eventually spent seven months in San Quentin on drug charges and died of AIDS in 1995. At the end, Brigham writes, the man who invented the high five "could barely lift his arm."

For every Burke who was out, there were dozens in the closet. There have been many false starts. In 1984, rumors flew around the Summer Olympics in Los Angeles that two prominent U.S. gold medalists were going to come out. Pressure from sponsors allegedly kept them quiet. One of them, diver Greg Louganis, had a very public coming out a few years later, but the second athlete has still not made a public declaration.

The Nineties Bring Change

The 1990s saw increased visibility of gays and lesbians in society. And sports, though still lagging behind the culture, started to have their coming-out party.

In 1992, former NFL lineman Roy Simmons came out on *The Phil Donahue Show*. Simmons then lapsed into obscurity for more than a decade before writing a book in 2006 that chronicled his fight with HIV and detailed a life of drug addiction and wild sexual escapades.

In contrast to Simmons, Billy Bean was as wholesome as mom and apple pie. A nine-year veteran of Major League Baseball, Bean was inadvertently outed when the *Miami Herald* revealed his sexual orientation in a profile of his partner, who had opened a restaurant. This led to a front-page story in the *New York Times* on September 6, 1999, where Bean said, "For nine years, I felt as though I had one foot in the major leagues and one on a banana peel."

Bean's story struck a chord because by all accounts he was the all-American boy—good-looking, polite, athletic, a model student—the kind of man mothers dream of their daughters marrying. "Class act, everybody loved Billy on the club," Jim Riggleman, Bean's manager with the San Diego Padres, told the *New York Times*. "It surprised me that he's gay, but it doesn't diminish my feelings. He was one of the most plea-

Billie Jean King said the change has to come not from gay athletes, but their straight counterparts. "We need the straight guys to stand up," she told the *New York Daily News*, "and say, 'You're gay and I don't care. As long as you can play football or baseball and you're a good person, it doesn't matter. Now let's go out and win some ballgames.'"

surable guys to manage. He was such a good guy that I think it would have been all right on the club. The news crews, that might have made it tough."

Since coming out, Bean has gone on to write his autobiography and become a sought-after speaker, his days in the closet forever over. In 2006, he competed as an openly gay athlete in the Gay Games tennis tournament and served as one of the event's ambassadors.

The Outsports Revolution Begins

The beginning of a new century saw an explosion of attention to gays and lesbians in sports. A lot of credit goes to the Internet, which has made it much easier for athletes to connect and their stories to spread.

In 2002, former NFL defensive lineman Esera Tuaolo came out simultaneously on Home Box Office's (HBO) *Real Sports* and in the *New York Times*. Outsports had the story the same day, and within days Tuaolo had received more coverage than he had in nine years of playing. He has become a very visible spokesman for gay issues and in 2006 wrote his autobiography, *Alone in the Trenches: My Life as a Gay Man in the NFL*.

At the 2006 Gay Games, Tuaolo was in tears as he accepted his gold medal for being part of the winning Outsports flag-football team. "It was great, an incredible experience," said Tuaolo, who played for five NFL teams and made one Super Bowl appearance. "At the Super Bowl, I couldn't really be myself; I couldn't really share my life with anyone. But being myself, being free in the Gay Games, was totally a lot better than the Super Bowl."

Tuaolo never came out while playing. Still only a handful of male athletes in other sports have come out while currently active, including

Esera Tuaolo played nine years in the NFL but says playing flag football in the 2006 Gay Games was an athletic highlight.

Photo by Jim Buzinski

Outsports Breaks the Amaechi Story

Outsports had a major hand in breaking one of the biggest stories in the history of gays in sports: The coming out of former NBA player John Amaechi in Februrary 2007.

Outsports had heard rumblings of Amaechi's impending announcement and book, *Man in the Middle*, to be published by ESPN books, in early 2006. But it wasn't until December 2006, when Amaechi called Cyd from London one afternoon hat they had the chance to talk to Amaechi directly. Amaechi told Cyd about the limited publicity he had been able to set up himself, so Cyd introduced him to publicist Howard Bragman, who had handled the coming out of Esera Tuaolo, Rosie Jones, and Sheryl Swoopes.

The whole story was supposed to drop February 12, the night before an episode of ESPN's *Outside the Lines* in which Amaechi was to announce that he is gay. However, many media outlets started snooping around, and a couple of them (namely Deadspin.com and *Sports Business Daily*) published Amaechi's name online on February 6. While Outsports had agreed not to run the story until February 12, the publishing of Amaechi's name changed all of that, and Outsports had the first full story confirming Amaechi's announcement and excerpting from the book later that night.

Roberts, English soccer player Justin Fashanu, figure skating champions Curry and Rudy Galindo, 2000 Olympic diver David Pichler, and six-time Olympic equestrian Robert Dover.

The Internet also spawned a burgeoning trend of nonelite athletes sharing their stories. In 2000, the story of Corey Johnson, an openly gay high school football player, was unique enough to warrant a front-page article in the *New York Times* and a feature on ABC's *20/20*. Just a few years later, these kinds of stories, of athletes coming out in high school and college, are so ubiquitous that Outsports has a section devoted to them.

It is starting to become routine for some in the mainstream media to write about gays in sports—so routine that several polls have been conducted of players and fans. For example, a 2006 *Sports Illustrated* poll found a majority of players in pro baseball, football, basketball, and hockey would welcome an openly gay teammate. Another poll found that two-thirds of fans said they would accept an openly gay athlete.

The Next Generation

At the 2006 Winter Olympics, American figure skater Johnny Weir caused a buzz with his flamboyant personality and his professed love for shopping and fashion. It caused no end to speculation about Weir's sexual orientation ("Johnny are you queer, boy?" the *Washington Post* asked), but he wouldn't take the bait.

"People talk," Weir wrote in his online journal prior to the Olympics.

Outsports broke the story of John Amaechi coming out in February 2007.

Photo by David Myrick, grooming by Cynthia Griffin

Figure skating is thought of as a female sport, something that only girly men compete in. I don't feel the need to express my sexual being because it's not part of my sport and it's private. I can sleep with whomever I choose and it doesn't affect what I'm doing on the ice, so speculation is speculation. I like nice things, and beautiful things, so if that is the only way people are determining that I swing one way or the other, then to me, that's sad. You can't judge a book by its cover, ever. I never get angry about things because it's human nature to be jealous and rip people to shreds if you don't like them, regardless of the subject. I am who I am, and I don't need to justify anything to anyone.

The discussion of Weir's sexual orientation became news precisely because he and his handling of his sexuality are so unusual. The media have shied away from even asking the question of most jocks, but few jocks are as ballsy as Weir, or as out there ("He's Here, He's Weir" was the segment title of an NBC feature on the skater during the Olympics). In 2006, even asking a male athlete about their orientation was still enough to cause a stir.

The situation has been somewhat different for women. Navratilova was able to come out and still be successful. Pro golfers Karrie Webb, Muffin Spencer-Devlin, Patty Sheehan, Kelly Robbins, and Rosie Jones all came out (or, as in Webb's case, were outed) while still active, and women's pro basketball superstar Sheryl Swoopes came out to a flurry of positive publicity in 2005.

Professional tennis player Amelie Mauresmo was out for several years yet still thrived as an athlete, winning the Australian Open and Wimbledon singles titles in 2006. Most notable about her triumph was that the media focus was on her play, not with whom she had sex.

Still, the Amelie Mauresmos of the world—proud, out jocks who let their play do the talking—are still extremely rare. More common is the reaction of professional baseball catcher Mike Piazza, who felt obliged to call a press conference to declare he's straight after a blind item appeared in the *New York Post*'s Page Six. To Piazza and many others, being perceived as gay in sports is still a bad thing. Despite progress on the collegiate level, the pros still remain a tough sell.

OUTSPORTS

Flashback
#10

MARCH 13, 2002

Helen Carroll: A Tireless Advocate for Gay, Lesbian Athletes

Jim Buzinski

Ashly Massey, an eighth grader in California, was forced to spend two weeks in the principal's office while her classmates were in gym class. Her offense? She disclosed she was a lesbian. The student had been sent to the principal's office because the physical education teacher was uncomfortable with Massey's sexual orientation. The teacher's action, while morally offensive, was also likely illegal under California law.

Ashly Massey's story became national news when the American Civil Liberties Union and National Center for Lesbian Rights (NCLR) sued the Banning School District on her behalf late last year. The case is still pending.

To Helen Carroll, coordinator of the Homophobia in Sports project at the NCLR, Massey's case is a textbook example of the prejudices confronting gays and lesbians on a daily basis, especially in issues regarding sports. And it's this prejudice that Carroll is determined to meet head-on.

"I'm just an old basketball coach," Carroll, fifty, said in a self-deprecating way that belies her effectiveness as an advocate. In her job with the NCLR, Carroll is at the forefront of fighting discrimination against gays and lesbians in high school, college, and pro sports. "I'm not a lawyer," Carroll says, adding that she acts as an intermediary with the center's lawyers and the offending athletic department and officials. She might not be a lawyer, but her background has extensively prepared her for the challenges she faces.

Carroll's long career as a basketball coach and college athletic director gives her credibility when examining complaints. She speaks the language of the locker room and the coach's office. Her 1984 University of North Carolina at Asheville team won the National Association of Intercollegiate Athletes (NAIA) women's national college basketball championship, making her the first woman to win an NAIA title. From 1988 to 2000 she was the athletic director of Mills College in the Bay Area.

In dealing with schools and sports organizations Carroll's goal is always the same: no athlete should be harassed or discriminated against because of his or her sexual orientation. The NCLR, a small nonprofit based in San Francisco, will cajole, educate, and, if necessary, threaten legal action to create a tolerant atmosphere. "If there are no consequences [to homophobic behavior], you can educate out the wazoo and it doesn't matter," Carroll said of the need to threaten litigation.

Positive Momentum

Carroll sees the issue of gays and lesbians in sports as having a "momentum that is going so quickly." In alluding to former NFL player Esera Tuaolo's public coming out last year, Carroll notes that "the public is seeing out football players with kids." Tuaolo and his partner are parents of twins.

"Before two years ago, we had a lot of individuals like Patty Griffin at UMass and Mike Muska at Oberlin College who were doing great work individually," Carroll told the *New York Daily News*. "Now we are pulling all those resources together to really change the atmosphere for lesbians and gays in sports. That has really set the ground work for change." In addition to the Massey case, Carroll has been involved in a variety of issues that show the extent of homophobia in the sports world:

• Cindy Butz, a member of the Philadelphia Liberty Belles of the women's pro football league, charged an assistant coach with sexually ha-

About Helen Carroll

Family: I am definitely a Southern gal born and raised in Tennessee, where everyone's grandmother played great basketball so the sport's heritage is strong. My family is comprised of my former partner and myself sharing the raising of our 4-year-old twin daughters, Mica and Savannah, with their "aunties" Jenean and Laurie (who watched them being born and are an everyday integral part of their growth). My stepson Brian, 15, completes the picture.

Hobbies: Raising the twins as we play all kinds of sports (plus some dress-up!). Sea kayaking, hiking, and, of course, basketball. Just being still and reading is a fun activity.

Favorite Sport to Watch: Once being a coach, it's hard to watch and not be directing the action; however, women's college basketball in person and on television has great strategies and play.

All-time favorite game as a coach: In the National Association of Intercollegiate Athletics (NAIA) national basketball championships, we won the 1984 national title in overtime with a long outside shot in the final seconds of overtime. That made me the first woman in NAIA history to coach a national basketball championship title team. What a game!

rassing her because she is a lesbian. As part of the settlement brokered by the NCLR, sexual orientation will now be included in the team's antidiscrimination policy.

- A standout player on a Division I women's college basketball team in Colorado was removed from the team and forced to miss her senior season for creating dissension. Her crime? Wearing a gay pride T-shirt. She is seeking to get her scholarship money back.
- A lesbian soccer coach at a community college was harassed by the football coaches. The athletic director was very proactive and decided to hold diversity training. "It wound up being very positive," Carroll said.

These cases represent some of the challenges faced by gay and lesbian athletes as they struggle with reconciling their sexuality in often hostile

Athlete Helen coached that she is most fond of: Actually, it is every young person I had the opportunity to coach as each of them brought such special gifts to the team and to me as a person; they continue to do that. Sheila Ford does come to mind—a 6'4" woman who led the nation in rebounds (all basketball levels, NCAA, NAIA, and men's professional) her senior year. An amazing fact is that other colleges did not recruit her because they thought her large size would keep her from being a great athlete. She completed her senior year as Most Valuable Player of the Nation.

Current athletes Helen admires: Jennifer Azzi, former Stanford basketball standout now with the WNBA [Women's National Basketball Association], and Teresa Weatherspoon, also with the WNBA. They tried to make a professional basketball league with a new model; they took the chances when the NBA did not, setting the stage for pro women's ball. Of course, the American Basketball League didn't make it due to many reasons, but we were able for a short time to live that excitement with the owners, coaches, and players of that league. I also really admire how the Women's United Soccer Association has developed its professional teams.

environments. Men and women face different challenges, Carroll said. "There's a lot of harassment in men's athletics. A lot of the hazing has to do with homophobia in sports." A key to overcoming this ingrained prejudice is for coaches "to set an atmosphere on the team so each player can play to the best of their ability."

The former coach is convinced that change starts from the top, which is why she is dismayed and angry at the so-called negative recruiting that takes place in women's athletics. The issue became mainstream news following a major story in the *Washington Post* in January. Basically, negative recruiting involves a coach subtly (or not) implying that a rival is gay in an attempt to scare the parents of a recruit. Carroll was quoted in the story as calling it the fear of the gay "boogeywoman" who will make their daughters choose a lesbian sexual orientation. Negative recruiting is the "biggest drawback to getting Division I coaches to come out," Carroll told participants at the Outsports convention in February. Women already struggle to get head coaching jobs and don't want a public declaration of being a lesbian to be one more reason to deny them a job.

Carroll sees the *Washington Post* story as a landmark in airing the issue talked about before only in the shadows. It named names and has led to a discussion of the topic among NCAA coaches and administrators. HBO is conducting research to do a segment on the subject for its *Real Sports* series.

Climate Warms Up

The raised public consciousness is one reason Carroll sees the cultural climate for acceptance of gay and lesbian athletes going from cold to lukewarm. She cites as a positive the NCAA including sexual orientation in its nondiscrimination clause.

Her background as a coach and athletic administrator has made her acutely aware that dealing with homophobia on campus has to be addressed in a general discussion of discrimination. "How do you discuss the subject [with a team] without it taking over the program?" Carroll asks. Too intense a focus can be a distraction, and she encourages coaches to bring it up in their first team meeting of the season. "We can deal with 75 percent of the problem simply by mentioning sexual orientation" to athletes, she added.

Carroll is flexible enough to realize there is no one-size-fits-all approach to dealing with a prejudice that has long haunted athletics. And she is not naïve enough to think the problems will go away simply with visibility. The "old coach" who once took a losing, rudderless program to a national title realizes there are no shortcuts and no substitute for hard work and perseverance. "I'm in it for the long haul," she said.

IT'S NOT A GAY THING;
IT'S A GUY THING

It's as much a precursor of spring as baseball in Florida and Arizona. The 2006 edition weighed in at 228 pages, loaded with ads from mainstream advertisers such as Apple, Verizon, Best Buy, and HBO. It is a major source of revenue for Time-Warner, with spin-offs that include television and the Internet. It is the annual *Sports Illustrated* swimsuit edition.

Predictable are the letters that appear a few weeks later in the magazine from people complaining that the publication is trying to corrupt their young sons. The letters have become almost an inside joke. More representative are letters from red-blooded American men who say the issue is a perfect antidote to the winter blues. The issue is such a well-established part of the sports media scene that every year the Associated Press writes a story about the latest publication. No one tries to suggest that *Sports Illustrated* is somehow less journalistically sound because it runs 200 pages of scantily clad models.

Outsports runs photo galleries. Beautiful photo galleries of men and women playing football, swimming, diving, cycling, running—you name it. Outsports also provides photo links to pictures of elite athletes. In contrast to *Sports Illustrated*'s swimsuit edition, whose models are virtually all nonathletes, the photos on Outsports are exclusively of athletes, people actively engaged in their sport. Yet Outsports is occasionally accused by some of running titillating photos that (they claim) undermine the journalistic integrity of the web site.

It is the classic double standard that Outsports and many other gay publications have had to live with for years. When a mainstream magazine shows photographs of women wearing next to nothing, it's boys being boys. When Outsports or *Out* magazine does it, in the eyes of many it's scandalous.

A Closeted Pro Athlete Has a Bone to Pick

A prime example of the double standard is a letter from "Timmy," an anonymous e-mailer to Outsports who said he is a closeted professional athlete. Regardless of whether he is a pro athlete or not, his views were articulated forcefully enough that they helped frame the debate of what Outsports sometimes hears:

> Timmy: I've been reading Outsports.com for quite some time, but this is the first time I've written. I am a gay professional athlete, and I'm in the closet to almost everyone I know.
>
> I'm writing to offer some kudos and some criticism. I hope you'll take it with the sincerity that I intend.
>
> First, I'd like to say that I think that it's great that a site like Outsports exists. The number of hits you receive, the traffic on your bulletin boards, etc, surely must show you that there's a need for a site like yours. . . . It's clear that you're not eager to "out" anyone, or inflame rumors about who might be gay and who might not be. (even though I'm sure you hear all the same rumors that I do, if not more.)
>
> I do believe, however, that there are a few elements of the website which greatly hurt your credibility, and if you've truly got a long-range goal for the acceptance of gay athletes, you should consider a re-haul of your site.
>
> As I'm sure you know, one of the main things we've got against us is the perception by the public that if we're gay, we'll want to "sexualize" our sport. According to what THEY think, locker room showers aren't about getting clean, they're about scoping out naked guys. A football center isn't snapping a ball, he's letting the quarterback see what it'd look like to fuck him. Slapping a basketball player on the ass after a good play isn't camaraderie, it's a come-on. Wrestling isn't merely wrestling. . .
>
> You know what I'm saying.
>
> So when someone visits Outsports, they've got these pre-conceived notions about what a "gay athletics" movement is all about. Unfortunately, a first visit to your site only confirms these notions. The first thing they're going to look at, naturally, are the photos. Your site, unfortunately, is filled with photo galleries that clearly show athletes in sexualized poses, or hot guys with their shirts off, etc. . . .
>
> This site isn't about taking athletics seriously . . . it's merely jerk-off material.

The very first photo gallery—rugby players grabbing each other's ass? Nine photos of water polo players hugging and kissing? I do realize that these photo galleries are probably your most POPULAR, which is why they're on the homepage. . .

But do you honestly expect "straight america" to take us seriously when this is the first image we're putting out about ourselves? Images speak far more loudly, and more potently, than any article that you put on your site.

I appreciate the inherent humor in the absurdity of how some manners are accepted (an ass slap in a game) while others are taboo (an ass slap in a bar), but we don't need Outsports to illuminate this for us. We need to be taken seriously, and your photo galleries blow our credibility. If every issue of *Sports Illustrated* were filled with lucid, scantily-clad pics of Maria Sharapova or Anna Kournikova, do you think it would be taken seriously as a magazine for real athletes?

Again, I do realize that these galleries are probably popular, but if you're determined to keep them, I'd like to urge you to bury them

No publication should need an excuse to run this picture of an Outgames swimmer.
Photo by Cyd Zeigler Jr.

deeper in your site. Just because they're popular doesn't mean they're GOOD (porn sites are, after all, the number one search on Yahoo.)

From a branding perspective, you really ought to consider designing your site—it looks a little old and clunky, and therefore, unprofessional. And when you do, PLEASE prioritize intelligent, authentic content for athletes like me over jerkoff material for horny guys with locker room fantasies.

Thanks for reading, and good luck with everything.

—"Timmy" (not even close to my real name.)

Outsports sent this response:

Thanks so much for your e-mail. We really appreciate all the kind words you had about Outsports.

We did want to address, though, the substance of your concerns about the site. Namely, our use of photo galleries. While we certainly understand your point, we respectfully disagree.

We regularly watch "Pardon the Interruption" on ESPN. You can't get any more mainstream than Tony Kornheiser and Mike Wilbon from the *Washington Post*. It is one of ESPN's most popular shows and gets critical acclaim. Yet on a regular basis the two of them talk about all the "hot babes" they see. Whether it's Marat Safin's girlfriend or the female Indy 500 driver or an actress from "Desperate Housewives," the two of them go on and on, always showing pictures of what they're talking about. A regular feature on MSN/Foxsports. com is a gallery featuring babes of the week, none of them athletes. One of the most talked about sports at the 2004 Summer Olympics was beach volleyball, not the men, but the women, scantily clad in bikinis (the men were required to wear shirts!). The mainstream media loved it. The staid and traditional NFL rakes in millions each year selling calendars, posters and videos of cheerleaders, most of whom couldn't tell a football from a highball. And, of course, *Sports Illustrated*'s most popular issue each year is a swimsuit edition.

Jeremy Bloom and Terrell Owens, two mainstream athletes, have pictures on their sites that are much more provocative than anything found on Outsports. All of the above can easily be considered "jerk-off material." It truly is in the eye of the beholder.

We see a huge double standard in criticizing Outsports for showing images that are found regularly in newspapers, magazines, on the Internet and on television. We are credentialed for every event we shoot and have found athletes overwhelmingly cooperative. You cite examples of water polo players hugging. These are great images. The same images were found on the official site of the tournament sponsor. The "ass-grabbing" on the rugby pitch is actually fairly common, ruggers have told us, and it happened on the field. Our photo galleries are a blend of action shots and more candid shots, but all are taken within the context of the events.

Are the pictures meant to show attractive athletes? Of course, but what's wrong with that? It's better than [rotund Philadelphia Eagles coach] Andy Reid in tights. People have been admiring the athletic form since ancient times. The examples cited above are not meant as an "everybody does it" defense; rather, we see nothing wrong with it.

You were dead on about the quality of our content, which is why we are frequently quoted by the mainstream media. We have tremendous credibility, and that is because of the quality of the stories we run. ESPN ran a feature on an openly gay lacrosse player. They got the story from Outsports, and we assisted the reporter who had questions on what language to use and how to frame the importance of this athlete's story. The fact that we have pictures of shirtless athletes did not lessen our credibility with ESPN or any others in the media. In fact, we would say that Outsports has greatly increased the visibility of gays and sports and driven the mainstream media to cover us as part of the mix; not bad for two guys doing this on a relative shoestring.

Your concerns, interestingly enough, have virtually never been voiced by the "mainstream." We hear these criticisms from time to time, but they mostly come from other gay people. This is actually understandable. People who are still struggling in whatever fashion with their sexuality, especially people in the often unforgiving world of sports, are much more concerned about how they are perceived by straight people. We get the sense sometimes that we must portray ourselves as celibate monks to satisfy these concerns. We would argue that Outsports is actually tamer than many other mainstream media outlets. The way to get straight America to take us seriously used to be up front and honest about who we are, and not buying into a double standard on what is and is not acceptable. In the minds of many it is totally unacceptable for two men who have lived together for 20 years to marry, but a man and a woman who met an hour ago can legally go down to the local courthouse and tie the knot.

Outsports has hundreds and hundreds of pages of content, with photos being merely a part. Our editorial vision is to provide a place for discussion of gays and lesbians in sports without any shame attached to that. We think that for the most part we succeed.

Sorry for going on so long here, but your letter was very provocative and got us thinking. Feel free to comment on this in any way you see fit. We ultimately may have to agree to disagree on this point, but I suspect that ultimately we have the same goals in mind.

Good luck in whatever sport you play and hope you're having tremendous success. Stay in touch.

—Jim

Timmy was not mollified and sent this follow-up:

Thanks for writing back at such length; I certainly intended my letter to be thought-provoking, so I'm glad you really thought things through.

I agree—we're essentially on the same page, and both want the same things; it's just a matter of how we achieve them. I also agree with you that Outsports is playing a crucial role in establishing the authenticity of gay athletics, without shame. This discussion is occupying a larger and larger arena, nationally (as you can see by Kraft Foods's response to the efforts to block their sponsorship of the Gay Games in Chicago), and I'm heartened to know that journalists look to you to lead the way in this discussion. You've got a role that will only increase in importance over the next several years.

Which is why it's so crucial that you get your act together now, before more and more people come looking—and never return for a 2nd impression.

I completely hear your argument on how ESPN, FoxSports, *Sports Illustrated*, etc. use "hot babe" pics to leaven their coverage of hardcore athletics—but there are *two inherent differences* between this content and yours, and I'd really like you to think it through, as you contemplate your site re-design:

1. These media outlets have brand recognition and mass-media credentials BEFORE they speak about "hot babes." Although the Swimsuit Issue is nothing new, most of the oogling-and-aaahing of hot women on TV sports programs is a reflection of the current decade's new acceptance of blatant objectification (which was VERY taboo in the 80's and early 90's . . . simply because it was perceived as sexist, until Diet Coke turned a male construction worker into an acceptable

role-reversal of equal opportunity catcalling). I'm sure you're savvy enough to know that the 90's emergence of gay culture (Mapplethorpe, muscle culture, etc.) has added to our new era's acceptance of objectifaction, period, simply because now, MEN can be objects too.

Outsports, however, does NOT have this lead-in of brand recognition and credibility. Instead, you've got the opposite perception: people arrive with a negative expectation, and they're looking to be proven wrong. Quite honestly, you've got a tougher road than *Sports Illustrated* will ever have, and they don't need to make such a brazen

This Gay Games VI wrestler finds time to relax on the mat.

By Brent Mullins

effort to win over the mind of the viewer, the way that you do. Just keep that in mind.

2. The major inherent difference between Outsports and the other sport media you mention, however is this: they've got a built-in "context shift" whenever they transition from discussion about real athletics to a mention of hot babes—simply because they CHANGE GENDERS. We don't have this same automatic shift of thought. For us, the same photo that depicts hardcore, devout athleticism—say, two guys wrestling with all their might—could be inspiring to one viewer, but erotic to another. In mainstream sports media, the VAST, VAST, VAST percentage of their content—which they use to establish the bulk of their credibility—is about men. And, these men are not sex objects to their viewers.

Then, after 45 minutes of sports coverage, they pause, make a fun comment, and "lighten their programming" with a little diversion—a hot babe. *Sports Illustrated* builds their cred with a year of hardcore coverage, then features ONE issue of women in swimsuits. There's a frame around it, a set of quotation marks. The "jerkoff material" is called out as just that, BEFORE they broadcast it.

Because of these inherent differences, I'd like you to really consider how you depict gay athletes. If you want to "lighten your content" the way that *Sports Illustrated* or ESPN does (they do have an online poll every year for "hottest athlete"), I'd like you to strongly consider putting it into a whimsical, fun-loving "frame." Separate it, visually, on your site. Put it someplace special. Give it some context; call it for what it is, without shame, and you just may achieve what you're looking for. I think the main reason why your current format hurts your credibility is because you've got clear jerkoff materials smushed right up against pics that depict our athleticism, and your messages get muddled.

It's simply editorial sloppiness, on your part, and in the way that Outsports has grown organically from a small site into something larger, it's par for the course. But now's the time to clean up the messages, and know what you're really saying.

Don't overthink this; of course it's difficult to know what's jerkoff material to one guy and a political statement to another, but you're smart, I'm sure, and you'd be wise to save some photos for a separate photo album or website area.

And please . . . don't make it the most prominently featured area of your site. Keep in mind that its our skills, our passion and our commitment that's going to win over the minds of those Kraft higher-ups who decide to sponsor [the Gay Games], not our collection of near-naked foreign water polo players whose hugs and kisses are mere expressions of their cultural norms.

—"Timmy"

Outsports got in the last word, and Timmy was never heard from again:

After reading your latest, we find we disagree with almost all of it.

You wrote: "Outsports, however, does NOT have this lead-in of brand recognition and credibility. Instead, you've got the opposite perception: people arrive with a negative expectation, and they're looking to be proven wrong."

Who arrives with a negative expectation? You, perhaps? Almost everyone else arrives and says, "It's about time." We wrote in our last e-mail that we have more than established our credibility. One sign of this is the respect we have garnered from the mainstream media, which regularly cites us, quotes us, and uses us as a resource. Ask the people at ESPN or the *New York Times* or dozens of other media outlets about our credibility. We would not be sought out as often as we are if we had no credibility. It's also why we have won journalism awards, beating out the likes of Newsweek online. We are not worried about our credibility.

In addition, our photo galleries are not the most prominent part of our site and they are on separate pages. As for Kraft, they have reiterated their support for the Gay Games and know what they are sponsoring. They get it.

You use the words "shame" and "jerkoff material" and "sex objects" in your e-mail. This may say more about you than about Outsports.

Thanks again for writing. You are very articulate and write well, even if I disagree.

—Jim

What Is It with Gay Men?

Interestingly, comments such as Timmy's are most often expressed by gay men. In running Outsports, we have heard almost none of the same complaints from mainstream, that is, straight, readers or reporters; it seems as

It's no shocker that this "cheap but not easy" photo was one of Outsports' most popular Gay Games pictures.

Photo by Cyd Zeigler Jr.

if they get it. People like Timmy are likely dealing with fear and a certain sense of what might be called internalized homophobia. This is quite understandable, especially for athletes or anyone else who is in the closet. When discussing gay men in sports, so much of the reactions from other athletes, media, and fans deal with the issue of the locker room: the concern that a gay jock will stare at and ogle his teammates in the showers. It perpetuates the stereotype that all gay men are hypersexual and will jump the bones of any man who has a pulse.

Esera Tuaolo has said that he was extremely careful to avert his eyes in the locker room, lest anyone suspect him of looking. Tuaolo was a three hundred–pound nose tackle who was as tough as anyone, yet even he was aware of the possible dangers that could face an openly gay man in a professional sports locker room. After Tuaolo came out, LeRoy Butler, a former teammate, offered his support but also echoed what he said many other players would feel about having an openly gay teammate: "A lot of guys would be upset. Particularly because football players shower together. I'm sure a lot of guys are looking back right now and wondering if Tuaolo was checking them out. For many players—and for many heterosexual men in general—it's distressing to know that a guy you're sharing soap with is gay. I have to admit, if I knew an openly gay guy was in the shower, I would not be in a rush to go in there."

Of course, the argument that gay men can't control themselves is nonsense. Ian Roberts knocked down this argument with simple logic: "I take offense at the old locker room argument which assumes a man cannot, in any circumstances, control his urges. Any self-respecting human being can respect the rights and ways of another human being. The idea, then, that gays can convert, or want, heterosexual guys, is ludicrous. We want to play the game, not the field."

Relating this to Outsports, it seems that some people can't take their eyes off the pictures that are posted on the web site and assume that everyone else is equally obsessed, ignoring the other award-winning content on the site. The mentality mirrors in many ways the arguments about jocks showering together, replete with the same stereotypes and ignorant assumptions.

Yet people have no problem going to *Sports Illustrated*'s web site, which features dozens of photo galleries, including such eye candy as "NBA finals cheerleaders," "Soccer wives and girlfriends," and the ubiquitous swimsuit models. *Sports Illustrated* regularly features galleries of females with only a passing connection to sports, picked for their looks and not their skills. In contrast, one never sees galleries of hot male athletes; galleries with men all feature them playing their particular sport. No one claims that *Sports Illustrated* is shirking its journalistic duties. These galleries are pleasant diversions from a web site with thousands of pages of content. It's the same with Outsports.

It's not a "gay thing," it's a "guy thing." This is not to say that women don't enjoy a picture of a hot jock, be it male or female. It's just that there is seldom the same clamor for such. Men are simply more visual than women. As the *New York Times* said, "Male arousal, studies find, is strongly visual, and when men engage in sexual activity or even anticipate it, brain structures once thought to have little connection to sex spring into action. The same brain regions, however, remain relatively quiet when women are aroused. . . . One reason for the powerful response to visual stimuli in men. . . . could be cultural. Men tend to be inundated with sexual imagery and, possibly, are more likely to seek it out."

This explains why *Sports Illustrated* and other mainstream web sites such as ESPN and Fox Sports regularly run galleries of hot babes but seldom of hot men (unless it's of these men in action). The editors of these web sites know that the vast majority of their audience is composed of heterosexual men for whom these galleries are an added bonus. Flip that around, and you have Outsports.com. The editors of all the sites are simply giving readers what they want. Luckily for the men and women who like looking at photographs of beautiful athletes, Outsports isn't going to succumb to Timmy's requests anytime soon.

OUTSPORTS
Flashback
#9

July 10, 2002

Double Standard Still Rules: Why Mike Piazza Got All the Attention while Sue Wicks Was Ignored

Jim Buzinski

A baseball player in New York calls a press conference to declare his heterosexuality, and the story fires up the sports world. A female pro basketball player in New York tells a magazine she's a lesbian, and the public yawns. The reactions to Mike Piazza and Sue Wicks confirm that there's a double standard when reporting on the sexuality of male and female athletes. The media—and by extension the public—seem much more fascinated with the identity of gay male athletes. The reactions point out the stereotypes that both gay male and lesbian athletes still confront as they struggle for acceptance. Although a bit simplistic, the biases boil down to this: many female jocks are presumed lesbian unless otherwise proven; male jocks are presumed straight unless there is a public declaration to the contrary.

Wicks, a player on the New York Liberty of the WNBA, came out publicly in an interview with *Time Out New York*. When asked if she was a lesbian, Wicks said: "I am. Usually I don't like to answer those kinds of questions, because you worry the issue might become so much bigger than the sport. As an athlete, it's a little annoying when that becomes the point of interest. But I would never avoid that question, especially in New York. I think it's important that if you are gay, you should not be afraid to say who you are."

The reaction? There was none. In a database search on Dow Jones Interactive of six thousand top publications, I could find one reference to Wicks's statement, by Judy Van Handel (herself out) in a WNBA notes column in the *Boston Globe*.

Contrast this with the outpouring of interest in Piazza's statement that he wasn't gay. We at Outsports did at least twenty-five interviews with print and broadcast reporters, including seven appearances on various sports talk shows across the country. In addition, virtually every major media outlet weighed in on the subject, interviewing players, former players, management, and fans.

Outsports can plead equally guilty. Although we mentioned and applauded Wicks's coming out and have assigned a writer to profile her, we did relatively little compared to Piazza. Even our active reader Discussion Board has been virtually silent regarding Wicks.

Part of it was the intense media focus on Piazza, combined with discussions of press ethics for how it unfolded (in a *New York Post* gossip column). Part of it too was that Sue Wicks is not a household name and plays in a league that gets little exposure. But part of it was that we also bought into the notion that an out lesbian pro athlete simply isn't as big a story as the possibility that a male pro will one day come out.

For starters, there have been active lesbians playing pro sports. Martina Navratilova is the most famous, but the list also includes Amelie Mauresmo. Carol Blazejowski, a former player who is the general manager of Wicks's New York Liberty, is also out. In contrast, there is no out male athlete on any pro sports team or on the pro tennis or golf tours.

Reinforcing Stereotypes

Gay men and lesbians are each hurt by the stereotypes. Although it is widely presumed that there are many lesbians in pro basketball, golf, and tennis, the hierarchy of each is still publicly and relentlessly heterosexual.

Anna Kournikova, she of the zero tournament wins, is featured on the cover of *Sports Illustrated* for her suggestions of foreplay and not her forehand. She makes it okay for men to watch women's tennis. In contrast, the out Mauresmo is dogged by unproven claims of steroid use, which would imply she is somehow less than feminine for being muscular. It's a claim I haven't seen hurled at the equally muscular but presumably heterosexual Williams sisters.

At the collegiate level, straight female coaches tout their marriages and children to prospective recruits and their parents, sending the message that they are not "one of them." Even the WNBA, whose crowds are heavily lesbian, has a spotty record of reaching out to its fan base. The Liberty's refusal to hold a gay night (something done with other franchises) prompted a group called Lesbians for Liberty to give up trying this year, according to the *New York Blade*. If a team with a lesbian general manager and an openly lesbian player in very gay New York City is resistant, it shows how much progress still remains to be achieved. The situation means that lesbians, even if present in large numbers in a sport, still have an incentive to hide or downplay their sexual orientation.

The need for Piazza to call a press conference to declare his heterosexuality (even though he was not named in the gossip item) aptly sums up the situation for gay men in sports. Even rumors are seen as career and especially endorsement threatening. The closet rules, and the mainstream can hold on to the last bastion of hypermasculine heterosexuality in society. Until barriers in sports are broken down and people can be honest about who they are, expect these stereotypes to persist. And expect the double standard to apply.

THE MEDIA'S FUMBLING
OF GAY SPORTS

More than maybe any other question, Cyd and Jim get asked why they started Outsports.com (though, "Is [so-and-so hot athlete] gay?" is a close second). The answer is simple: because there was no media outlet at the time that catered to gay sports fans and athletes. No one had yet been able to tap into the growing nexus of gays and sports, and very few had even tried.

It seemed no one in the media really cared. The gay media were much more interested in talking about New York's Fashion Week, the latest in the Ellen–Anne Heche saga, and what circuit parties were going to be over the top in the coming year. Sports were relegated to small corners of the *Advocate* and were highlighted only when a major news story that simply couldn't be ignored hit. To be sure, they covered the fanfare surrounding Billy Bean and Martina Navratilova, but that was much more about the gay media's obsession with attractive men and celebrities than any interest in sports.

Plus, there was still the dominant notion that gay people, particularly gay men, simply don't care about sports; it's fashion and gossip about B-list celebrities they most want to read about in the pages of the tabloids that cater to them. Or so the story went.

Brendan Lemon was the editor of *Out* magazine, the number-one gay men's lifestyle magazine, from 2000 to 2005. Lemon brought national attention to gays in sports when, in 2001, he revealed in an editorial that he was in a relationship with a Major League Baseball player. But Lemon brought a lot more than stories of late-night phone calls to the mix. A lifelong sports fan, he also brought a sports-friendly sensibility that was sorely lacking and largely disregarded in the gay media. "Probably 10 to 15 years before I was at *Out*, gay publications barely covered sports at all,"

Lemon told Outsports, "I think because that generation associated team sports with being picked on in school. People in the gay media tended to be people who probably weren't big on sports as a kid, and they saw it as part of what was pushing them down."

While Lemon was at *Out*, he produced two sports issues (which included his revealing editorial, among other things). He felt it was important, at the turn of the millennium, to start embracing sports for a couple of reasons. "Sports are so important in our culture that it seems to me im-

Chuck Booms, straight comedian and former cohost of Fox Sports Radio's *Kiley & Booms*

I think it's homophobic to have your policy on anything gay be avoidance. And that's what I think happens a lot in sports radio. They're not necessarily gay bashing, but they just avoid it. By purposely or consciously staying away from topics that should be talked about, you're as bad as the people who gay bash.

portant that we cover that just as we would cover the relationship between gays and religion, politics, or show business," Lemon said. "And also, I'm very interested in sports myself and I knew a lot of other people who were gay who were interested in sports, and I didn't feel that their interest in sports were showing up in gay media very well."

Since Lemon's departure from *Out* in 2005, the magazine has continued to embrace sports-focused articles and columns. Although it still may not be at the level of a straight-male lifestyle magazine such as *Maxim* or *GQ*, it's a big improvement over the 1990s and earlier.

Despite the gay media's largely blasé attitude about sports, it was at least marginally better than the sports media's complete lack of interest in gay issues. If you asked the average sports reporter in the late 1990s what he thought of gay professional athletes, he probably would have asked, "Are there any?" Today, the media are becoming a lot more savvy on the issue.

We have various incidents to thank for that. Whereas major gay sports incidents that necessitated media coverage through 1998 could be counted on one hand, there was a watershed of gay moments in sports from 1999 to 2002 that forced the sports media to take notice that this issue now mandated their attention:

- In 1999, Billy Bean came out of the closet. Though Bean wasn't well known for his ball playing, he became a media darling and put a fresh face on the issue of gays in sports.
- In December 1999, Atlanta Braves pitcher John Rocker made homophobic and racist comments to *Sports Illustrated* that grabbed the attention of many and got people wondering, just how homophobic is your average professional athlete?
- In early 2000, the story of openly gay Massachusetts high school football captain Corey Johnson grabbed headlines.
- In June 2001, Lemon's column revealing his relationship with an unidentified Major League Baseball player hit.
- In May 2002, the *New York Post*'s gossip column, Page Six, ran a blind item claiming that a certain local baseball player was gay. All attention focused on Mike Piazza, who held a press conference declaring his heterosexuality, causing a torrent of coverage.
- In October 2002, Esera Tuaolo came out of the closet in a segment of HBO's *Real Sports*.

The coming out of Bean and Tuaolo are appropriate bookends for those three years of gay sports stories, particularly when you look at how

The story of former high school football captain Corey Johnson made a lot of waves in the media in 2000. He has since been the commissioner of the New York Gay Football League and won a Gay Games gold medal for football in 2006 with Team Outsports.

Photo by Ross Forman

the sports media handled each. Bean's story was largely relegated to the news and lifestyle sections of magazines and mainstream TV news shows. Although the sports media certainly acknowledged Bean's story, many of them approached it with a "well, isn't that interesting" perspective, maintaining that a gay man in professional sports was an aberration.

By the time Tuaolo came out, the three years between his and Bean's similar revelations had grabbed the attention of the sports media, this issue was not going away, and we have seen only the proverbial tip of the iceberg. The story was embraced by major sports magazines, televised sports shows such as HBO's *Real Sports with Bryant Gumbel*, and the sports sections of newspapers. Whereas Bean's coming out in 1999 was a "culture" story, Tuaolo's coming out in 2002 was a "sports" story.

A key development in that period was the launching and development of Outsports.com. While all of those news stories were popping up, Outsports became the first widely read news outlet to focus specifically on gay issues in sports. What that meant was that the sports media finally had a resource to turn to when researching a story. Instead of having to write in a vacuum, sports journalists could now turn to Outsports to find sources and background information for their stories—and they do so regularly. The existence of Outsports also gave notice to the rest of the sports media that these issues had context and legs, and that each news item was contributing to the bigger story of gays in sports.

Recently, other gay-rights groups focused on media attention have followed Outsports's lead. The Human Rights Campaign (HRC) now regu-

Brendan Lemon

I think that's been the really good thing that Outsports has done, and less so other entities of the gay media, is you give permission to people who are gay or bisexual to talk about sports in a way that isn't girlie. That's what it was before. You either talked about figure skating or you talked about team sports in a way a girl would talk about it.

larly tackles sports issues, and the sports media have begun reaching out to the HRC for comment and direction on gay sports issues. The Gay and Lesbian Alliance Against Defamation (GLAAD) had largely left sports issues to Outsports, utilizing Outsports as a resource for media when sports issues arose. With the hiring of former Tempe, Arizona, Mayor Neil Giuliano (who as mayor presided over the stadium that was home to the Fiesta Bowl, the Arizona Cardinals, and Arizona State University and has extensive relationships at many levels of sports) as its president in late 2005, GLAAD has started focusing more on sports. Giuliano has even created a GLAAD sports desk, the first of its kind, to educate the sports media on gay issues.

Just as gay blogs are often ahead of gay magazines on the news curve, they're also following Outsports's lead in covering sporting items. Until 2006, Towleroad.com, one of the most-read gay blogs on the web, featured sports only when there was a direct gay tie-in (for example, when Sheryl Swoopes came out). But Towleroad owner and editor Andy Towle now covers some sports news that he thinks will interest his readers, not just when an athlete calls someone a "fag." Although he won't report on the score of the Poinsettia Bowl, in December 2006 alone he did give some airtime to the Heisman Trophy race and the now-infamous brawl between the Denver Nuggets and the New York Knicks, and he even claimed to enjoy playing *Madden Football* on Nintendo's Wii. In 2006 he also started a feature called "Sportrait" in which he featured a picture of an athlete from a recent match. This probably shouldn't come as too much of a surprise. When he was the editor of *Genre* magazine in 2001, Towle hired Cyd to launch the first-ever sports section of a gay magazine, identifying then that there was a growing interest in sports in the gay community.

Michael O'Keeffe, New York Daily News

There are some sports reporters who have long been interested in delving into areas of sports not widely covered. One of the best is Michael O'Keeffe at the *New York Daily News*. O'Keeffe is a different kind of sports reporter. Although he's certainly interested in A-Rod's hitting percentage, he'd be much more apt to dive into a deep conversation about racial profiling by the New York Police Department.

O'Keeffe got into journalism because he wanted to pursue activist journalism, initially reporting on civil rights violations for *Rolling Stone* and the *Village Voice*. He ended up in Denver covering University of Colorado sports. "I thought sports journalism was frivolous," he told Outsports. "I was kind of full of shit. I thought I should be in Nicaragua reporting on the Sandinista crusade to educate children. I thought covering the University of Colorado football games was pretty pointless. But really, I was stupid to think that because some of the issues that have come up with the University of Colorado in the last few years were happening in the '80s [when I was there]," referring to the sexual-misconduct allega-

The arrival of Outsports on the media scene helped alter the way the mainstream sports media covered gay issues and the way gay publications covered sports. Before Outsports.com, there was no singular source where media professionals could research gay issues in sports, and there were very few national sources for quotes, comments, and interviews. Hundreds of media outlets have utilized Outsports and its two cofounders as resources, including:

Sports Illustrated	ESPN
ESPN the Magazine	CNN
HBO's *Real Sports*	Logo
New York Times	*New York Magazine*
Chicago Tribune	*Boston Globe*
Miami Herald	BBC Radio
The Howard Stern Show	Fox Sports Radio
San Francisco Chronicle	Salon.com
Advocate	Planetout

In addition, Outsports has broken many stories that attracted national attention, including the NFL's list of words you can't put on the back of any customizable NFL jersey, including *gay* (despite the fact that the last name of a player in the NFL was "Gay"), New York Giants tight end Jeremy Shockey's homophobic comments on *The Howard Stern Show,* and the refusal of a rugby team composed of New York Fire Department firefighters to play against a gay rugby team.

tions that rocked the Colorado football team in the first few years of the new century. Behind all of the touchdowns and cheers and bowl games, there was a deeper story about top-notch football players sexually harassing women that was just waiting to be uncovered by a reporter who did some digging.

Unfortunately, O'Keeffe's observation just about sums up most of sports reporting: frivolous. In defense of sports journalists, it actually serves one of the great purposes of sports. Sports are, most of the time, nothing more than an entertaining diversion. Ten bucks for a bleacher seat, $5 for a Dodger dog, $5.50 for some beer, $20 for parking, and you've got yourself three hours of respite from your own hectic life where you can watch grown men toss around a little white ball on the grass and try to hit it with a bat. For sports fans, the last thing they want with their sports is a big helping of politics or reality.

Most sports reporters are, to a large extent, sports fans with a voice, and they don't want "life" interfering with their sports any more than the guy at Dodger Stadium. The average reporter covering a team wants to talk football, make pseudofriends with the coaches, and get close enough to a college player or two who might end up in the NFL and score him some tickets; he doesn't want to have to deal with chicks complaining about the antics of the football team . . . or gay men and lesbians pushing social change in the NCAA.

They Got the Beat

The beat reporter was, at one point, most every sports fan's deepest connection to the team she loves. The beat reporter covers a team, follows the team to every game, stays in the same hotel as the team, follows the team to the locker room, and, if he's doing his job right, gets to know every coach and player so that he may, when the time is right, get the scoop of a lifetime.

As kids growing up, many soon-to-be beat reporters become enamored with a sport or a sports team. They could be a Red Sox fan in Boston, a Bulls fan in Chicago, or a Niners fan in the Bay Area. For whatever reason, they're the kid wearing the jersey of their favorite players to school every other day, or the one who knows the batting average of everyone in the starting lineup of his favorite baseball team for longer than he's even been alive. They dream of one day not necessarily being the guy who catches the game-winning touchdown, but being the guy who gets the exclusive interview in the hours following someone else doing it.

To be a beat reporter, you've got to love what you do. And that's how

When German-based magazine *Der Spiegel* ran a four-part series about gay players in German professional soccer leagues, one of the closeted players told the magazine, "There are journalists who know that I am gay, but they keep it to themselves. However, they expect in return that I will regularly give them other information."

ESPN: Opening Doors for Gays in Sports

Although it may seem oxymoronic to some, ESPN, "The Worldwide Leader in Sports," has become a real leader in the treatment of gay people in sports. ESPN's gay-positive record is exemplary, especially in light of much of the rest of the mainstream sports media. What sets it apart is that it doesn't just avoid homophobic rhetoric but actively engages the gay community.

- ESPN first aired its groundbreaking *Outside the Lines* special, "The World of the Gay Athlete," on December 16, 1998. That was followed by a second *OTL* special, "The Gay Dilemma," on June 3, 2001.
- ESPN was a sponsor of the Gay Games in 2006, and ESPN Mobile sponsored a basketball team that participated in the Games; that team was captained by *ESPN the Magazine* basketball editor LZ Granderson.
- ESPN has recruited at conferences for the National Lesbian and Gay Journalists Association.
- ESPN was honored at the 2006 Commercial Closet's Images in Advertising Award for "Outstanding Business-to-Business/Trade Ad."

many sports reporters get their start in sports—they make one team their entire business. Johnny missed hitting the cycle by one double? Got it. Paul has a stomachache and is listed as probable? All over it. Tom's girlfriend's dog had puppies, and he might be a little distracted by it for the big game? Yesterday's news. The beat reporter makes every little tidbit of information he can glean from the players and management his business.

These beat reporters from Kansas City to Seattle to Buffalo are privy to more information about the individual athletes than any other reporter. And many of them know gay athletes. They know they're gay, they know whom they're sleeping with, and they won't tell. A beat reporter considers himself part of the family, and his ability to get the big story depends on the team looking at him the same way. If he ever divulged the private information of an athlete's sexuality, not only does that reporter risk being blackballed by the athletes and the club, but he also runs the risk of alien-

- Several ESPN hosts, including Trey Wingo and Sean Salisbury, are on record as being gay friendly.

  ESPN senior vice president of news Vince Doria told Outsports:

  > People want to make the association that locker rooms in sports are not necessarily receptive to gays and lesbians. But there's never been that extension [at ESPN's Bristol, Connecticut, headquarters]. It's a very open place. There are a lot of people of various different persuasions. While some people may want to take ESPN and attach it to the sports landscape, we are much different. There isn't a locker room mentality up here. We have a lot of former players and coaches who work up here as analysts, and part of the introduction to this place is that they are crossing into another world up here. It is not an extension of the locker room. It's a workplace that is very sensitive to issues of race, gender and sexual orientation.

ating every athlete he could ever want to interview. If he'll reveal a secret as deep as a player's sexuality, chances are he'll view other deep, dark secrets as child's play.

Although O'Keeffe has never been a beat reporter, he said that this line of thinking is "old school." There was a time, before the Internet, that beat reporters were every fan's connection to the team. Now, with so many more media outlets, the player–beat reporter relationship is watered down, he said. Some beat reporters continue to go out of their way to protect the athletes they've come to know and rely on. Then there are others who understand that, in this world of fast-growing media outlets, it's their ability to identify and report a good story, not their willingness to buddy up to particular players, that will land them a job at a bigger-name media outlet.

Still, whether they fear reprisal from athletes and teams or not, there are few sports reporters who want to breach the subject of an athlete's sexual orientation, especially when he's in the locker room after a practice or a game and the athlete is standing there in nothing but a towel.

The Big Question

Is it even appropriate for a reporter to ask an athlete if he or she is gay? "I think that's an appropriate question," O'Keeffe said. "But, in a locker room, it would be a really hard question to ask." O'Keeffe knows first-hand. When Piazza held his press conference in 2002 to announce that he is straight, O'Keeffe was hanging out "off-duty" with some friends at Yankee Stadium when the call came in: go ask some of the Yankees about the issue. O'Keeffe tried to figure out who would be most likely to answer the question. He settled on Robin Ventura. Ventura responded, "I'm not touching this one with a ten-foot pole," and then turned and walked away. Ventura's response doesn't necessarily point to an unwillingness to discuss gay issues, but an unwillingness that many athletes share to say anything that could be construed as political. After *SI*'s infamous 1999 interview with Rocker, everyone saw what might happen if you said the wrong thing to the press.

Undaunted, O'Keeffe then tried Mike Mussina. O'Keeffe said Mussina prides himself on being one of the thinkers of the clubhouse. Although he may not be the proverbial rocket scientist, O'Keeffe said, Mussina is a smart guy. "The thing that I remember was asking him, 'Do you think you'll ever have a gay teammate?'" O'Keeffe recalled. "And I thought his response was really cool. He said: 'What makes you think I haven't already had one?'"

Also that year, O'Keeffe came face-to-face with the possible physical pitfall of asking athletes unwanted questions when he approached then New York Knick Mark Jackson with a question about Ernie Lorch, the founder of the Riverside Church Amateur Athletic Union (AAU) basketball program, which is one of the best AAU programs in the country. The program has produced such NBA players as Jackson, Chris Mullin, and Ron Artest. In 2002, former players started to come forward, accusing Lorch of molestation; he stepped down from his Riverside position that year. When the story was heating up, O'Keeffe asked Jackson if he had any insights into the charges. Mind you, he didn't ask him if he had been molested or if he was gay; O'Keeffe simply asked him if he had any information about it. "I thought he was going to put me through a locker," O'Keeffe remembered. "He got really angry about it."

What will stick in most reporters' heads of these three stories is the

Kevin Kiley and Chuck Booms were two of the first strong drivers of bringing gay content to sports radio. When *Kiley & Booms* was based in Washington, D.C., they had a weekly segment called "Gay Thursdays," in which they would bring a gay person on the show to talk about gays in sports. The most memorable appearance for Booms was two gay basketball players in Boston, Marc Davino and Steve Harrington. "Part of it was funny, in that they were telling us the names of some of the teams," Booms remembered. You can only imagine what those names might have been. "But then one of them told a story of having to go to his prom in high school when he knew darn well that he was gay, and having his father say, 'I think you're going to marry that girl,' so then it became really compelling, too."

When the show moved to Fox Sports Radio, they brought in Cyd, who did a weekly segment called "Cyd's Fag Five," in which he picked five NFL games against the spread. "I don't think there's any question we wanted to get people thinking," Booms said.

> We didn't want to force our beliefs on anyone; we just wanted to force the subject matter. And the saddest thing with homosexuals in this country is that, from the time they realize that they're gay to the time they come out, they have this horrible, hiding, incubation period that is incredibly uncomfortable, and it's not fair to expect any human being to live that way. We wanted to make sure that we dedicated some part of the show so that there wasn't that feeling anymore of having to hide. And it wasn't just targeted to the individual homosexual; it was families, brothers, sisters, because they're also told to be bottled up and not talk about it. We put it out there in a funny way, sometimes a serious way, but we always wanted to make sure the subject matter came off as normal. And by doing it that way, I think we affected a lot of people around the country who were left thinking, "Maybe I've been a little goofy about this for the last ten years."

one involving Jackson. Wanting to avoid being put through a locker by these players who are both potential sources for quotes and stories and also the icons they and their kids look up to, many sports reporters have come up with the ultimate excuse. "It doesn't matter if the guy's gay" has become the accepted professional cop-out for "I don't really want to know if the guy's gay."

And so the athletes and the reporters have created a nice symbiotic relationship surrounding the issue. The athletes need the reporters to stay in the headlines, and the reporters need the athletes because they want to keep their jobs; the athletes don't want to be asked about their sexuality, and the reporters don't want to ask.

What is curious, however, is why neither side wants to touch the subject. Why would a straight athlete be afraid of simply saying, "Gosh, good question. You know, I'm not gay, but thanks for giving me the chance to clarify that issue." And why are reporters scared to ask the question? It's the same reason many athletes don't want a gay player on their team: guilt by association. Even the simple question "Are you gay?" to an athlete can make him feel as though his manhood is being called into question. And if you somehow threaten the perception of his masculinity, you leave yourself open to being tossed (literally) into a locker.

Outsports repeatedly asks athletes and other sports professionals if they are gay, if only to get the question out there and get people in sports used to hearing and answering it.

Radio Opens More Minds

Radio is a slightly different story, and the biggest reason is the medium itself. The medium of radio, particularly talk radio, is more like the Internet than it is like television and print in that it is highly interactive. Sports talk radio offers listeners the opportunity to be heard and interact with newscasters and newsmakers. Callers with questions can ring the station and drive the topics of discussion; that means what's discussed isn't always planned, and those conversations can lead into uncomfortable waters for both the host and the interviewee.

Chuck Booms, the comedic, conservative half of the highly rated *Kiley & Booms* show, which ran on Fox Sports Radio until late 2002, said that the people who called into the show when they aired some of their gay content were generally either gay-positive or simply inquisitive about the issue. "Management and upper management were way more skittish than the general public," Booms said. "They thought advertisers would bail."

There are some real good guys in sports radio, and Dave Tepper, formerly of ESPN-Austin and now producing a sports show in Houston, is one of them. He's funny, warm, welcoming, gay-friendly—and it doesn't hurt that he's easy on the eyes, too.

Why are you so gay-friendly?

"I'm just an open-minded person. I think part of it comes from living so long in the Los Angeles area. Growing up, I had a lot of people pounding into my head what's right and what's wrong, and I just got real tired of it. I've just never had a problem with people in the gay community. If you've got a problem with gays and you're working in Los Angeles, you've got a big problem."

Have you found a lot of gay-friendly people in sports radio?

"No. I think a lot of people—the guys on our show are certainly open to the angle, but it's something they're not even aware of. They think sports are just something for the straight man."

Do you find a lot of homophobia at ESPN-Austin?

"I think you hear a lot more negative stuff about race than you do about sexuality. Austin is pretty open-minded. There's a pretty big gay community out here. And, if you don't like it, you'd better leave."

You've done a bunch of 'gay' programming on your show. Have you ever gotten push-back on it?

"There are a lot of problems and people asking, 'Why do this?' before, but everyone loves it after. I haven't had any problem with the callers or in the station; in fact, they generally call up and like it."

Radio is also much like the Internet in how much space it has to fill. The sports section of a newspaper is generally a dozen pages a day. *Sports Illustrated* might fill a hundred pages in a week (and half of that is ads). Even twenty-four-hour ESPN fills a lot of its time with repeats of *SportsCenter* and entertainment shows such as *The Contender*. Barring the broadcast of a game, sports talk radio stations have to fill twenty-four hours a day with sports news and discussions. That means that fewer topics can be taboo, including gay issues.

This isn't to say it's all love and roses. Although the topics broached by sports talk radio may be more diverse, so are the opinions expressed. It's not uncommon to hear uneducated, antigay rhetoric from hosts and listeners on sports talk radio; antigay language that might be subdued by an editor at a newspaper or on *SportsCenter* can make it on-air in radio.

Plus, whereas sports radio may be more open in terms of topics than other sports media, as Booms said, management can still be wary of gay topics, and gay-related programming can easily be quashed by the hosts, the producers, or management.

OUTSPORTS
Flashback
#8

MARCH 20, 2002

Out and Proud at the Worldwide Leader in Sports

Bill Konigsberg

I spent the last night of my ESPN career at a bar in Plainville, Connecticut, drinking beers with my soon-to-be ex-coworkers. It was a bittersweet experience.

On the one hand, I was sad to be leaving a place that had come to be like a second home to me. It was as if a part of my identity was being stripped from me, and I wondered how I would feel the next morning, when I was no longer an ESPN employee.

Not to mention very hung over.

On the other hand, it was a time for celebration. I was moving on to an exciting opportunity, as a writer at the Associated Press in Hartford. More important, I had accomplished a goal that had eluded me for so long: I had found a way to be Bill, the sports guy, and Bill, the homosexual, simultaneously.

It was a night for laughter. Early on, my buddies Woj, Rico, and

Wayne set about to teach me how to talk like a straight guy:

"Fuckin' A!" I repeated, mimicking Rico's inflection. "Nice rack."

"What else?" Woj asked.

"Um, hold on a sec . . . ," I responded. Focusing on the waitress, I scrunched up my face like it was hard for me to say. "Nice pooper?"

A roar of laughter enveloped our side of the table. Wayne wasn't buying my innocence on the subject. "Oh, right, like he's never thought that before."

At which point a geyser of beer came spewing from my nostrils.

Mature? Not quite. But what was so great about this evening is that it left me knowing for certain what I had suspected all along: I might be different, but whether or not I was gay didn't matter. Here I was living it up with my sports buddies, and I was one of the guys.

How did I get there? Not sure, really. Many people come out in far more conducive environments than ESPN, with far worse results. Somehow, it turned out great in this instance.

March 1999

It was my first month at ESPN, and I was constantly anxious. Not only was I trying to live a double life, but I was trying to do it while working in studio production as one of the guys who creates the highlight packages for *SportsCenter*. This was not the most sophisticated group of people I was working with. Mostly just out of college and male (there were about eight women out of more than one hundred employees), these guys constantly threw the word *fag* around the screening room, and everything that was lame, or bad, was called "gay." It was not the best place for me. I mostly stayed to myself and got the reputation of being a hardworking, quiet type. Ironic, since I'm more of a hedonistic loudmouth, but that's another story.

Cracks were forming in the façade. One day in the screening room we were talking about Jewish ballplayers. Steve Sax was named, as was Shawn Green. Now I've had many a speculative conversation about ballplayers before, but rarely has it been about their religious orientation.

"Gabe Kapler is gay," I said. It just slipped out. I'd meant to say, "Gabe Kapler is Jewish," but who says such things?

A couple of people looked at me quizzically.

" . . . and Jewish," I finished softly.

June 2000

I was now working in studio research, which meant I was one of the ten guys who created the "Did You Know?" and "Inside the Numbers" segments. I was much more comfortable with my surroundings by now, had plenty of friends, but I still wasn't open about being gay. My pal Todd was becoming a problem, because he always wanted to talk about girls. I'd put him off for nearly a year, and he was getting fed up.

"What are you, gay?" he'd say, a sneer on his face. Honestly, I don't understand why this was such an outlandish possibility, but to him I guess it was. Finally, to get him off my back, I changed the gender of my boyfriend, Richard. He became "Rachel" in a few conversations. I felt slimy, but I hoped it would get him to stop pestering me. It did.

However, a couple of things around that time pissed me off. First, in a meeting for the late *SportsCenter* broadcast one day, the Ladies Professional Golf Association (LPGA) came up. Trey Wingo, an anchor, started in on "the lesbian problem" in the LPGA, and how it was getting out of hand. Apparently, he was at an LPGA tournament one day when some woman was wearing a shirt that said "Yes I am!" and as he told us about her at the meeting, he said, "Yes, we know!" Someone asked him if there was "a gay problem" in the Professional Golf Association (PGA), to which he commented, "Of course not!"

Trey is a good guy, but I sensed he was a problem for me. When I'd work with him directly on a show, he had a tendency to say things to me like, "I love you, Koni," "You are so sexy," that type of thing. He was joking, but it bothered me because it hit a little close to home, and I wasn't sure if he was doing it because he thought I was gay or he thought I couldn't possibly be gay. I still don't know.

In a show later that week, Kenny Mayne did an auto-racing highlight, and at the end when the pit crew was celebrating, hugging each other, he said in that dry tone of his, "The pit crew. They're gay." I understood it was a double entendre, but something bugged me about the comment. What made it funny, of course, was the impossibility that a pit crew could be composed of gay people. And I was getting sick of hearing that.

I set up a meeting with the head of studio production to voice my concerns. I came out to him and told him that his department was a walking lawsuit. The word *faggot* was being thrown around with regularity, not to mention inappropriate comments on the air.

His answer was to set up sensitivity training. To me, nothing is more of a joke than sensitivity training, but I let it go. I began looking for work on the Internet side, and was hired there in August.

May 2001

I'd found a good home at ESPN.com. The people there were more sophisticated, I found, and I could see myself having a life there. I told two friends about myself, and they were supportive, and I was even playing softball in the company's day and night leagues (a perk of working at ESPN is that it's considered normal to play softball at eleven in the morning on a weekday on a regular basis).

On May 22, I read Brendan Lemon's article in *Out* magazine about his baseball-playing boyfriend, and it struck a chord with me. Have you ever had a moment in your life when everything turns on its head? In my mind, my life was fine, but I knew I could never mention my sexuality or my sports career would be history. In a split second, that all changed. What would happen if I just refused to lie anymore? Not that I was openly lying, but by not divulging an important truth, it felt that way.

I decided to see what would happen if I put myself out there in my truest form. The worst, I realized, would be that I'd find myself looking for work elsewhere. I decided to test my inner strength.

I wrote a column about what it was like to be gay in the world of sports. I wrote it lightning quick, in about ten minutes, and took it into the office of one of the senior editors. I said to him, "You're about to think I'm crazy. But I want you to read this." And I walked out. I came back ten minutes later, and he said unflinchingly, "I think we shouldn't change a thing."

That was the beginning of two days of craziness. There were phone calls to the head of the department, a lot of closed-door conversations, calls to public relations. I was asked, over and over, if I wanted to put myself through this. "I'm ready," I said.

This all sounds so silly to me now. I was an assistant editor, not a million-dollar athlete. But I kept hearing that it was something that would break new ground. Bring it on, I thought.

It was set to hit the front page of the site, in conjunction with a package on gays in sports that they'd built, at noon. The final conversation I had was with the department head, who sat me down that morning and told me to expect hate mail, hate calls, and possibly physical violence. I told him all I expected was their total support, and he said I had it. My two best friends took me to lunch, knowing that when we came back it would all be different.

More than one hundred e-mails awaited me when I returned. To my surprise and delight, every single one of them was positive. I'm not kidding. The first one I read was from my buddy Woj: "Great article Koni, that took some balls," it said. "Now on to important stuff: Are you gonna trade me Larry Walker or what?"

Another classic, from Andy, who sat a few cubicles away: "Nice ruse to get on the front page." I went over to him, and we shared a laugh, and I told him that I'd been trying to get on the front page for a long, long time. Management had turned down my "I'm tall" angle, I told him.

Many were from coworkers registering their surprise and offering me congratulations and support. Some friends told me they had never known anyone who was gay before. I reminded them, gently, that they had.

Surprise of surprises, I got a note from *SportsCenter* anchor Bob Ley. Because he's a staunch Republican, I'd certainly not expected much from him, especially since he had never been too friendly to me when we'd worked together. One of my first days there, I was reading a notice on a door leading to the newsroom, and he came up behind me and yelled, "Well? Are you gonna open the door or what?" He wrote me an e-mail congratulating me and praising my column as "the most eloquent he'd seen on the subject." He and I spoke several times after that, and I will always respect him for his supportive reaction.

One memorable note came from someone within the company that I didn't know. I was surprised he sent it, since I then had his name. It said something like, "Your article really meant something to me. I've been having trouble with my wife, and this put things in perspective for me." I assume he was telling me he was gay and about to tell his wife. I reached out to him with a reply but never heard back. Alas, he's probably just one of the incredible number of married gay guys in Connecticut. It's truly amazing the number of married men here looking for other men.

Hardly an Issue

Curiously absent: hate mail, hate calls, violence. Did I get looks in the cafeteria? Absolutely. But in my entire time at ESPN, including out on the softball field where anything goes, I never heard a negative word directly from anyone.

In the following weeks, a funny dichotomy formed. At ESPN.com it was hardly an issue, and it was business as usual. If anything, people seemed to feel closer to me. On the production side, however (both are located in the same complex in Bristol, Connecticut), it was another story.

Possibly because I was less outgoing for much of my time in production, possibly because television is a less "enlightened" place than is an Internet site, possibly because this particular group has existed since 1979 without a single out gay person in their midst, it was tense.

One day I was in the television newsroom, and Wingo came up to me. I was on edge, feeling very much as if everyone were peering at me (probably because they were). People who had always come up to me and said hello were suddenly not doing that. Trey walked up to me and put his hand on my shoulder. "Koni! Great article, buddy. That took some serious balls."

"Thanks man," I said.

"You know, one of my best friends is gay. He's great. We play golf all the time," he said.

"How nice for both of you," I thought. I'm mostly kidding. Really, I was grateful that he had come up to me and said what he did. That's the kind of guy he is, though. Even though he said some things that upset me at one time, I'll remember Trey as very good-hearted and warm.

From that point on, I was much, much happier at work, much more comfortable. I became the designated homo, meaning any gay political or watchdog group with an ax to grind came to me with their stories. That was a mixed blessing. It was nice to be able to help, but I hated feeling obliged to take an activist stance, since I'm hardly an activist. I took it on the chin and did my best to help people when I could.

The memorable moments are too many to list. Actually, I went weeks at a time without my sexuality coming up at work, which was fine with me. I was pleased, however, that I could make offhand comments from time to time, and heartened to know that my friends weren't enjoying Bill the Shadow Person, but Bill the Real Person. That made me very happy.

The final memory, other than the going-away party I mentioned earlier, was a pre-going-away party a few nights before. About ten of us were having dinner, and we were trying to organize what kind of pizzas to order. One was called the "Wooster St. King."

"Will you eat the king?" the wife of a friend asked me earnestly.

There's nothing like a good belly laugh with friends.

And yes, of course I would.

OUTSPORTS GUIDE TO ENTERTAINMENT

One of the first features Outsports ever ran was "The Ten Best Sports Films for Gay Guys." It wasn't a listing of films that dealt with gay issues in sports, but rather one reader's list of his favorite sports movies that had some added interest for gay men. Some simply satisfied the "hot" factor, whereas others were a bit more schmaltzy and tugged on the heartstrings.

It was Outsports's first really popular feature, and one that helped the community at Outsports grow quickly in its early days. Outsports readers wrote in with favorite sports movies of their own that they wanted to point others to.

The feature's popularity was no big surprise. Entertainment has long been a place gay men and lesbians call home. From the high school drama club to high-level Hollywood executive positions, entertainment is considered by many a "gay industry." It's partly because of the more open attitude of most people producing theater that gay people have flocked to entertainment like no other business and have developed screenplays. It's also in large part because of the power of entertainment to help lose yourself, forget about the fight you had with your boyfriend, and focus on the fictional football game being played out, to the hilt of the dramatic, in front of you.

For those people who aren't interested in sports, these movies can also be a great entrée into them. With vivid characters and dramatic or comedic story lines surrounding them, sports in movies are a lot easier to swallow for the gay people who want to have nothing to do with them. The intricacies of sports in movies are also generally toned down a bit to make them accessible to the broadest audience possible. Even if you don't know what "3rd and 5" means, the movie's characters will hold your hand and guide you all the way.

Mainstream Sports Movies for Gay Viewers

Although virtually none of these movies has gay characters, many of them have themes that gay people will find familiar. Whether it's Jamaicans in the Olympics or a woman in boxing, a man struggling to reconcile his life with the Church or two boys trying to win their father's acceptance, sports can be a microcosm for the same struggles gay people endure, and these movies are some of the best of those stories.

Bang the Drum Slowly (1973). A Major-League story of the friendship between a star pitcher (Michael Moriarty) and his favorite catcher (Robert De Niro) as they both cope with the sudden diagnosis of the catcher's terminal illness. There's a surprising amount of humor and lightheartedness in the film, and De Niro's award-winning performance is incredibly memorable.

Breaking Away (1979). Four friends in rural Indiana attempt to come to terms with life after high school; one of them, Dave Stohler, immerses himself in Italian cycling, picking up an Italian accent, shaving his legs, and even pretending to be an Italian exchange student. And none of that sits well with his father. A heartwarming coming-of-age story.

Bull Durham (1988). You'd think a movie about sex, sports, and poetry would be starring Jake Gyllenhaal and Heath Ledger. Instead, this classic sports comedy surrounding the then single-A baseball team the Durham Bulls follows a local vixen (Susan Sarandon) who attaches herself to a new rookie every season, this time glomming on to now-long-term partner Tim Robbins's character. The movie offers such pearls of insight as: tying a man to your bed and reading him Walt Whitman isn't a form of torture; it's foreplay.

Caddyshack (1980). Although it may be tough for anyone, gay or straight, to watch Rodney Dangerfield, this was his crowning glory. The screwball comedy about the brash new member of a country club and the destructive gopher has "drop-dead laughs" and is regarded by some as not only one of the great sports comedies of all time but one of the great comedies of all time.

Chariots of Fire (1981). Two athletes strive for personal glory in running for Great Britain at the 1924 Paris Olympics. The two boys must deal with discrimination and anti-Semitism as they chase their Olympic dreams. Winner of the 1981 Academy Award for Best Picture.

The Endless Summer (1966). The original great surfing movie, filmmaker Bruce Brown follows two surfers in search of the perfect wave in California, Hawaii, Australia, and other surfing hot spots around the globe. Complete with tons of toned male bodies wearing only a pair of soaking-wet board shorts.

Hoosiers (1986). In small-town Indiana in 1954, basketball is king, rumors spread like wildfire, and nobody likes a city-slicker coach whose tactics are unorthodox and whose compassion is sometimes ruthless, sometimes insane. Regarded by many as the greatest basketball movie of all time, it's chock-full of stereotype bashing and overcoming prejudice. It's hard not to cheer for the underdog in this flick.

The Natural (1984). The movie has been panned by many critics but remains a favorite for sports fans. About the resurgence of a once-forgotten ballplayer named Roy Hobbs, it has a sex scandal, cheating, Wilford Brimley being mean, a swelling score that you'll be whistling long after the end credits, and a home run for the ages. Oh, yeah, Robert Redford and Kim Basinger are hot, too.

North Dallas Forty (1979). The movie follows a Dallas professional football team (loosely based on the Cowboys of the 1970s) and its aging star, Phil Elliott (Nick Nolte). The story dives into the use of drugs, sex, and intrateam rivalries and offers a blueprint for how a sports team could go about getting rid of a gay player it didn't want.

A River Runs Through It (1992). For those who wanted to see more of Brad Pitt after *Thelma & Louise,* they got it a year later in *A River Runs Through It.* And long before the vistas of *Brokeback Mountain* swept audiences away, it was the images of rural Montana, shot on location, that viewers lost themselves in. With themes of religion and family strife, and starring a rebellious son (played by Pitt), it's easy to sink into this gorgeous movie. As an Outsports reviewer put it, it's "a marvelously moving movie about men."

Rudy (1993). A lot of movies go over the top with the underdog story. This one, based on a true story, tells it as honestly as possible, with one underdog kid just wanting to play a down for the Notre Dame Fighting Irish football team. Samwise—er—Sean Astin is also cuter and more likable than ever.

Slap Shot (1977). A slapstick comedy featuring Paul Newman, the movie follows a soon-to-be-defunct minor league hockey team and one player's struggle to save the franchise. The team is full of misfits, one man's wife is a lesbian, and there's enough gay dialogue to fill a John Waters movie. Incidentally, Newman made this movie shortly after he let his option on *The Front Runner* run out.

White Squall (1996). Okay, it's not the best movie in the world. But

Ridley Scott's high-seas yachting adventure has Scott Wolf, Ryan Phillipe, and about eight other young men running around shirtless and wet for half the movie: more eye candy than Chelsea's Eighth Avenue on a hot July day.

Gay Sports Movies

Although the list of great sports movies of gay interest could go on and on, the list of movies specifically about gays in sports, or even sports movies including gay people, is short. The dearth is, on the one hand, surprising. Movies thrive on the buildup of tension and drama—and throwing a gay basketball player onto a straight team and into a locker room has those things in spades.

Cyd's Top Five Sports Movies for Gay Fans

5. *Cool Runnings* (1993). It's Disney's broad comedy at its best, following the journey of the first Jamaican bobsled team to compete in the Winter Olympics, in 1988. As the Jamaicans train and race with constant barbs about how they don't belong, you see this movie is about a lot more than just racism. It's not often you find a sports movie that hits the theme of being an outsider as well as this film, and it does it with humor and poignancy.

4. *Field of Dreams* (1989). What gay man doesn't long for a closer relationship with his father? What man doesn't, for that matter? As the viewer follows Kevin Costner's Ray Kinsella in his search for answers, he finds himself wandering through his own life's struggles. Sometimes pooh-poohed as a sports movie, along Kinsella's journey is revealed a wonderful mystery encircling the dark, "ancient" history of baseball. And the ending is one of the great payoffs of all sports movies: "Build it and they will come."

3. *Bend It Like Beckham* (2003). Although there is only one small gay character in the movie, rumors abound in the story about two girls in love. In its own funny way, it tackles head-on the notion that if a girl plays soccer, she must be a lesbian. In the end, this feel-good flick about a girl living in a traditional Indian family in England, who just wants to

On the other hand, it's understandable. In Outsports's experience, it's been even harder to find a gay athlete who's working in the entertainment business than it is to find a straight man in West Hollywood. People write what they know about, and when gay people make movies, they're usually about coming out or someone in the arts. The most heralded of the genre, *Brokeback Mountain*, was put together by straight writers, a straight director, and straight actors.

There are certainly some very good sports movies made by gay people. But by and large, as with any sports movie created by people who don't fully understand the sport or who have not played it at a high level, the sports aspects of the movies are often a little lacking.

Yet there are a bunch of movies that do stand out for their stories, their

play soccer like gay icon David Beckham, is a testament to one person's will to overcome the prejudices and traditions of a past generation. Though you'll want Joe (Jonathan Rhys Meyers) to be the "surprise" gay character, don't get your hopes up.

2. *Remember the Titans* (2000). There was a time in America when it wasn't gays who weren't wanted in the locker rooms; blacks were the pariahs. This movie is based on the true story of a coach who broke that rule and a team that followed his lead. At a deeper level, it centers on a high school football team that turns prejudice on its ear, with strong themes of acceptance and brotherhood, and is as powerful as they come. It also features some great music and a cute kid from California who doesn't mind kissing other boys.

1. *Million Dollar Baby* (2004). "There's a magic in fighting battles beyond endurance. It's the magic of risking everything for a dream that nobody sees but you." I think every gay person can relate to that. Regarded as one of the best sports movies of all time, the 2004 Best Picture of the Year Oscar winner centers around a woman dedicated to boxing, and a sport that doesn't want her there. Gay Christians will find Frankie Dunn's (Clint Eastwood) internal struggle with the Church familiar territory.

characters, their performances, or even the occasional brilliant sports moments:

Beautiful Boxer (2003). A Thai film based on the true story of transvestite kickboxer Nong Toom, the story follows Toom from childhood, to teenage traveling monk, and then to powerful kickboxer hoping to earn enough money to become a woman.

Beautiful Thing (1996). On the outside, Jamie and Ste are nothing alike, except for living in the same run-down apartment building. Whereas Ste is a soccer jock, Jamie skips school to avoid sports. When they are thrown together, though, they find themselves hopelessly in love with one another. A true-to-life story about young teen romance.

Billy Elliott (2000). This British film, nominated for three Academy Awards, follows eleven-year-old Billy Elliott as he follows his love of ballet out of the boxing ring. Although there is little talk of Billy being gay, the hints are certainly dropped, culminating in the final scene of Billy, several years later, and another man performing Matthew Bourne's all-male version of *Swan Lake*.

Brokeback Mountain (2005). The most heralded film of 2005, the movie, which spans twenty years from the 1960s to the 1980s, chronicles the lives of two cowboys in love and their struggles to come to terms with their own feelings for one another and the lives they feel they must lead. Although there isn't a lot of actual sports participation in the movie, it is set against a backdrop of rodeo and fishing.

Broken Hearts Club (2000). Acclaimed director Greg Berlanti's first film centers around a group of West Hollywood friends who play on a softball team together. The movie is a testament to the power of friendship and the role a strong group of friends can play in the lives of gay people.

Cock & Bull Story (2003). The story of several "straight" men's struggle with society's homophobia and the secret desires locked inside of them. It's not the best movie in the world, but if you can stomach the violence, homophobia, and dreadful dialogue, it's got some hot boxers in just their briefs and shorts (unfortunately, the movie's star, Brian Austin Green, is not one of them) and does make a strong attempt to tackle what is behind homophobia in sports.

Get Real (1998). This coming-of-age story follows British prep school student Steve as he falls in love with the class jock, John, who is falling in love with Steve in return.

Guys and Balls (2004). A mildly entertaining story, but you just might cringe at how bad the soccer is. Still, the story of Ecki's (Maximilian Bruckne) banishment from his soccer team in Germany because he's gay and his attempts to put together a soccer team made up entirely of gay players has its moments.

The Iron Ladies (2000). A fun, whimsical look at the true story of a Thai male volleyball team that goes on to compete for the national championship. The catch: the team is almost entirely made up of gay men, transvestites, and transsexuals. It's a fun little romp whose tone is driven by the whimsy of Jung (Chaicharn Nimpulsawasdi), the transvestite who can't seem to stop smiling.

Like It Is (1998). Craig is a bare-knuckle fighter in Blackpool, England. Matt is a young music producer in London. When the two meet, sparks fly; but can their relationship withstand a litany of problems? The odds aren't on their side.

Maggie & Annie (2004). Life gets more complicated when Annie, married with a daughter, meets Maggie, athletic and openly gay, at softball practice. A night of dancing and, of course, drinking eases them into each other's arms.

My Life on Ice (2003). An exceptional foray into film vérité, this wonderfully charming movie follows young Etienne and his self-proclaimed "year of love." A figure skater, Etienne has to navigate his athletic endeavors, a close friendship with Ludovic (who is more interested in girls), his handsome teacher, his doting mother, and seeing them all find love before he does.

Personal Best (1982). One of the most well-known gay sports movies of all time centers on female runner Chris Cahill and her love affairs with her male coach and another female runner.

Ring of Fire: The Emile Griffith Story (2005). This compelling documentary tells the story of boxer Emile Griffith, who killed Benny "Kid" Paret in the ring in 1962 in response to Paret's prefight taunts of *maricon* (Spanish for "faggot"). Griffith does not acknowledge being gay in the documentary, but his comments and those from others seem to make it clear.

The Slaughter Rule (2002). Set in wintry Montana, the story follows a cute young football player (Ryan Gosling), who is cut from his high school team just days after his father's death. He's discovered by down-and-out six-man football coach Gid Ferguson (David Morse), who has a not-so-well-kept secret. When Gid falls for his player, everything changes.

Straight Acting (2005). A lively documentary about one man's journey to rugby manhood. Filmmaker Spencer Windes was inspired by the death of Flight 93 passenger Mark Bingham (the inspiration for the biennial gay rugby tournament the Bingham Cup) and decided to, despite being overweight and in bad health, take up rugby. The film also introduces the viewer to gay rodeo and some of the colorful faces in that sport.

Summer Storm (2004). This German movie about a young rower and his coming-out story doesn't exactly get the rowing right, but it nails the angst of coming out and being in love with your straight best friend. It focuses on young Tobi and his crew team, who must race a gay crew team from Berlin during summer camp. The reactions of the straight rowers to the gay rowers run the gamut of possibility, and it shows how people are willing to treat perfect gay strangers better than the people closest to them.

When Beckham Met Owen (2004). This Chinese movie follows the growing attraction between two thirteen-year-old boys, David and Michael, and their fascination with soccer and their English soccer-superstar namesakes, David Beckham and Michael Owen.

You'll Get Over It (2002). This wonderful coming-of-age story revolves around Vincent, a star swimmer on his high school team. When Vincent meets Benjamin, suddenly life, including the relationship with his girlfriend, gets more complicated.

Gay Sports Books

As with all gay stories, Hollywood is often reluctant to put millions of dollars behind gay sports movies because of the perception that only gay people would see them. Although several gay-themed movies—*Philadelphia*, *Brokeback Mountain*, *In & Out*, and *The Birdcage*—have found box-office success, there are still a surprisingly low number of gay and gay sports movies being produced.

Luckily, there are books. With a much lower financial investment, publishing companies have been allowing authors to tell their gay sports stories for decades. Although the must-see movies are driven by titles, the must-read gay sports books are dominated by a few authors who have immersed themselves in the subject.

Just as you could fill a warehouse with X-rated gay sports movies, the number of erotic books about gays in sports is huge. From personal accounts to personal fantasies, these books let readers explore that side of the locker room and sports that so many wouldn't half mind being a part of. Although there aren't as many mainstream books on the subject, many of those that are published are some of the best, most evocative works in gay literature.

None is more heralded than Patricia Nell Warren's classic, *The Front*

The 1974 publishing of Patricia Nell Warren's groundbreaking novel *The Front Runner*, about a gay runner who goes to the Olympics, was the first hugely successful foray into gay-sports entertainment. An estimated 10 million copies of the book have been sold worldwide.

Art courtesy of Wildcat International Press

PATRICIA NELL WARREN

the Front Runner

A NOVEL

THE MOST CELEBRATED
GAY LOVE STORY EVER
20th Anniversary Edition

Runner. The best-selling gay-themed novel of all time, with more than ten million copies in print, tells the story of up-and-coming gay distance runner Billy Sive and his quest for Olympic gold. Kicked off his track team, he and two of his friends find Harlan Brown, a distance coach at a small liberal arts college in New York. What transpires over eighteen months and three hundred pages is one of the great gay love stories ever told.

Warren has followed up her classic with two sequels, *Harlan's Race* and *Billy's Boy*. Another of Warren's gay sports novels, *The Wild Man*, follows a matador in Spain. Warren is also a featured columnist on Outsports and is the author of a regular series on the site about the history of gays in sports. Her in-depth look at athletes from Martina Navratilova to groundbreaking jockey John Damien was compiled in 2006 into *The Lavender Locker Room*, which chronicles three thousand years of gays in sports.

Another groundbreaking set of novels is Dan Woog's *Jocks* and *Jocks 2*. These books chronicle the stories of a couple dozen gay athletes from many sports and various levels of sport. Some of them are completely closeted, whereas others are completely out. Woog, an openly gay high school soccer coach in Westport, Connecticut, knows a thing or two about the plight of gays in sports and has been writing on the subject for years.

Randy Boyd has also been writing about sports for years. His award-winning novel *Uprising* revolves around three closeted celebrities, one of whom is a pro athlete, who are trying to kill a U.S. senator. *Walt Loves the Bearcat* is a fantastical story of one man's long-term love affair with a quarterback. Boyd is also a contributor to Outsports, writing mostly about basketball and racial issues, two subjects he has been immersed in all his life.

There is also an incredible group of biographies and autobiographies that are at the top of the must-read list for gay sports fans. The most important historically is *The David Kopay Story*, published in 1977 and reprinted in 1988 with a foreword by storied sportswriter and broadcaster Dick Schaap. The book is David Kopay's story of a tortured childhood, finding glory as a football player at the University of Washington, and nine years as a journeyman in the NFL during which he played for six different teams. While he was making headlines and earning a place in NFL history, he was struggling with his sexuality in private. From relationships with teammates to his marriage to a woman, the book has changed the lives of many who have read it.

One of those people is another former NFL player, Esera Tuaolo. Tuaolo's biography, *Alone in the Trenches*, follows much the same path as Kopay's story, along with a heavy dose of religion. But whereas Kopay's story ends with him alone, searching for something more, Tuaolo's book has a finality to it: not only does he have a "husband" and two kids, but they were the reason he came out in the first place.

The Front Runner Movie

The best-selling gay novel of all time is, as author Patricia Nell Warren likes to call it, one of the great movies that's never been made. Recently, however, particularly with the success of *Brokeback Mountain,* Warren has fielded an innumerable number of questions about the future of *The Front Runner* as a film, and her hopes have been raised that this groundbreaking novel will someday be a major motion picture. It has a rocky history, the option rights having been sold to Paul Newman in 1975 and then changing hands until 2002 when the rights came back to her. Warren said that the biggest stumbling block to the movie getting made is the budget. "It's not a low-budget movie," she said. Whereas *Broken Hearts Club* was about an amateur softball team that you could film on any baseball diamond in Los Angeles, *The Front Runner* is a film about the Olympics—and that kind of event, with its size and scope, costs money to portray. Still, with the success of *Brokeback Mountain,* which was made for about fourteen million dollars, the prospects are growing stronger that she will, in fact, finally get the movie made.

Pat Griffin's Strong Women, Deep Closets

Few lesbians in sports have been as open and brave for as long as Pat Griffin. For more than twenty years, she has been leading seminars for players, coaches, and sports administrators at universities across the United States. In *Strong Women, Deep Closets,* heralded as one of the most honest, most revealing portrayals of homophobia in women's sports ever written, she brings her incredible history as an athlete to bear: she played basketball and field hockey at the University of Maryland, she coached both sports at the high school level, she was a member of the 1971 U.S. Field Hockey team, and she won a bronze and a gold medal at the Gay Games in 1994 and 1998, respectively. Among her many other incredible projects, Pat is presently a consultant with the Women's Sports Foundation and has created a powerful program called It Takes a Team: Making Athletics Safe for Lesbian and Gay Athletes and Coaches.

One of the earliest gay-athlete biographies was *Big Bill Tilden: The Triumphs and the Tragedy.* Published in 1975, the book chronicles the tennis legend's rise as one of the first great tennis players and his fall from grace amid sexual scandal. Although forgotten by many of today's sports fans, Tilden is arguably the greatest openly gay male athlete of all time and was named to ESPN's Top 50 North American Athletes of the Twentieth Century. Set mostly in the 1920s and '30s, the book offers an insight into the homophobia of American culture long before the gay-rights movement.

Other popular biographies include Billy Bean's *Going the Other Way* and Eric Anderson's *Trailblazing: The True Story of America's First Openly Gay Track Coach.*

QUEER EYE FOR THE SPORTS GUY

Sports are a lot more than scores and statistics; sports offer everyone a way to connect to them, if they're willing to look. The Olympics with their hard-luck stories, shown in five-minute sepia-tone vignettes with sweeping scores and poetry written by Maya Angelou, which often engage even the strongest sports detractor, are the ultimate example. People living in Pittsburgh, when the Steelers are in the Super Bowl, find themselves inextricably tuning into their first football game of the year to see how their city's team fares. In today's media-hyped world of athletics, there are a lot of reasons to watch sports other than simply watching the sports.

When Cyd and Jim first created Outsports.com, many people looked at them with a cocked eyebrow when they said the site featured, among other things, mainstream sports "from a gay perspective." That could be a story that centers around sex (the Duke lacrosse rape case comes to mind), humor (everyone loves a good Terrell Owens pom-pom story), or flamboyant characters (such as NFL wide receiver Randy Moss).

And for many gay men and lesbians, part of experiencing sports from their own perspective is enjoying the physical beauty of the athletes while watching the competition unfold. Each sport offers something different to see, and a big part of that is driven by the uniforms that adorn the athletes.

The look and style of most sports' uniforms are driven by practicality. In sports, performance is king, and the attire draped on players is generally determined by a decision about what will best help the athletes achieve their best.

It's no coincidence that there's a direct reverse correlation between the perceived masculinity of the athletes in a sport and the amount of equipment—and what that equipment looks like—that the athletes wear.

It's hard to believe a time when goalies didn't have a mask protecting them from pucks flying at them. Though many gay men might prefer to see more of the players 'faces, they'd be seeing lots of black eyes and chipped teeth without the masks.

Photo by Ross Forman

Two of the more physical sports, both of which are deemed masculine sports by most of society, feature uniforms that include heavy padding and masks that turn each player into little more than the number on the back of his jersey. The equipment for both hockey and football has developed over the years to reflect the increasing brutality of the respective sports and the growing strength and speed of the men playing them. It's too bad, really. The men who play these two sports are some of the most handsome of all athletes; to be covered up by all of that padding, with all the TV cameras zooming in for close-ups, is unfortunate.

It's the face masks, though, that are the most prohibitive, though very necessary, piece of equipment. Search Google in hopes of finding a picture of the face of most any professional football player or hockey player, and odds are the best Google will come up with is a mug shot (photographed, clearly, by a straight guy) from the league's web site. You'll get a lot of pictures of them with their face masks on, but a picture of NFL wide receiver Brandon Stokley's handsome mug is harder to find than a good quarterback on the Chicago Bears.

The Gay Softball World Series is one of the premier events on the gay sports calendar. The North American Gay Softball Organization includes 50 leagues in 35 cities in the U.S. and Canada.

Photo by Brent Mullins

A member of the Cardiff Lions kicks the ball away against the Washington Renegades in Bingham Cup 2006.
Photo by Cyd Zeigler Jr.

This flag football player from San Diego can get changed and make a phone call at the same time. He participated in Gay Super Bowl III in Boston.
Photo by Brent Mullins

This professional beach volleyball player shows his athleticism at an Association of Volleyball Professionals event on the beaches of Southern California.

Photo by Brent Mullins

This rower guides his boat at the Montreal Outgames 2006.

Photo by Cyd Zeigler Jr.

Sprinter Stefan Tärnhuvud from Sweden awaits the passing of the baton during a relay at a 2006 meet between Sweden and Finland in Helsinki.

Photo by Olavi Kaljunen

Members of the Hungarian water polo team celebrate a world title at the 2004 men's finals in Long Beach, California. The photo gallery from the event, showing elite players from six nations, was the most viewed in Outsports history.

Photo by Brent Mullins

An Italian water polo player surveys the scene at the 2004 world finals in Long Beach.

Photo by Brent Mullins

A player at the Long Beach event during warmups. Water polo is a fast-paced and intense game with much of the action happening under the water. Players wear two pairs of trunks since they often will lose a pair when the action gets hot and heavy.

Photo by Brent Mullins

Petar Mrcela from Croatia at the 2006 European Short Course
Swimming Championships in Helsinki, Finland. The event brings
together the elite swimmers from Europe.

A player performs a uniform check on a teammate during the 2005 International Rugby Board Sevens tournament in Carson, California. While this mainstream event is popular, the sport is also growing in the gay community.

Photo by Brent Mullins

Of course, it's hardly a fashion statement the players in these sports are trying to make; they're looking to stay safe. Hockey players used to never wear masks. They didn't even exist for years after the game was invented. And even after they had been created, players argued that the masks obstructed their view, and, hey, they were tough guys; they didn't need no stinking protective masks.

With all the machismo melting the ice in hockey, it's no big surprise that the person credited for being the first hockey player to wear a mask was a female goalie from Queen's University in Ontario, Canada, Elizabeth Graham, who in 1927 put a fencer's mask on to defend herself. That's right: before Graham had the good sense to put a mask on, even goalies with pucks whizzing past them opted to play without anything protecting their faces. What might be even more shocking is that, even after 1927, goalies in the NHL didn't wear masks regularly until Montreal Canadiens goalie Jacques Plante decided that his broken nose, jaw, and skull were enough and first donned one in 1959! Even hockey players figured out, at

Sports jerseys, hats, and uniforms are big business. Not only do the apparel companies know it, but marketing executives at pro teams and colleges know it, too. It's the number-one reason the need for stylish, highly marketable logos and uniforms is so huge in sports. Every year, professional and collegiate teams take a hard look at their look and assess what they can do to sell more merchandise. It often takes the form of slightly changing the team's uniform or logo. It's so common and such a big business that ESPN.com's Page 2 has a columnist, Paul Lukas, devoted to tracking uniform changes in his "Uni Watch."

NFL rules allow for a uniform change every five years. Good thing, otherwise teams would likely change the expensive jerseys of their favorite players every time they signed a high-priced rookie. Although teams have a "home" uniform and an "away" uniform, the NFL allows teams to use a third uniform style in two games per year, an option that many teams, looking to get a third jersey on the market, exercise.

The NFL isn't the only league looking to add new merchandise to the shelves. In the NBA, for example, the Los Angeles Lakers several years ago introduced a new white uniform, in addition to their yellow-home and purple-road unis, that they wear only in home games on Sundays.

some point, that it's not so easy to pick up chicks when you're missing two teeth, have a broken nose, and you're sporting a black eye.

Football players, too, once ran into one another at full speed without something to protect their faces. Until 1951, face masks weren't even legal in college football; that's more than seventy years after the first American-style college football game was played. Though the utility is clear, college football would be even more watchable for many gay men if the fit twenty-year-old players didn't have plastic bars obstructing our view of them.

Luckily, no other sport is as confining to the spectator's eyes as hockey and football. In fact, some of them are downright revealing.

The Tighter the Better

The bikini swimsuit, known by many people as simply a "Speedo," in this country is the ultimate gay athletic wear. Speedo is simply the brand name for the most popular men's bikini, but, as a photocopy has long been called a Xerox and tissues are known simply as Kleenex, the brand name has stuck to represent the whole range of swimsuits that most straight men wouldn't be caught on the same beach with.

Unfortunately for the lookiloos, the demand for full-body racing swimsuits (left) has increased.

Photo by Cyd Zeigler Jr.

Although straight men in much of the rest of the world have made these "banana hammocks" their swimwear of choice, most straight guys in the United States wouldn't go near them. However, with the growth of metrosexuality, the recent phenomenon that has more and more straight men caring for their bodies and dressing with the fashion sense of gay men, the attitude toward the show-all swimwear is changing a little, as some men are starting to don tight square-cut swimsuits. But the Speedo, which lets everything hang out and most clearly defines the shape and size of the package it holds, is still off-limits for most American men.

It's understandable why so many straight men are a little scared of the Speedo: wearing one does take a little extra work. Even a guy with a decent-size gut can look okay in a pair of board shorts. But you put the same guy in a Speedo and wham: people start moving their blankets away, looking the other direction. It gets ugly.

Although any half-naked body looks better when it's been pumping iron and burning body fat regularly, to look good in just a few inches of stretchy fabric, a body with sub–15 percent body fat is quite nearly a must.

Thankfully nothing will ever fully replace the classic "Speedo" (here worn by gay former Rutgers swimmer Sean Smith).

Photo by Cyd Zeigler jr.

Although male athletes for years have put up this more-masculine-than-thou front, many of them are now finding they can get more attention—and probably get more chicks—if they style their hair a bit and use moisturizer. Many athletes in recent years have also found that, in an era when marketing and commercialism are more powerful than ever before, with more media outlets popping up every day, looking good in front of a camera can pay big rewards. Some of them at the forefront of metrosexuality, who have been able to cash in on their good looks and sense of style, have included:

British soccer star *David Beckham,* whose hair is more talked about than his bending kicks, and whose wife happens to be singer-cum-fashion-designer Victoria "Posh Spice" Beckham.

Dimming tennis star *Andy Roddick* is one of those rare break-through athletes who is able to grab the admiration of straight guys for his athletic prowess and the attention of straight women and gay men with his style, his smile, his hair, and his willingness to take his shirt off.

Derek Jeter. The most popular man in New York sports is all Bronx when he's playing baseball, but the SoHo in him comes out when he hits the town. Stylish with perfectly manicured eyebrows, he's the toast of the Big Apple even though he no longer has Mariah Carey on his arm.

To be sure, not every gay man opts for a Speedo when hitting the pool. But whether they wear Speedos or not, it's hard to argue that most don't like watching fit men swimming, diving, or walking around the pool in them. Sure, there's something to be said for leaving a little to the imagination, but there's also something to be said for seeing a lot of skin on a beautiful specimen with a well-contained package.

In the past few years, the beauty of the Speedo has been under attack in the swimming world. Companies (including Speedo, unfortunately) have developed longer form-fitting shorts and leggings that many are claiming make the body flow more smoothly, thus more quickly, through the water. Swimmers from high school to world-class have jumped on the new swimwear. Australia's Olympic gold medalist Ian Thorpe was one of the first to adorn not only the leggings but also a full-body suit. Others such as American Olympic gold medalist Michael Phelps have oscillated between the longer swimwear and the short bikinis, with Phelps even appearing on the cover of *Time* wearing nothing more than revealing Speedos.

The divers have avoided the trend toward covering up. Diving, of course, is very different from swimming, particularly in the way victory is won. Whereas success in swimming depends solely on an athlete's ability to swim a certain distance faster than everyone else, diving is a judged sport, and presentation is key. Gay men can take solace knowing that diving judges, and probably divers themselves, think the smaller Speedos are more sexy than their longer cousins; for the sake of a few hundredths of a point, divers won't be donning Lycra pants or full-body suits anytime soon.

Water sports aren't the only ones with Lycra-based uniforms. A bunch of sports feature skin-tight outfits in hopes of cutting down wind resistance. It's hard to believe that a runner sprinting halfway around a track might reduce his time by dropping the shorts and slipping into a one-piece that might as well have been painted on. Although most distance runners have opted to keep the shorts (you really can't argue that the time of a two-mile run around the track, often won by several seconds, would be affected by cutting down a little wind resistance), sprinters have almost all taken to the tightest uniforms imaginable.

No sport is more homoerotic than wrestling. The skin-tight uniforms and the positions competitors end up in certainly contribute to that.

Photo by Cyd Zeigler jr.

There are some notable exceptions to the idea that athletes in more "masculine" sports wear more equipment—and, again, it's always for utility.

Few sports are viewed as more rough-and-tumble (quite literally) than wrestling. Generally regarded as the oldest sport in the world, it features men grabbing one another, tossing each other around, and mounting each other like they were in a porn video. And all they wear to separate themselves is a singlet that's tighter than a Hulk Hogan full nelson.

Australian Rules football just might have the gayest uniforms in all of sports. Although seeing the packages kept firmly in place by bikini swimsuits and other form-fitting uniforms of crew and track is great, Aussie Rules football sets itself apart with sleeveless shirts that any muscled hunk would be proud to wear down Santa Monica Boulevard.

Even übermasculine football does feature skin-tight pants in part to give potential tacklers less to grab onto.

The Iconic Jockstrap

Probably no single piece of athletic wear is more iconic of the athlete than the athletic supporter, or jockstrap. The jockstrap was invented in 1874 by a man named C. F. Bennett to offer some much-needed support for bicycle messengers traveling over Boston's cobblestone streets. Bennett went on to create what became the Bike Company, which is the industry leader in jockstrap manufacturing.

Jockstraps were the forerunners to the briefs, which most recreational athletes today use for support. But briefs don't offer all of the protection that jockstraps can. Many jockstraps are designed to hold a

In a sport that is often decided by tenths of a second, rowers wear some of the most form-fitting uniforms in sports.

Photo by Cyd Zeigler jr.

hard cup that slides into a front pouch and gives further protection to the family jewels.

For sports, they became an obvious fit. For running and tennis and other noncontact sports, the jockstrap prevented the bouncing around of certain balls that just don't feel great when they're being jostled over the course of a two-hour run or match. Today, most athletes engaging in non-contact sports forego the jockstraps for the supportive briefs, though some do still prefer the jockstraps, as they keep everything in place a little better than the briefs.

For contact sports, it's a whole other "ball game." The ability of a jock-strap to hold that supportive cup is key for those athletes who are being pushed, shoved, jumped on, and tackled. Many football, basketball, soccer, rugby, and hockey players wouldn't be able to get through a couple of games without collapsing to the ground in agony without that hard-plastic cup. Although it's a coincidence that the jockstrap was created in the same year that the first college American-style football game, between Harvard and McGill in 1874, took place, it isn't a coincidence that the creation of the jockstrap, along with other padding, allowed the game to become more violent and hard-hitting than otherwise would have been possible.

Athletic supporters aren't just for guys. Women have what is commonly called a jillstrap. Although the men's version is in part for comfort, keeping things from bouncing around (just as women's sports bras do for them), the jillstrap's function is exclusively protection, as there's not much to keep in place there.

Basketball's Changing Hemline

In possibly no sport have uniforms changed as much over the past twenty years as in basketball, but then, few sports' cultures have changed as much as basketball, either. When you see footage of Larry Bird and Magic Johnson lighting up the scoreboard in the 1980s, you'd swear they have a camel toe, the shorts are so short. Whether it was flattering or not, the players in college and professional basketball wore their hair longer than their shorts.

But in the early 1990s, as the era of Magic and Bird waned, the culture of basketball shifted as well. Instead of college graduates and corn-fed boys from the Midwest, young men from the inner cities, and increasingly some with no college education whatsoever, began dominating professional basketball. The hairstyles got shorter, and the shorts got longer. In the early 2000s, some teams started abandoning the standard tank top for tops that looked almost like sleeveless tees, offering a bit more cover for the shoulders. The more homoerotic-fearing urban culture has, like its signature clothing lines Fubu, Sean John, and Phat Farm, demanded more cover for the brothers.

Women Get Loads of Eye Candy

Although there's certainly plenty of eye candy in sports TV for gay men, it's the lesbians who get catered to. Lucky for them, they have the same objects of their affection as straight men—and straight men are the direct target market for most sports, sports networks, and their advertising campaigns.

It's no accident that the uniform for women's beach volleyball has devolved into the bikini, and FOX and NBC, which broadcast some women's beach volleyball tournaments during the summer, couldn't be happier. They have developed advertising campaigns highlighting the scantily clad women diving after balls in the sand.

Women tennis pros show off plenty of leg, as most wear skirts so short they may even be illegal in a Hooters restaurant. Just as men's uniforms are largely designed for utility, these short skirts allow the women to move laterally as freely as possible, and many lesbians aren't complaining.

Unfortunately for women seeking equality in sports, this is how they're often marketed: as sex symbols first, athletes second. Although it's a shame that female athletes are not taken more seriously as athletes, it's a problem many gay men wish male athletes had: being forced to show off their bodies to sell tickets. But as long as straight men are the target market for most sports, that's not going to happen anytime soon.

The NFL (No Fun League)

Although each sport has its standard uniform, each team and player adds their own colors and personal style to the basic uniform—some more successfully than others.

With such a variety of uniforms worn in different sports, it should be no surprise that sports gear is a popular focus for many fetishists. From wrestling singlets to dirty socks to used jockstraps, there seems to be a fetish involving some form of sports apparel for everyone.

NFL Coaches Back in Black

The best fashion statement of 2006 wasn't Johnny Weir's "Camille," it was San Francisco 49ers head coach Mike Nolan in a suit. The NFL has long mandated that all coaches wear league-approved attire on the sideline of games. Until 2006, the league had failed to approve any suits because Reebok, with whom the NFL has a partnership, did not make suits. But after Nolan petitioned the league for two years to wear a suit, Reebok came up with one. "It's the league's call," Nolan said. "They tell me what I wear and when I wear it. I just hope they don't put me in a Speedo." Jacksonville Jaguars head coach Jack Del Rio followed suit (pun intended) later that weekend.

It's hard for most team athletes to venture away from the team uniform. The NFL (called by some the No Fun League) is notorious for fining athletes who stray away from the designated uniform. It's so common, they have an official policy on it: generally, the first uniform offense is a fine of five thousand dollars; the second is ten thousand dollars.

- In 2002, the NFL fined Philadelphia Eagles wide receiver Shawn Dawkins for wearing black shoes in a game instead of white ones (which he couldn't find before the game started).
- Also in 2002, the NFL fined Atlanta Falcons quarterback Michael Vick for wearing red socks that showed above his white socks. The NFL rescinded the fine after some embarrassing public relations on the issue.
- In 2005, the NFL fined Washington Redskins running back Clinton Portis for wearing dark socks and shoes. His fine was twenty thousand dollars, ostensibly five thousand for each sock and each shoe.
- In 2006, the NFL fined then-rookie New Orleans Saints running back Reggie Bush for wearing Adidas cleats during a preseason game. The NFL allows players to wear only Nike or Reebok (guess with whom the league has lucrative contracts).

Individual-Sport Athletes Break Out

In individual sports, athletes are more able to show off their own personal style. Clay-court specialist and French Open champion Rafael Nadal has raised eyebrows with his choice of match attire. Several players in recent years have foregone sleeves for a little more freedom in their swings, and, as added benefit, everyone watching gets to see a bit more of their bulging biceps. But Nadal looks more like a twink on Chelsea's Eighth Avenue when he dons the sleeveless tee with his odd choice of Capri pants. Will Leitch of Deadspin. com hit the nail on the head when he wrote after Nadal's 2006 French Open championship, "I just can't support a guy who wears his sister's pants."

Jesper Parnevik has certainly made a name for himself in golf, and not just for his solid play. The Swedish golf pro can often be spotted on the golf greens from three counties away thanks to his Day-Glo pants. Although Parnevik's choices sometimes include sunshine yellow or lime green, it has been his hot-pink pants that have gotten him the most attention. Add to those his funky checkered sweater vests and his baseball caps with the bill turned inside out, and you'd assume he was blind—if he couldn't hit a green in regulation. It shouldn't be a surprise that Jesper is the son of Bo Parnevik, who is a legendary comedian in Sweden. Dad's sense of humor apparently rubbed off on his son a bit more than the fashion industry would have liked.

Red Is the New Black

For decades, sports teams had two uniforms: one was white (or very light), and the other was dark and representative of their team or school colors (for example, purple for the Los Angeles Lakers, cardinal red for USC, dark blue for Georgetown). However, many teams in the past ten years have been abandoning their school colors when they select their dark jerseys and opting for black. When Duke basketball adopts it (which they have), you know it's already come and gone. Still, team after team, particularly in basketball, is coming out wearing black. The decision for many has been to look more "intimidating" on the court or the field, but

In 2006, the NFL changed the uniforms of its referees in part to give them a more distinctly NFL look. Unfortunately for the league, many have quipped that they now look more like jockeys than officials.

THE FLATTERING POSERS

Although Outsports.com started in November 1999 as a place for its two founders to talk about the NFL, it took only a couple of weeks for new readers to start asking for more features. The request sent in the most was for an interactive area of the web site where athletes could meet other athletes.

Outsports quickly developed "The Clubhouse," where people could post information about themselves and their sports interests and where members could find other men and women to play basketball and watch hockey with, whether it was as friends or in an effort to develop something more.

But it isn't just athletes who want to meet and date athletes. Other than people of very particular interests, you don't hear many people, in the general public or gay community, say, "Gosh, it would be so hot to find a Sondheim fan to date," or "I had this incredible dream last night of sex with a delectable pastry chef." It is the bedding of an athlete, with a toned body and a winning attitude, that has come to be the ultimate conquest in today's gay culture.

That fantasy has made being an athlete, or being perceived as an athlete, a hot commodity. Athletes and nonathletes alike spend a lot of time, money, and energy building up appearances of a track-sprinting, ball-catching, route-running, pass-throwing jock.

The A&F "Jock"

Cyd remembers his single days and one particular "jock" at the gym. Gorgeous. Looked like an Abercrombie & Fitch jock; dressed like an Abercrombie & Fitch jock. For months, Cyd had wanted to talk to him, and one day he finally got his chance.

They were both working out their upper backs, and he was on a machine that Cyd wanted to use. Aw, shucks. Cyd went up to him between sets and asked if he could work in. Not only did a purse fall out of his mouth, but so did a compact, a pair of high heels, and a bottle of Nair.

Not to be daunted by his voice and sudden feminine mannerisms (Cyd had, in fact, dated several guys in the past who would fit much better in *A Chorus Line* than on a football team), Cyd marched on, working in between the A&F jock's sets. Cyd had played gay football for

How to Go from Poser to Player in Three Easy Steps

You've already got the body, the looks, and the gym clothes, now take the next step and become a jock. Here are three things you can do to jump-start your transformation:

1. Dive into a sport. Although weight lifters and runners can certainly be athletes, neither "lifting" nor "running" makes you a jock—these are everyday occurrences that even our moms do. From tennis or ice hockey to basketball or football, there are a lot of options you have to back up your outward jock persona. Learn the rules, learn the big names and best teams of the sport, and don't just watch other people play it; take to the field or court yourself. Even if you're not very good, if you're playing, you're a jock.
2. Educate yourself on nutrition and fitness. Beyond just looking good, jocks build their bodies for health purposes and to perform better in their sport. Part of that is not just taking to the gym floor and following the instruction of a trainer but also learning how your body works, what to do to improve how it functions, and why to do it.
3. Diversify your training. Just hitting the gym and lifting weights won't make you a jock. Cross-training, involving both short- and long-distance running, swimming, biking, and footwork drills, is something that many great athletes take advantage of and will fine-tune your body and your skills into that of a true jock.

With bodies like this, it's easy to see why the jock image is so sought-after by gay men. This Gay Games athlete certainly had reason to go shirtless.

Photo by Brent Mullins

several years, and he knew there were plenty of nelly queens who could dunk on his ass. So Cyd kept admiring the guy's strong legs, partially covered by his shorts; his biceps, bulging out of his tank top; and his beautiful blond hair, barely visible beneath his cap. The tank top said "Abercrombie & Fitch Football." Seeing the opportunity, Cyd asked him, "Do you play football?"

"No, I just liked the shirt."

And don't think for a second that it wasn't the word *football* and all of the tough, hard-hitting images it conjures that were the real reasons the guy liked the shirt.

There's nothing wrong with wanting to be thought of as an athlete. In fact, genuine athletes find it quite flattering. Sure, it's a little disappointing to think you've found another gay jock only to find out he's a poser. But in a gay culture that puts so much emphasis on what's on the outside and so little focus on what's on the inside, it's not a big surprise that gay men and lesbians might put on some of the muscles and wear the clothes of an athlete with little else to back it up.

The fact is, athletes are revered in our society. They are put on a pedestal for their athletic ability, their beautiful bodies, their "bling bling," and even their intelligence (some more than others).

At an early age, kids (and not just American children but those from around the world) learn just what it means to be considered an athlete. At the high school level, and even earlier, they see that the kid who catches the game-winning touchdown or hits the championship-clinching home run is made into an instant celebrity by the school and locals. And maybe most important, he gets all the sex he wants with whomever he chooses.

In college, the big men on campus aren't the drama students or the ones on the dean's list. The students everyone is talking about are the ripped, handsome athletes who show up on the front pages of newspapers and whom ESPN commentators Chris Berman and Dick Vitale are anointing with clever nicknames.

Our culture worships athletes like the Greeks once worshiped the gods. Is it any big surprise that gay men, like so many others from high school students to business executives to construction workers, see the social value of being seen as an athlete, or at the very least associated with sports?

Consider the fact that athletes and sports have long been dubbed "off-limits" to gay men. The notion of sports and the gay community mixing has been around only since the 1970s and started to become truly accepted by the public only in the late 1990s (and, in truth, many pockets of society still fail to recognize the gay sports nexus). The idea of a gay man somehow getting in the pants of a real red-blooded athlete had long been thought impossible. This "forbidden fruit" for gay men has added to athletes' allure and their sexual appeal, just as that "hard-to-get" buxom blonde is near the top of most straight men's wildest fantasies.

It plays back into the cult of masculinity that has dominated civilization for millennia and has been firming its grip on American gay culture more and more in recent years. What better way to raise your stock in that culture than build up some biceps, throw on a Steelers tank top, and learn the meaning of terms such as *free safety* and *offensive line*? The easiest way to pass the "no fats, no fems" test on so many Gay.com personal ads? Hit the gym and buy a South Carolina 'Cocks hat.

Still, while investing all that time and energy to look the look, the posers miss out on all of the fun of sports. From the exciting games to the camaraderie to the positive self-worth catching a touchdown or watching your favorite team win the big one brings, there's a lot more to being a jock than just sporting the muscles, the muscle T, the Nike Airs, and the mesh shorts.

THE RUMOR MILL

Outsports has a policy to never out an athlete. Coming out is a big step in someone's life; for a public figure to do it, it can be overwhelming, and for someone in sports to do it, well, according to many straight players, it can be career altering. Although Outsports has certainly been among the first, if not the first, to report on some athletes being gay, Outsports has never done so without their consent or without it being reported in other venues. This policy has allowed Outsports to talk with some athletes who might otherwise be wary of talking to the press

Brendan Lemon

My sense of the world of pro athletes who are gay or bisexual is much less black-and-white than it used to be. So much of the attention to gay pro athletes has been, "who's gay, who's gay," and my experience of them has been much less categorical. I'm not saying that every team sports athlete I know who has slept with men is bisexual. But my perception of it, my personal experience of it, is much more bisexual than what gay sports fans might want to hear.

Sports are very much about yes or no, black or white, won or lost. And I think that mentality carries over to sexuality, it's very much either or. And for most athletes I know who have been expressive or open or had experiences sexually, that's not how it works for them. Of the gay or bisexual pro athletes that I've met or know, about half of them are married to women or they have girlfriends. And that's something that neither the gays nor the Middle American sports fan wants to think is true.

about their sexuality. Outsports will always respect each individual's choice to come out how and when he or she chooses.

It might be tempting if a videotape surfaced of John Rocker in a compromising position—for someone to have spewed venom about gay people and then turn out to be gay themselves, that would be a story not even Outsports could resist. But, barring that, Outsports won't be following the lead of Perez Hilton and other gay bloggers in deciding when it's the right time for other people to come out.

That doesn't stop some others in the sports media, and many fans, from talking about the rumors of who's gay. When David Kopay came out in the mid–1970s, it was widely accepted that no one in sports was gay. Now, thirty years after Kopay's revelation, the rumors about pro athletes being gay are too numerous to detail in a single chapter. Most of these rumors are either based on a loose set of facts run through sixty degrees of separation or very active imaginations—hardly the kind of rumors to be dealt with here.

Outsports certainly talks about rumors, too. When something is being openly discussed in the public, it would be foolish for the World-wide Leader in Gay Sports to not comment on it. However, there's a big difference between discussing a rumor and outing someone: the former is usually based on conjecture, the latter on personal information. Saying "Hey, the friend of my hairdresser's sister told me Troy Aikman's gay" isn't outing him (in fact, it's likely just wishful thinking). Claiming "I slept with Troy Aikman, and I know him to be gay" is a whole other matter.

Wishful Thinking

We have gotten e-mail after e-mail, question after question, from gay men all over the world asking, hoping, praying that their favorite athlete is gay. It seems like Outsports has heard a random, baseless rumor or gotten a question about virtually every single elite white male athlete who's at least semiattractive, and Outsports has heard rumors about many elite black, Asian, and Hispanic athletes, too. Because many people still have the antiquated notion that every woman who plays sports is a lesbian, Outsports has heard plenty of rumors about female athletes as well. Interestingly, though, the rumors about women seem to come with a tone of a little less titillation and a little more fact.

There is no reason to believe any of the wishful-thinking rumors heard about any of a host of professional athletes including football players Brian Urlacher, Peyton Manning, and Joey Harrington; tennis players Jan-Michael Gambill and Rafael Nadal; basketball players J. J. Redick and Mark Madsen. Some of these men may be gay. However, the adage that "He's too hot to be straight" simply doesn't hold water.

With that said, it's certainly no crime for gay people to hope that the

Odds on Who's Gay

In October 2005, on the heels of Sheryl Swoopes's announcement that she is gay, Oddjack.com offered up its odds for five athletes to be the next prominent male athlete to come out of the closet:

*Kordell Stewart,*former NFL quarterback, is the subject of some of the most-discussed gay rumors in all of sports. Odds: 1/5 (and, as Oddjack.com said, a "prohibitive favorite").

Tony Stewart, NASCAR driver, has been rumored to be gay, and rumored to have had a gay relationship before he began driving, for years. Odds: 3/1.

Bruce Chen, MLB pitcher, was rumored to be the boyfriend of Brendan Lemon. Odds: 6/1.

Mike Piazza was the centerpiece of a gay rumor printed by the *New York Post.* Odds: 8/1.

Peyton Manning, Indianapolis Colts quarterback, has been very chummy with oft-rumored country singer Kenny Chesney. Odds: 14/1.

The great snarky sports blog Deadspin also asked its readers which of these five athletes was the most likely to come out first. The tally:

1. Kordell Stewart, 27.3 percent
2. Mike Piazza, 26.4 percent
3. Peyton Manning, 23.8 percent
4. Tony Stewart, 14.4 percent
5. Bruce Chen, 8.1 percent

Some of the write-in names for Deadspin's poll: NFL quarterback Jeff Garcia, Chicago White Sox manager Ozzie Guillen, former MLB players Brady Anderson and Todd Zeile, and NASCAR driver Jeff Gordon.

athlete they've had their eye on for some time is actually willing and available to them. After all, most of these rumors have no foundation in reality and are the innocent whims of men and women who simply have too few role models and gay objects of their affection. Some have had a brief encounter with an athlete and are convinced that the athlete they saw gave

Jim Buzinski, August 12, 2004

Terrell Owens should be the last guy inferring that someone is gay. He fits several gay stereotypes: He's single and flamboyant and totally obsessed with his body. He loves parading around during practice clad in form-hugging Lycra warm-up clothes even in the coldest of weather. He also did the gayest thing I ever saw on a football field when he shook pom-poms after scoring a touchdown in 2002. I wished the *Playboy* writer had asked Owens if he ever went on the down-low.

them "a look," or the athlete was seen coming out of a gay dance club, or the person has a friend who swears he hooked up with so-and-so. Some of these are true; most are not. Weeding through the good and the bad is impossible.

It's only been the past ten years that these gay rumors about athletes have become increasingly present. As more and more athletes have come out, our culture's acceptance of the fact that gay men and women are playing sports at an elite level has turned into speculation of who's sleeping with the quarterback, and more and more people are talking about it.

Probable Actions

One of the more common rationalizations for thinking an athlete is gay is based on "probable actions." There can be absolutely no basis for many of these rumors other than a single infamous incident, an athlete's mannerisms, or his personal grooming.

We often hear "Oh, he's so gay" about male athletes who somehow defy the normal stereotype of the butch, masculine athlete. NFL wide receiver Tim Dwight shaves his legs; tennis player Andy Roddick dresses to the nines and shows his midriff; NFL quarterback Joey Harrington plays the piano. Gay, gay, and gay, according to many gay fans who often look for one chink in the masculinity armor. Of course, these are some of the same fans who get upset about people stereotyping gay men as unathletic Marys who wax their eyebrows and listen to show tunes.

Jeff Garcia

Still, to many fans, as former San Francisco 49ers wide receiver Terrell Owens said, "If it looks like a rat and smells like a rat, by golly, it is a rat."

Those were Owens's comments when asked by *Playboy* if his quarterback while with the 49ers, Jeff Garcia, is gay. The implication of his statement about the quarterback he had often criticized was clear: Owens wanted people thinking Garcia is gay. The truth is, many already did think that. Garcia's speaking voice sounds like he just stepped out of the Café in the Castro—it's a little high and a little lispy—and the "probable actions" philosophy points directly at Garcia. Owens quickly backpedaled after taking heat for his comment, saying Garcia had a girlfriend (no doubt Owens knows how tried and true that defense is).

Interestingly, Owens himself has been a focus of gay rumors that have graced the e-mail account at Outsports. Given his constant obsession with his body (which is sculpted like that of a Greek god), his narcissistic attitude with the media, the way he struts around wearing the tightest clothes known to man, and the style with which he shakes a pom-pom, you can understand why.

"I've heard the rumor myself that I'm gay," then San Francisco 49ers quarterback Jeff Garcia told Matt Maiocco of the *Santa Rosa Democrat* in 2004. "That is not the case. I've had girlfriends in the past and I do want to be married some day. . . . Somebody saying it obviously doesn't have any clue as to who I am as a person and, secondly, speaks from a sense of having jealousy for what I've been able to attain as a person and is trying to knock me. Well, they're not knocking me."

We hear more gay rumors about NFL quarterbacks, such as Garcia, than any other group of players. Part of that is certainly the wishful thinking; there is no more important position in all of team sports than the quarterback in football, and that allure is as powerful for high school cheerleaders as it is for grown gay men. The probable actions of NFL quarterbacks are also brought to light more because of the high media scrutiny of the men in that position.

The Other Quarterbacks

The granddaddy of all the gay rumors is Troy Aikman. There is no professional athlete in the United States about whom Outsports has heard more rumors than this Hall of Fame and former Dallas Cowboys quarterback. The unique thing about Aikman is that the rumors don't just come from gay men; straight people get in on the act, too.

Jim and Cyd are often invited as guests on radio shows across America. Although Texas has a reputation of being antigay, sports radio shows in Houston, Austin, and Dallas have invited them to talk about gay issues in sports and have done so with open arms. Quite often, the discussion turns into them asking them to name names—who's gay in sports? Although they never reveal information about the athletes they know to be closeted, they certainly have some fun leading them on and talking about the fact that they know there are gay athletes in every major sport. "Who, Troy Aikman?" is the inevitable response. "We've all heard that."

Outsports has heard rumors of Aikman being in relationships while at the University of California at Los Angeles (UCLA), coming in and out of various gay clubs, and spotted at the house parties of prominent gay men. These are, of course, just rumors; Outsports has never spoken to a single person who has been able to say they were there or that they themselves had sex with the Hall of Fame quarterback.

The rumors gained mainstream traction with the 1996 publication of sportswriter Skip Bayless's book *Hell-Bent: The Crazy Truth about the Win-or-Else Dallas Cowboys*, about the tumultuous months following the Cowboys' Super Bowl XXX win. In the book Bayless directly addresses the gay rumors about the star quarterback. In response, Aikman reportedly asked a lawyer how much it would cost to punch Bayless in retaliation.

(It should be noted that Bayless, along with his *Cold Pizza* compadre Woody Paige, has among the most laughable of reputations of all sportswriters in America, in part because of his assertions about Aikman in his book, and in part because of statements and rants that many consider a bit loony, such as his assertion that the NFL should get rid of field goals and point-after-touchdown kicks.)

Rumors have also abounded for years about former San Francisco 49ers quarterback Steve Young, who was inducted into the Pro Football Hall of Fame in 2005. These rumors have plagued the two men likely for much the same basic reason: they were both single for, according to societal standards, far too long for a straight man. "There is a certain level of

Kopay on Aikman Rumors

The outspoken Kopay answered reader questions for ESPN.com on December 18, 1998. One reader asked him about his reaction to Bayless's assertion that Aikman is gay.

> To begin with, people always ask about Aikman or Steve Young or Joe Montana—they always pick out the most dynamic, successful men. Is that fuel for their own fantasies? I don't know. They never pick out the ugly ones.
>
> I think Skip Bayless has a screw loose. I had an incident happen when I was getting on the airplane. The last person on the plane was Troy Aikman. I introduced myself to him and said I owed him an apology, because I said something I regret saying. Troy is a very handsome man and would be anyone's fantasy, whether from the gay or straight world, and I had said something off the cuff in doing an article for GQ magazine, because everyone's always asked me about the gay quarterbacks when I played. He asked me, "Would you be interested in having sex with Troy Aikman?" And I said the answer was yes. And he wrote that in the magazine.
>
> Which wasn't fair, because it might have put more pressure on Troy. Gay men and women don't always know who is gay, but I'm often very accurate. To this day, I don't believe Troy Aikman is gay.

expectation about any unmarried man in this society that goes into their late 20s or 30s and doesn't get married," agent Leigh Steinberg, who represented both Hall of Fame quarterbacks during their careers, told ESPN in 1999 when asked about the rumors surrounding two of his highest-profile clients.

Interestingly, Aikman and Young both married a woman within a month of each other in 2000: Young to former model Barbara Graham on March 15 when he was thirty-eight; Aikman to Rhonda Worthey, a former publicist for the Dallas Cowboys, on April 8 when he was thirty-three. Both men have children with their wives.

One of sports' most acknowledged gay rumors popped up in 1999, just as Outsports got its start, about then Pittsburgh Steelers quarterback Kordell Stewart. Rumors about his sexual orientation have been rampant among Steeler fans (even long after he left the team) for years. It's been discussed on sports talk radio (the nationally syndicated *Jim Rome Show* for one), and there was even a mention in *Sports Illustrated*. Type "Kordell

Cyd Zeigler, April 12, 2000

Aikman, 33, certainly silenced the rumors by his marriage Saturday to former Cowboys publicist Rhonda Worthey, 31, in a private ceremony in Dallas. After all only straight people get married.

Stewart gay" on Google, and you'll find more than twenty thousand results on the search, including ample chat room discussions and article mentions. The most specific rumor: that Stewart was arrested by an undercover cop one evening for soliciting sex from a male prostitute. However, no police report has ever surfaced to verify this.

Stewart has been unusually circumspect when asked about being gay, not denying it but simply saying he won't discuss his private life. He gave these rather interesting comments to KDKA radio, when the rumors reached their most frenzied moments in the midst of his having an awful season: "I was a guy who stood up in front of the team and just said, basically, this is what's going on," Stewart said in December 1999. "A rumor is a rumor, you look it up in the dictionary it will tell you exactly what it means. I'm Kordell Stewart, the guy who worked with you guys and . . . has made some great plays around this place. And I don't want any fan or any knucklehead outside of this organization make you feel any differently about me as a player. The rumors can be real nasty sometimes, believe me. When you're out there on the field and you hear some of the things that are said, it can be real nasty. . . . It can cause you to be bitter."

There was no doubt that Stewart's on-field performance was terrible in late 1998 and '99, when the rumors coming out of Pittsburgh gained momentum, following a sensational '97 season that saw the former University of Colorado star take the Steelers to within three points of the Super Bowl. Pittsburgh fans can be fanatically loyal, but also turn on a underachiever with venom. He rebounded late in 2000 and led the Steelers to the AFC Championship game in 2001 before being shipped out of Pittsburgh after the 2002 season.

Page Six "Outs" Mike Piazza

Mike Piazza was allegedly "outed" in the *New York Post*'s Page Six in 2002. Overnight, people—straight and gay—were suddenly privy to the rumor that has followed Piazza since his playing days with the Los Angeles Dodgers in the '90s. Although many were hoping that America would finally see its first openly gay active professional athlete, instead there was quite another first: a press conference, called by Piazza, to "come out" as straight.

Outsports doesn't know if Piazza is gay, but there is certainly reason to hope he's not. It would be a shame to have seen a gay athlete feel such incredible pressure from a rumor that he's gay to call a separate press conference to distance himself from something that defines him. Other gay athletes simply have to not talk about it or invite the occasional cheerleader into their beds to throw off the scent. But if Piazza is gay, to feel the need to publicly say he's something else would be a very sad commentary on our culture indeed.

Whether he is or isn't, the length to which he went to publicly declare his heterosexuality shows that it still might be years before an active pro athlete comes out. In fact, that happened in 2002, and gay people are still waiting for an active out male athlete five years later. It's not crazy to think that press conference may have a part in that.

Other Major League Rumors

Major League Baseball player Gabe Kapler made a name for himself by modeling in *Gym* magazine in the late '90s wearing nothing more than tight square-cut swim trunks that barely left his religion to the imagination. Because he was willing to bare almost all, and because he has a body for days, and because the magazine was thought to be soft-core porn for gay and straight-but-looking men, the rumors started that Kapler himself was gay. It was based on nothing more than his appearance in one magazine, and there is absolutely no reason to believe the rumor is true.

Yet it stuck so much that Kapler opted to decline respectfully from a phone interview with Cyd in 2002. Cyd was writing a feature article for *Genre* magazine about athletes whom gay men idolize for their sex appeal. Tennis pro Andy Roddick, NBA star Wally Szczerbiak, and Jeremy Bloom were featured, along with others including Kapler, who was playing for the Colorado Rockies at the time. Kapler told Cyd in a phone con-

In ESPN's 1998 *Outside the Lines* special, "The World of the Gay Athlete," former NFL wide receiver Ernest Givins, who spent nine quality seasons with the Houston Oilers, talked frankly about the widespread rumor that he is gay.

ANDREA KRAMER: Had these rumors always been out there about you?

ERNEST GIVINS: Definitely, yes.

KRAMER: You've heard them?

GIVINS: I've heard them.

KRAMER: So I'll ask you, are you gay?

GIVINS: No.

KRAMER: If you were, would you tell me?

GIVINS: Yes, if I were I would tell you.

KRAMER: I think that the strange thing, and you seem to be aware of this, is that the rumors have been out there for so long. How can that be?

GIVINS: How could that be? Because, one, when they have Super Bowl parties I don't go, one, when they have major type events I don't go, another thing, when they have things that involve with a lot of players, I don't go. So everybody feels that if I'm not a part of something that's major, and I'm not

versation that he was not gay and that he had no problem with gay people or gay people looking at him; he had just been hounded by teammates so badly for that *Gym* magazine photo spread that he didn't want to be plastered in another gay-targeted magazine, which could ignite another round of endless harassment.

Many gay men, like some of Kapler's teammates and colleagues, took that photo spread and began the rumormongering that Gabe "the Babe" Kapler was gay, despite absolutely no other evidence to back it up. Kapler has been married to his wife, Lisa, since 1999 (the same year the *Gym* magazine spread hit newsstands). They have two sons and together created the Gabe Kapler Foundation to end domestic violence, of which his wife was once a victim. Of course, the rumors have never taken any of this into account.

Former major leaguer Brady Anderson, who spent most of his career with the Baltimore Orioles, is generally considered one of the more attrac-

> a part of something that's "outstanding," then I'm hiding
> something. I'm not hiding anything. I'm not hiding not one
> thing at all. They can say whatever they want to say.
>
> **KRAMER:** You've taken young receivers under your wing.
>
> **GIVINS:** Yes.
>
> **KRAMER:** Rumors abound, "Ernest is hitting on the young guys."
> Do you hear that?
>
> **GIVINS:** Yeah.
>
> **KRAMER:** Is being gay one of the worst things that could be said
> about an athlete?
>
> **GIVINS:** Yes.
>
> **KRAMER:** If somebody said Ernest Givens hit his girlfriend, it
> wouldn't be as bad as somebody saying Ernest Givens is
> gay?
>
> **GIVINS:** Right. If they say, I found Ernest Givens driving at 140
> miles an hour, get pulled over with cocaine in his car, or
> whatever the case may be, that's nothing. They say, one,
> we see that and hear that every day with athletes. But when
> you start stereotyping athletes, start putting that gay thing
> on them, that hurts more than anything. That hurts more
> than anything.

tive men to have played Major League Baseball in the past ten years; he's also one of the most-rumored players to be gay.

The famous black-and-white picture of Anderson, wearing nothing but spandex shorts and leaning against a baseball bat, at a time when virtually no professional athlete (except Kapler) would be caught dead in that kind of a photo, surely fueled the speculation that Anderson is gay.

The problem with this rumor is that Outsports knows for a fact that Anderson dates women—and he doesn't just do it for show. In 2003, he dated a semipro female boxer, who is a friend of Cyd, to no fanfare. Of course, this doesn't mean that Anderson isn't gay (though, to be fair, it doesn't mean he's straight, either).

Cyd's Take on Johnny Weir

My guess is Johnny Weir is as gay as balloons, and he keeps coming out to us in just about every media interview he does. To come out, you don't have to call a press conference and say to the world, "Yep, I'm gay." I think if you got Johnny to talk off the record he'd probably say, "Are you an idiot? Did you not see the outfits I've been wearing? Did you not see me on NBC? What, do I have to spell it out for you?" Just because he hasn't said the words doesn't mean he hasn't told us. Weir seems completely comfortable with everyone else talking about his sexuality. He just isn't interested in talking about it. He's much more interested in shopping, listening to Christina Aguilera, and trying on sunglasses.

Beyond Weir's over-the-top style, the fact that he is a figure skater is supposed to be the proof that he is gay. Many look at all athletes in a variety of sports as gay, and figure skating tops the list. Scott Hamilton has been the focus of gay rumors for years, and he has denied every one, at one point becoming a bit homophobic, as he admitted in his autobiography, *Landing It.*

Male gymnasts are also supposed to be gay, and the rumor mill focused its energies in mid–2004 on Olympic gold medalists Paul and Morgan Hamm. Not only do the twin gymnasts compete in what is perceived to be a "gay" sport, but their voices are also very high for their age; their voices, coupled with their height (they are both five-foot-six), make them seem younger and, by society's standards, more feminine. Thus, of course, the rumors.

"That rumor doesn't bother me," Morgan told Outsports in late 2004. "It's almost flattering. It makes me feel that we are reaching all kinds of people and touching them."

The "Gay" Sports

On the flip side, it's hard to believe figure skater Johnny Weir *isn't* 100 percent gay. With all of his antics at the 2006 Winter Olympics, and the blog entries and fashion shows since, he seems to relish in flirting with coming out but not quite going over the line. He's probably the only nonhomophobic athlete Outsports would actually consider "outing," simply because he is, for all intents and purposes, out. All you have to do is look at the coverage of Weir at the Winter Olympics. NBC went so far as to call one of their segments about the flamboyant figure skater "He's Here, He's

"How great is it that they're not gay?" Daniel Hamm, the gay uncle of Olympic gold-medal gymnasts Paul and Morgan Hamm, told Outsports in 2004. "We in the gay community keep putting pressure on gay athletes to come out. We should be putting pressure on the straight athletes to come out and take a stand and say, 'I applaud my gay team-mates. They should be able to bring their partners to games, and it should be OK.'"

Weir," obviously a play on the famous "We're here, we're queer" chants of gay activists.

Morgan was right on: with their good looks and fame, they were a popular target with gay rumormongers for quite a while after their gold-medal Olympic performance. Although they have a gay uncle and a lesbian aunt, each of the twins said he is straight. When interviewed by Outsports in 2004, they were both dating girls.

Rumors can be a fun diversion or a product of fantasy. And even more fun than the fantasy, sometimes, can be the athletes' attempts to quash the rumors about their sexuality. Outsports will continue to report on rumors as they hit the public consciousness, but we won't start them. Perez Hilton is doing a nasty job of that all by herself.

OUTSPORTS

Flashback
#7

JULY 29, 2001

Who Is and Who Isn't?
Speculating about Sexual Orientation
May Put Some People Off,
but It's Understandable

Jim Buzinski

During the cold war, Kremlinologists in the United States regularly got out their magnifying glasses to study pictures in *Pravda*, the Soviet Union's official newspaper. By analyzing who had joined—or who was missing from—the podium at various parades and functions, these Soviet experts would attempt to dissect the shifting power structure. The speculation was necessary because of the extreme difficulties of gathering much information from independent sources in the Soviet Union.

In many ways, gay sports fans have become the Kremlinologists of the twenty-first century, as we try to divine who on the fields of play shares our orientation. We're reduced to reading tea leaves, looking at a jock's marital status (as if that means anything), mannerisms, the way he talks, his choice of clothes, and our not-always-reliable "gaydar."

The reason for all this guessing is clear: athletes remain buried deep in the closet. The number of out athletes couldn't fill a book larger than *Great German Comedians*. And virtually all of these athletes have come out only after retirement. With everyone hiding, we've all become detectives. Seeing jocks we know to be gay getting engaged or married only adds fuel to the fire.

This is not a ringing defense of speculation but rather an attempt to understand it. The constant guessing, parsing, and throwing out of names of entire football teams get old fast and are generally pointless. The "evidence" is often so scant that Judge Judy would dismiss the case before the first commercial break. I would rather focus on the courageous athletes who have come out and made a difference, such as Corey Johnson, Brandon Triche, and Mark Welsh.

Speculation on who's gay and who's not has been everywhere of late—on discussion boards (both on Outsports and on mainstream sites such as ESPN.com), in print, and on sports talk radio. The catalyst was Brendan Lemon's column about his affair with an unnamed major league player.

The fact that Lemon's player remained anonymous caused all the guessing, even among other major leaguers. It's human nature, and not limited to gay men, as the frenzy over Gary Condit and Tom and Nicole demonstrates.

A need for validation fuels much of the speculation of gay sports fans. We do not require openly gay athletes to validate our existence, but symbols are important.

The black civil rights movement did not need Jackie Robinson to play in the major leagues; nothing was going to hold back the demands for equality. Robinson, though, was important to show the white world that blacks could compete as their equals. Billie Jean King performed a similar role for female athletes when she trounced Bobby Riggs.

I see a similar analogy regarding gay athletes. Most homophobic slurs directed at men revolve around demasculinization: Sissy. Wussy. Throws Like a Girl. These are all lies and slanders that we as gays know are far from the truth, yet they continue to hold a powerful grip on attitudes. These stereotypes also affect young gay athletes who see no role models to emulate and believe that hiding is the only option. The cycle then continues.

How shocked would society be if they knew some of their star players, some league most valuable players (MVPs) and Hall of Famers, were homosexual? Perhaps not as shocked as we—or the gay athletes—imagine.

One way of reducing the shock value is by discussing the topic. This was the greatest service performed by Lemon's column. When a sports talk radio station in Huntsville, Alabama, is talking about gays in pro sports, it shows it's not an alien concept and has moved into the mainstream.

Once the Soviet Union fell and Russia became more open, there was no more need for magnifying glasses. Once our society becomes more accepting and athletes feel comfortable proudly coming out, there will be no need for speculation.

PART II

ELITE ATHLETES
AND BIG-TIME SPORTS

THE WAVE OF OUT YOUNG JOCKS

Although the world of sports is the last closet in Western society, that is becoming less and less true at the high school and collegiate levels. The situation is changing among these younger athletes, and mainly of those in "nonglamour" sports such as skiing, softball, lacrosse, or tennis (unfortunately, for the time being, the closet is still, for the most part, shut on collegiate jocks who participate in the two major sports—football and basketball—and in baseball, which is huge is some parts of the country).

For many of the college and high school athletes who have come out, it was a decision they don't regret. "I came out in the beginning of my sophomore year here at Cal, and in retrospect it was one of the best decisions I've made," said Graham Ackerman, a captain on the University of California at Berkeley gymnastics team. Ackerman won an NCAA title in floor exercise in 2005, was a two-time NCAA champion in 2004, competed in the 2003 World University Games in Korea, and has placed in the top three at U.S. Nationals. "I credit the upperclassmen at that time a great deal with smoothing out the entire process as it was very new to all of us," he said in an interview with Ryan Quinn for Outsports, himself a former college athlete. "As it turned out, I couldn't have asked for a better reaction from my teammates. Because we spent so much time together in and out of the gym, it was not a huge surprise for most of them. The process has been a great learning experience for myself, my teammates and my coaches."

Athletes who have told their coming-out stories report near universal acceptance and a sense of relief that their secret is out. Quinn, who skied for the University of Utah, credits the Internet with making it easier for college jocks to connect. "The Internet has done wonders for gay people," Quinn wrote in an article for Outsports.

The ability to anonymously read articles and participate in message board discussions allows an athlete to explore his identity in ways that he otherwise might have kept closed off, even from himself.

For gay college athletes, this cloak of anonymity has jump-started a coming-out momentum that's long overdue. A community of openly gay college athletes has emerged on the Net, and the transition from online curiosity to full disclosure with teammates has been positive in almost every case.

In the past two years I've spoken with and received e-mails from almost 36 gay athletes who want to come out but who first want to bond with other gay athletes and share their experiences. The Internet is the most convenient setting for this exchange.

Ackerman made a splash in 2004 with a coming-out story in *Instinct* penned by soon-to-be-crowned Perez Hilton. Ackerman is a three-time NCAA champion gymnast.

Photo by Cyd Zeigler Jr.

There has been some research into gay athletes on campus, most notably by sport psychologist and sociologist Eric Anderson, and also by former Seattle Pacific University graduate student Mike Bryant. In a research paper, Bryant surveyed 115 self-identified gay male athletes who played at either the high school or the collegiate level in team contact sports: basketball, football, baseball, soccer, lacrosse, field hockey, ice hockey, rugby, and wrestling. These sports were chosen, Bryant said, because of society's assumed masculinity of anyone playing them.

Bryant, who has played basketball and volleyball and now coaches both, has been out since he was twenty years old. He instinctively knew gay men could also be good athletes, but even he was surprised by some of the findings. The one that most sticks out is that 75 percent of those surveyed said that in high school they were either the best player on their team or better than average. Of those who played on a college team, 68 percent said they were best or better. "Best" was defined as the team's leading scorer, MVP, or team captain, whereas "better" meant being a starter and major contributor. "This surprised me the most because I was kind of a skeptic myself," said Bryant, a Washington State native. He then recalled his 1998 gold medal–winning volleyball team from Gay Games V in Amsterdam that had two players who had been U.S. national team members. Bryant himself was in the "better" category, but his experiences showed how hard it is for many to reconcile an elite athlete being gay. "My high school reunion a couple of years ago confirmed to me that my high school friends and teammates thought that I might be gay while we were in school together," he said. "I was never social outside of school and I never dated girls. But, as many of my former friends attested, they could never really figure me out, only because I was a starting forward on one of the best high school basketball teams in the state."

For those athletes who are better than average, Bryant writes in his research paper, "the confidence in their abilities and contributions to their teams may . . . lend support to their belief that because they are better, nobody will learn of their homosexual identity. At the same time, sport is fulfilling its social and athletic purposes in the lives of those better athletes."

This desire to hide their sexuality was not as prevalent among the athletes in the survey as one might think it would be. Only 20 percent said they "participated in sports to hide the fact that I was gay or to prove to others I was straight." A slightly higher percentage agreed with the statement, "I used sports as a way to get physically close to other guys without them knowing I was gay." More than half said they participated so as to not feel isolated and to become part of a team. "It didn't shock me that most guys participated because they love sports, they love the purity involved in what athletics is. It's just something that is there," Bryant said.

Behind every statistic there is a story. Following are stories, in their own words, from college athletes who have shown it is possible to come out and to continue to participate in the sport they love.

Ryan Quinn: Earning His Team's Respect*

Every athlete reaches a point when they realize that sport is no longer an external activity in which they merely participate, but an actual part of their life. But for an athlete to be his best, the sport can be no more or less a part of their life than any of the other parts. But I haven't always known this.

Had someone asked me five years ago if I knew myself, I would have laughed, naïvely believing I did. But the laughing stopped when I discovered an inconsistency around me: I was attracted to other guys, and somewhere, a voice that I could never really believe, was saying, "I'm not supposed to want this." The confusion was not that the attraction felt strange or different. It did not. But I was reminded constantly that it *was* different. I was an athlete and I was not attracted to girls—as society clearly intended.

My response was to concentrate even more on athletics because it was the part of me that I understood. I was good at sports, and like all good athletes, I was accepted for that. For my final two years of high school it was easy to push aside anything that contradicted that existence. I never went through a period of doubt or depression. I enjoyed skiing and running and I enjoyed the friends and teammates that came with it, so it seemed pointless to challenge that despite what I knew was under the surface. I did not even say the words "I'm gay" to *myself* until my first year in college.

But once I did, I saw everything differently. I discovered that I did not fully know myself. And that thought was more disturbing to me than the fear of appearing different against the norms of society and sport. I came to Utah to ski; to win a national championship and to develop into my best. Somewhere in the confusion and self-isolation of the coming out process I realized that to be my best was not just to ski but to live. And not just to live but to live as myself. Suddenly I saw that I could not approach my potential as an athlete if pieces of myself were scattered. I had left some behind before, but this time they would all be faced equally.

Coming out to family and friends is terrifying. Coming out in the en-

*Quinn was a cross-country skier for the University of Utah

vironment known as Division I athletics is numbing. Honestly, I don't remember many of the details from two years ago, but the resulting effect of coming out to my team is very real and continues to awe me.

I was met not with hostility or even the surface-level gestures of tolerance. From my teammates I have received genuine interest, support, and mutual respect. While I give enormous credit to the secure and independent thinking people on my team, I also am beginning to see that my positive experience as an out college athlete is not entirely an accident, nor a stroke of luck.

Gay athletes are in a unique position because of the inevitable isolation. We are forced to constantly think about ourselves, making us acutely aware of our surroundings and our role in them. For me, this at first led to fear and uncertainty, but ultimately the introspection brought advantages that I now would not give up for anything.

"Ryan, Cross-Country Skiing, University of Utah, 2004," by Jeff Sheng, part of the series, "Fearless," a photography project on out LGBTQ high school and collegiate athletes. For more information please visit www. FearlessCampusTour.org

A common question I'm asked is, "Do you ever wish that you were straight?" No, not ever. "But wouldn't that make it easier?" Maybe, but not better. There is a value in such a high level of self-awareness that cannot be appreciated unless it is experienced. My greatest accomplishment is that, upon discovering that I did not know myself, I was not afraid to learn. Unfortunately, many people turn away from themselves and settle for what society will give them. But once I began to think about myself, I began to see that there was no contradiction, that I—all of me—was fully capable of being an athlete.

I am bothered by two misconceptions that define the role of gay athletes today. The first is that they do not exist. Fortunately, this myth is being dispelled more and more each year as athletes come out and the mainstream media presents their stories.

The second is a barrier that cannot be overcome until more athletes are out. It is the notion that if there is an athlete who is gay, and he or she does come out to their team, they will be met with homophobia and will experience such a struggle that it is not worth it. These were my perceptions before I came out. Now I see that there is something larger at work that transforms the struggle into an advantage, not just for the gay athlete, but for the entire team.

The heterosexist stereotypes and assumptions about athletes in our culture are very powerful, but I've found that the image of a person who has self-respect and honesty is far more so. Think about the people who are your personal role models—not distant people who have achieved this and that but people who you know, like, and admire. They are probably the people who are secure with themselves, who do not hide pieces of themselves because of what others may think, and would not ask others to hide.

In my experience, coming out to my team did not evoke homophobia, but rather inspired a new level of respect, both as friends and as teammates. I told them that I was gay. But what that really said was that I was committed to the team and the sport so deeply that I was willing to risk the honesty because it might make me better. My teammates did not waste any time stepping up to meet this gesture.

In the two years since, I have become so accepted by the team that my sexual orientation is discussed often and mentioned as having the same impact as the lives of my straight teammates. What impressed me the most is that the people around me did not shy away from the knowledge of me being gay. Everyone seemed to understand that in college sports, it's not about sex but about the skiing and about the team (the format of college skiing makes it very much a team sport).

I have heard the theories that individual sports are more accepting than contact team sports. Perhaps this is assumed true, but I think that's only because there are so few examples of athletes coming out in those sports. Either way, there is nothing inherent about team sports that make them more homophobic than individual sports. The latter still often has a team environment based around willful respect and the maximum performance possible from each team member.

The ski team at the University of Utah is historically a favorite among the nation's top ski programs. At the start of this season, Utah had won the NCAA Title 10 times, but none of them had come while I was on the team. This March(2003), after experiencing the disappointment of falling short for three years, our team won the NCAA Championship by the largest margin of victory ever.

To win a National Championship is awesome in itself, but to do it with your closest friends makes it that much more meaningful. At our team's celebration banquet that followed the final race and awards ceremony, the senior toasts and speeches began, as per tradition. As it came to be my time to speak, I could only think about the last two years—the years that I had been out to them and watched the environment around me rise to a new level of commitment. The other years—times of introspection, isolation, and fear—were not forgotten, but they had faded away. At the end of my toast I thanked them: "As skiers and teammates you all have been good. But as friends you have been amazing." I believe that every athlete—gay or straight—on every team should be able to say that. It is one of the most valuable outcomes that we can take from sport.

Since coming out I have had the opportunity to connect with other gay college athletes, both current and former. The overwhelming majority of them have had positive experiences with their teams and families. It is amazing to meet these people and to hear their stories, which are not unlike mine or the many other athletes who will come out in the near future. Many have received a flood of e-mails offering encouragement and asking for advice.

While this community is tremendous in its support and influence, it is not so in size. There is room for many more to be a part of what is the beginning of the end of homophobia and ignorance in sport. The greatest changes will occur not because of media stories or prominent athletes coming out but by individuals being themselves—their complete selves—and thus making an impact in the immediate environment around them.

Jordan Goldwarg: Jumping Off a Cliff*

When I look back over the past year, I'm amazed at how much my life has changed. Last year at this time, not only was I completely in the closet, but I had not even accepted myself as being gay. Today, though, I've fully accepted myself, and I'm completely out with all of my friends, my family, and most significantly, my ski team. What happened that changed everything?

Looking back now, I think I knew from a very early age that I was gay. I've always felt more attracted to guys than to girls, right from the time that I started feeling attraction. The problem was that I didn't see any other gay people around me who seemed similar to me at all.

Pretty much the only exposure to gay people that I had was through the media, which only reinforced in my mind stereotypes that I didn't fit into. I told myself that I couldn't be gay because I didn't *seem* gay, and there weren't any other gay men like me. Instead of accepting myself for who I was, I went into denial, making up many of the excuses that I'm sure other gay men have used, like, "This is only a phase" or "I just haven't found the right girl yet."

Even though this denial went on for years, I was lucky in that I had a lot of other stuff going on in my life that distracted me from thinking about it. I always kept myself busy in school, and I have a loving and supportive family and a close group of friends.

One of the most powerful things, though, was skiing. I had skied with my family pretty much since I could walk, and I started racing when I entered high school. There, I raced the Nordic (cross-country) events for both my school team and a club team outside of school. Skiing provided a focus in my life that made it easy to spend time thinking about the sport rather than agonizing over whether or not I was gay. At the time, I didn't think about the fact that my position as an athlete would later be one of the greatest barriers to my coming out.

When it came time to apply to college, I knew that I wanted to keep ski racing, so I began looking for schools with ski programs and found Williams College in western Massachusetts. It seemed to be a perfect fit for me, combining strong academics with a competitive ski team. I also meshed well with the coach as soon as we met.

My life at Williams was great right from the start. I loved my classes, my friends, and the location, and the ski team experience was even better

* *Goldwarg was a cross-country skier at Williams College in Massachusetts*

than I hoped it would be. The team was a lot of fun, forming the core of my social group, and I was also seeing steady improvement in my skiing. Always lurking below the surface, however, was the increasing knowledge that I was gay.

By the end of my sophomore year, I was starting to make some small steps toward accepting the fact. I would become comfortable with the idea of being gay for a while, but then something would happen that would push me back into denial. I still had a lot of trouble seeing myself as a gay man, in large part because I was an athlete and I didn't see any other gay male athletes around me. Through this time, I was still completely silent about the subject and none of my friends had any reason to suspect that I was gay.

Finally, in February 2002 (the winter of my junior year), things changed. While looking at Outsports.com one day, I came across the list of out athletes. Reading it over, I found that there was another Nordic skier on the list who was on the ski team at his college out West. This discovery was incredibly powerful. All of a sudden, it didn't seem like I was completely alone in my situation; here was someone else who had really similar interests and who was also gay.

I was able to get in touch with him through e-mail, and we began corresponding, which helped me first to accept myself as being gay and then to have the confidence to come out. Once I accepted myself, I quickly began to feel the need to start telling people and end the secret.

In April, I told my first friend (a girl), who was great about it—totally supportive and accepting. A few weeks later, I told a teammate (also a girl), who was also great. By June, when I went home after the end of school, I felt that I was ready to tell my parents. Even though I knew they would be totally fine with it, it was still probably the most difficult thing I've ever done. It was just such a big piece of news that I was filled with apprehension, wondering what their exact response would be. It took my parents some time to adjust to the idea that their son was gay, but they showed incredible love and support through the whole process, for which I consider myself incredibly lucky.

Coming out to people often felt like jumping off a 30-foot cliff into a deep pool of water. You think about it beforehand and plan how you want to jump. You know that it will almost certainly be safe, yet there's still an element of the unknown. When it actually comes time to jump, though, you can't really think about it at all because you'll chicken out. You just have to go on autopilot and take the plunge.

When I got back to Williams last fall, I soon realized that I wanted to come out to more people, including the rest of the ski team. I had come out to a few more people over the summer (including a couple of teammates), but most of my friends still didn't know. My sense of urgency was increased when I began dating my first boyfriend, since I couldn't stand the idea of living a double life. Most of all, I wanted my friends to know me for who I really am.

I still had lingering fears and doubts about telling the ski team, though. I really didn't think that my place on the team would be jeopardized in any way, but I was afraid that somehow things would be different and people would treat me differently than they had before. So I kept putting off telling the team until they were the last of my friends who didn't know. (One of the ironies of coming out for me was that it was often easier to tell people who I didn't know so well and harder to tell my closest friends—I guess I thought I had more to lose with those closer to me.)

Finally, I decided that I couldn't put it off any longer because it was really starting to eat me up inside, distracting me from my skiing and my schoolwork. I first told my coaches, who were great about it—they helped give me confidence to tell the rest of the team. A few weeks later, we had a training camp, which was a good opportunity to tell people since the whole team was together for a week. After dinner one night, I just said that I had something I wanted to talk about and told the team as a group. There was definitely an awkward silence afterward (this was not the usual post-dinner conversation), but later that night, people started asking me questions about being gay and telling me that they appreciated me telling them. They also told me that it didn't change their opinion of me at all.

Now that some time has passed since I came out to the team, I can see that all of my fears about coming out have not come true. Rather than changing my friendships negatively, coming out has actually allowed me to become closer to my friends since I can be completely honest and open with them now. My teammates even joke about my being gay now, which definitely shows me that they're comfortable with it and accept it.

I know that my experience is not the same as some other athletes' experiences with coming out. I think I'm lucky in that I compete in an individual sport (and one that happens to be pretty open-minded at that), since coming out in a team-sport environment definitely seems to be more difficult.

It is possible, though, to come out as an athlete and have a positive experience with it. I've gained much greater self-acceptance, and I don't have to waste huge amounts of mental energy anymore worrying about it and trying to hide it. The whole process has been incredibly liberating.

Matt Coin: Sharing a Secret*

The veterans on the team piled into the van I was driving for the final regular season road trip of the year from Santa Barbara to Stockton, Calif., this spring, leaving the rookies to drive with the head coach. We followed our coach closely and rode along in silence because it was early in the morning. When the van began to shake violently, everyone woke up and became alert.

Smoke enveloped the van as it began to sway, but I managed to regain control and pull over to a halting stop just short of a cliff. The entire team leapt out unscathed and moved away from the van, only to see that the right front tire had exploded and flown off of the wheel.

I called my coach; he pulled over a mile down the road, and walked back to meet us while we called for help. The university brought us a new van and we continued our drive up the coast. At first, my teammates and I were silent; more silent than before, but this time everyone was awake. After a brief lunch break, we piled back into the van and my teammates began to discuss the near disaster that we faced.

One by one, my teammates went around sharing stories that they never had told before and the bonds began to form stronger than ever. It was my turn. I reflected on what I had been through for the past month and the 180-degree turn my life had taken within days.

Growing up, I always knew that something about me was a little different, but I was never able to put my finger on it. Throughout high school, I was still unsure of what it was, but it was more out of insecurity and immaturity. I graduated high school and left New Jersey for Lafayette College in Pennsylvania to play tennis. I began to come to grips with the realization that I was attracted to men, but I believed that it was just a phase. After taking numerous psychology courses in my freshman year, I began to think that I could condition myself to like girls by dating them. By my sophomore year, it was all I could think about: I was gay and there was no way that I could change.

I did not know any gay men personally, but I did know that I was nothing like any of the gay men portrayed on television. No one had ever asked me if I was gay before because everyone just assumed that I was straight. I dated girls, played sports, and had male friends. However, I knew that I had to get a fresh start, so I transferred to UC–Santa Barbara to continue my tennis career. My two-year career at UCSB was humbled

*Coin played tennis for the University of California at Santa Barbara

by surgery on my left and right wrists, in addition to countless other injuries, including torn tendons and muscles. The surgery on my right wrist ended my senior year six matches into the season.

It is often said that things happen for a reason, but until February, I never believed that. Everyone always told me that I was the luckiest person alive: I won $4,000 on the *Weakest Link* and a new car on *The Price Is Right*, but the internal struggle that I battled with my sexuality and the countless injuries made me feel unlucky.

Tennis was the only outlet that I had where I could focus on something other than my sexuality, but now I was forced to come face to face with it; I did not know what to think or do. I had just recovered from the surgery on my left wrist and days later I received the news that I had to get surgery on my right wrist. I could not hold my sexuality in any longer and I revealed my secret to two close female friends of mine and their roommate, who was gay. I knew that I could trust them and each offered their support, which was something that I needed at the time.

As the captain of the team, I continued to go on road trips and be an active member of the team, but it became difficult to lead a life where some of my friends knew and others did not. Things progressed between my friends' roommate Josh and I, and all of the doubts that I had faced for years disappeared. I was certain that I was gay and that it was something I could live with.

I thought that I would just tell my three friends and then maybe one of my sisters, but within days, I told each of my close friends and all of my five siblings, but neither of my parents. I was becoming so comfortable with everything so quickly.

I told my mom that I needed her to come visit for my surgery, but really I wanted to reveal to her that I was gay. My mom is one of the most important people in my life and I have never lied to her about anything else. I needed her to know. I was afraid that if I waited to tell her until after my surgery, I would allow the medication to affect me too much. A few hours after she arrived, I said to her, "Mom, I am gay." It was the first time that I had uttered that sentence. Prior to telling my mom, I had always said, "I am coming out." While this may not seem like a monumental statement, it was for me.

Josh invited my mom and me over for dinner so I had to explain to my mom that Josh was more than a friend and that we were dating. She took everything very well considering the fact that she learned of my secret and met my boyfriend within minutes of one another. I let her know that it was OK if she needed time to herself, but she exclaimed, "I want to see him!"

Upon meeting Josh, my mom said, "How is your boyfriend better looking than all of your sisters?" I was excited that she was comfortable with the situation and it was a big relief.

The support that I received from my friends and family was overwhelming to the point that I was sorry that I had waited so long, but everyone has their time and it is important to be ready to come out so that you do not doubt yourself.

Each person I told was shocked, confused, and in utter disbelief, but my constant reassurance that I was telling the truth calmed them, and in turn, calmed me. I had never answered more questions about myself before, but I enjoyed every minute because it was freeing to finally be myself and express my true feelings.

I enjoyed educating people about all of the false stereotypes; the process made me learn a lot about my friends and family. I realized how truly special were the people I surrounded myself with. I was able to think analytically about homosexuality for the first time because I was able to accept myself as a gay man. However, I had not yet accepted myself as a gay athlete.

Telling my teammates, especially the veterans with whom I had already been through one season, was the scariest thing I have ever done. I missed playing tennis so much because of my injuries, but traveling helped me remain a part of the team. Would my teammates want me to leave the team? Would they be afraid to room with me on trips? I did not know what to expect, but I had to tell them, especially after what we had been through. My college career almost came to a close without some of the most important people in my life ever knowing such an important aspect of me.

I had played in matches when the team's fate came down to my court, and I knew that this situation was similar: I had to be confident and focus on winning instead of being afraid to lose, because on any team everyone has fallen down and needed to be picked back up.

All of those thoughts ran through my mind in the van as my teammates awaited my story. The thought of almost going over that cliff made me realize how fragile life was and how important it was to be myself. My team's attention focused on me and I tried to get to the point quickly so that they would believe me. I told them that I was dating someone and that it was a guy. Again, the shock and disbelief were rampant, but within minutes, I gained their trust and acceptance.

Not one of my teammates had an adverse reaction and when I told them who I was dating, a junior named Josh who had come to several of the matches, one of my teammates said, "Oh, the hot Abercrombie-looking guy?" I was flattered and replied, "That's the one."

I answered questions for the remainder of the trip and even throughout the weekend. I told my remaining teammates that same weekend and their reactions were similar to the others, but more importantly, so were their responses. I had not told my coach, Marty Davis, yet.

The season came to a close in disappointing fashion, as we lost in our conference tournament. The team was driving home together when he began to discuss the year-end banquet. Davis suggested that this year's banquet was going to be slightly more formal than in the past and he encouraged everyone to bring a date. I grew nervous as my teammates' eyes once again focused on me. I asked him whom we should bring and he said, "Well, only bring a date if you have a girlfriend or something like that." I replied, "I've got something like that," and after laughs from my team, the conversation ended.

The banquet is combined with the women's tennis team and I thought

Anthony Castro was an openly gay high school wrestler and football player.

Photo by Brent Mullins

Outsports Remembers: Anthony Castro

It's hard to write about a friend who has just died, but people need to know about Anthony Castro, killed in a crash in the Southern California mountains on January 21, 2007. He was nineteen.

Anthony was that rarest of people—an athlete out to his team. In Anthony's case, he was out in high school to his football and wrestling teams, out two most macho team sports. It took guts to take such a step but Anthony never thought too much about it—he was not ashamed of who he was and if you were uncomfortable; that was your problem.

My favorite Anthony story involves his senior year of wrestling. A fellow wrestler used to make snide homophobic remarks to Anthony. Rather than file a complaint with the school, Anthony addressed the problem head on—he challenged the wrestler to a put-up-or-shut-up match. It didn't take very long, as Anthony had the guy pinned in about twenty seconds. That stopped the heckling, and Anthony told me the guy quit the team.

Anthony was not a student in some L.A. Westside hotbed of tolerance. Rather, he lived in Banning, two hours east of L.A., in the desert and a rather "red" part of a very "blue" state. Being out in Banning, a pretty rough place, took some big cajones.

I first met Anthony in November 2006, when I received an e-mail from him about playing for our L.A. Motion gay flag football team.

> "Hi, I'm Anthony. I live in Banning, California. I am a gay athlete and still in high school . . . With no other gay jocks, I feel like I am the only one and it sucks cause I don't know any other guys that are gay like me. I play football, basketball, track, cheerleading and swim. I have been playing football since I was five. I am the tight end for my high school, free safety and kickoff and punt returner. I don't know why I told you this but there you go. LOL. You guys are the closest to me and I figured if I was going to be moving down there, I should find out about things that are going on. What are the age limits you guys need to join?"

At first I thought the letter was a prank—the odds of an openly gay high school player in Banning seemed remote and Outsports does get the crank e-mail from time to time. But I wrote him back with sincerity and was surprised when he showed up, as promised, a few days later. He had a build more like a linebacker than quarterback, but in just a few plays I could tell he had great skills. I could also tell he was a bit awed to be playing football with a bunch of openly gay guys.

"It was really fun," he wrote me a few days after his first game. "I told my wrestling coach that we better not have practice on Saturdays. He said why, so I told him I joined a gay flag football team. So he said don't worry we won't. So he was cool and I like it because it is fun playing with you guys."

We then saw him virtually ever week from then on and he showed a commitment that is rare. He was always the first to arrive despite driving two hours to get there. He especially liked the fact that he could be himself, flirt if he wanted and not have to worry about it. He took a liking to one of our players, JP, and they used to kid each other all the time about JP being a senior citizen (thirty-two looks like that to an eighteen-year-old).

"Hey, Mr. Hit Young Guy in the Nuts," he wrote JP after one game when JP guarded him and things got a bit rough. "Well, it was fun playing football, even though you hit me in the nuts. By the way, they still hurt like hell. Hope your boyfriend hits in the nuts or something."

Like most single eighteen-year-olds, Anthony was always on the prowl and wrote me "woe is me" e-mails as he pined for someone new who showed up at football. "I am not going to let him score on me unless it's in bed," he wrote about one lust object who was guarding him one week. His e-mails were a highlight for me and I felt like a big brother to him.

He also had a turbulent upbringing. He told me his mom rejected him for a time because he was gay, even though she lives with a woman (I never figured that one out). He wrote about seeing his dad in jail and having a relative with AIDS. He wound up with a legal guardian, Phil, who had a tremendously positive influence on him and was a key support for Anthony on and off the field.

Football was always a refuge for him, even as he endured

tragedy. "I am not doing so good," he wrote me last winter. "Two of my friends were shot and killed 2 days ago and another friend was jumped badly. I don't know what the world is coming to these days. I have been trying to not think about it, but it is hard. I mean, those are guys I helped out and they play football to stay out of trouble. I wish I could have been there for them. The guys came from rough lives and they told me playing football helped them out a lot to not think about drugs or anything. I am a little sad. Hopefully football will help take my mind off it."

One day at football last spring, he introduced me to a friend he had brought, Cody, a handsome, athletic twenty-four-year-old. "He's straight," Anthony whispered to me. Minutes later, I saw Anthony lying on the sidelines in Cody's lap, soaking up the SoCal sun. Straight, my ass! Cody was Anthony's new boyfriend and I could tell he was beaming. They were perfect for each other and quickly fell in love.

I knew things were serious when Anthony called me one Saturday to say he was going to miss football—he and Cody were going to Disneyland. A second time when they skipped football, JP wrote me sarcastically but with affection: "Lame excuse. I'm a lawyer and I can smell BS stories a mile away. This kid was sitting at home with his new love."

Anthony and Cody quickly became fixtures at football and other players gravitated toward them. They were fun and full of life and love, and Anthony (who could be grumpy at times) was a much looser person with Cody. When Cyd and I picked our Outsports flag football team for the 2006 Gay Games, Anthony was one of the first people invited.

The Gay Games were something special for Anthony. He was going to play in a tournament with other gay athletes and he could bring his boyfriend along without fear or shame. Younger than everyone else by six years, he became out team's little brother.

On the fields at the Gay Games, Anthony was a star. Playing receiver and defensive back, he caught the go-ahead touchdown in the gold medal game, and added an interception in the end zone to boot. In a close win a day earlier, he made a catch on fourth down that was so amazing that people just screamed "that's sick!" when he came down with it. Watching Anthony receive his gold medal from teammate Esera Tuaolo gave me goose bumps; two out jocks, separated by a generation but bonded nonetheless.

Anthony loved USC football, his 1999 Mazda Miata 10th anniversary edition, his No. 10 jersey and postgame trips to Tommy's burgers with Cody. I will miss him terribly.

Postscript: A week before his death, Anthony was accepted to the Fashion Institute of Design and Merchandising in Los Angeles.

A memorial service was held for Anthony at Banning High School on January 26, 2007. An estimated 500 people attended. The principal of Banning read aloud a love letter from Cody to Anthony. Michael Anthony Castro was buried January 20 in Santa Ana, California.

Anthony's story was read by thousands of people and generated much reaction. ESPN.com was moved to write its own column extolling his life. Outsports readers from as far away as South Africa wrote condolences. The notes editor/writer/blogger Andrew Sullivan wrote: "Castro is part of the next generation of gay men—out in high school, unafraid to be fully themselves, even if it means violating stereotypes."

Kevin, a young Boston gay man, said he cried upon reading Anthony's story: "I lost my close friend Hunter in a car accident in 1999 at the age of 19, and I always regretted not telling him who I really was . . . bit I visit his grave often, and even write in my journal addressing the entries to him. Maybe that's why this story touched me, the way Anthony passed, his age, our similar stories of experiencing the coming out in stages, and of course finding ourselves on the sports field."

Wrote another: "I just wanted to tell you, that I read your story about Anthony today at work and the tears were running down my face. Not only because the poor boy died, but because Anthony seemed like a kid that was on the right track and understood what it was to be GAY and an Athlete. That was tough for me, a little over 21 years ago. Though everyone knew that I was gay, it was not something I could talk about freely. I hope that your friendship with Anthony was blessed with his kindness and 18-year-old charisma. They are amazing at that age, yet so very fragile."

> And one mother with a gay son found Anthony's story hit home: "I read about Anthony . . . And I've been walking around the house with such a heavy heart, crying off and on ever since. I cannot believe the terrible pain I am feeling, the loss feels so close, almost as though he were my son."

about how the coaches, trainers, and alumni might react to my bringing Josh to the banquet. I decided to tell my coach so that everyone's attention could be focused on the banquet and not on Josh and me. He was glad that I told him and his support was overwhelming. He, unlike everyone else, treated the issue as if it was normal. He had not suspected, and maybe it was his shock, but he offered his support and told me to bring Josh.

I begged all of my teammates to bring dates so that Josh would not stick out and each promised me that they would. However, no one on either the men's or women's team brought a date . . . except for me! My coach did a great job of spreading the word to the other guests ahead of time and no one's jaw dropped.

The banquet went off without a hitch until the end: senior speeches. Most seniors fail to prepare and are put on the spot to give a speech. I came fully prepared and probably put more effort into my speech than I had into any paper in my four years of college. Of the approximately 35 people in attendance, there was not one dry eye by the end. I offered parodies of my teammates and coaching staff, but then spoke to them about the support that my teammates and coach had given to me over the past few months. I never directly said what their support was for, but the implication touched my team in a way that I never had before. I thanked them for understanding how difficult it was for me to watch from the sidelines, for keeping me as the captain, and most importantly for always trying to make me feel a part of the team.

It has been a very short amount of time that I have been open about my sexuality, but it feels as if a tremendous amount of weight has been lifted off of my shoulders. I am recently a college graduate and look forward to beginning a new chapter in my life in which I can be myself. I feel lucky and I know that not everyone will have as positive of an experience as I have had, but I can only tell my story, and hope that it offers someone a sense of security to know that there are openly gay athletes out there.

OUTSPORTS

Flashback

#6

FEBRUARY 27, 2002

Dwight Slater, Stanford Football

Cyd Zeigler Jr.

It's not love and roses for all collegiate athletes who decide to come out. One of the very few Division I football players to test those waters was Stanford's Dwight Slater, a redshirt freshman in 1998 when he decided to tell his head coach, Tyrone Willingham (who has since had stints at Notre Dame and the University of Washington), that he is gay.

OUTSPORTS: What position did you play? What kind of playing time did you get at Stanford?

DWIGHT SLATER: I played guard and center at Stanford. I only played my freshman season and was redshirted; therefore, I did not get any playing time.

OUTSPORTS: Where did you play high school football?

SLATER: I played football in Miami, Florida, at Miami Southridge Senior High, one of the better programs in the country at that time.

OUTSPORTS: In high school, what accolades did you receive?

SLATER: In high school I was All-County, All-State, both first team. I also received All-America honorable mention and recognition.

OUTSPORTS: What year did you start at Stanford?

SLATER: I started the '98–99 school year.

OUTSPORTS: How long have you known you were gay?

SLATER: In high school, I figured that I was at least bi. Didn't think about it before then. Then the summer before I arrived at Stanford, I realized that I was no longer bi, but gay.

OUTSPORTS: Why did you decide to come out to your team at Stanford?

SLATER: There was no specific event that prompted me to come out to the team. It was a culmination of homophobic conversations that I overheard. I began to feel cornered and became very depressed. I felt almost forced to come out. I just couldn't keep it to myself.

OUTSPORTS: How did you come out to the team?

SLATER: I told people who I felt would be sympathetic first. And they were for the most part. Later, there was an event in my freshman dorm, called Crossing the Line. In this event, they put a long piece of tape on the ground and ask a series of questions. If the question pertained to you, you crossed the line. I had heard beforehand that there were a few queer questions and decided this would be the way that I would come out. There were two other football players in my dorm. They actually took it pretty well originally, but within the next two days, the entire team knew.

OUTSPORTS: How was it received by other players? By coaches? By the administration?

SLATER: I told my head coach [Tyrone Willingham] first. I sat in his office for at least fifteen minutes in silence trying to muster the courage to just come right out and say it. He waited patiently for me. Then I just said it: "I'm gay." He sat there for a second, then asked, "Well, are you sure?" And I answered yes. Then from there is where it all started to go downhill. He handled my situation like any typical coach would. When faced with a problem, coaches make a game plan and want it followed through, no questions. He told me, first, go home and tell your family. Next, we will figure out how you will tell the team. Then we will get you back to practicing. Well, I couldn't see myself going home and telling my extremely pious and righteous family just like that. I had the biggest problem with telling them because I knew they wouldn't take it well (they didn't, incidentally). He tried to force me to tell them before I was ready. He then told all the other coaches, which I felt was a violation. The coach that recruited me thought he could help me hurry this process along by calling my dad and telling him that I was having a hard time and that there was something that

I needed to tell him. So my family was really worried about me and ready to get on a plane to come and get me. So I broke down and told my sisters. I never got the chance to tell my dad because one of the players told his mom, and his mom, who knew my father, called my father and told him. I'm still very upset with her. Shortly thereafter, I left the team.

OUTSPORTS: Do you think the fact that you are black played a role in the way Willingham, or other players, reacted to you coming out?

SLATER: No, I don't really think so. Willingham did liken his experience to how mine would be if I continued on the team. He said as a black man, when he played, he had to work hard to show that he was capable on the field and in the classroom. He had to work to disprove everyone's prejudices. He said that I would have to do the same thing.

OUTSPORTS: Was homosexuality ever discussed openly on the team? Conversely, how often did you hear terms like *faggot* and *sissy*?

SLATER: Those two words weren't used with frequency, but I did hear them. But there were several conversations that I overheard that made me uncomfortable. For example, "What would you do if your roommate were gay?" "I would move out." "I would kill him if he touched me." "There is no such thing as bisexuality. Either you suck dick or you don't." There were comments about orgies and the like occurring at the LGBT Center on campus. There were also running jokes about three or so guys on the team. Everyone contended that they were gay. They actually are not.

OUTSPORTS: Why did you stop playing?

SLATER: I left because each time I heard one of these conversations, I marked another group of individuals as insensitive and people with whom I can't be comfortable. By the end of that season I didn't have anyone that I could call a friend. I was very lonely and depressed. Then the coaches wanted to force me to tell my family, then told all the other coaches, my dad found out without me telling him. The attitudes of some of the guys clearly changed, and I didn't want to be involved anymore. I had to go.

OUTSPORTS: Did Coach Willingham ever talk with you after you left the team about you being gay, or about how he handled the situation?

SLATER: Nope. Not one conversation. This is partially my fault because I never outright told him that it was his pressure that made me want to leave the team. I wanted to do it before all of these panels and interviews started but just never got around to it.

OUTSPORTS: What has occupied your time since leaving the team?

SLATER: Well, I'm finishing at Stanford this June[2002]. I helped to start BlaQS (Black and Queer at Stanford). My studies, music (I'm a bassoon player), other organizations, and, of course, I had to work because I lost my scholarship after I left the team.

OUTSPORTS: Are you a fan of football? Of any other sports?

SLATER: Yes, I still like football very much. Mostly college. I'm still a big Stanford fan. Hard not to be. I also like basketball, tennis, figure skating, diving, gymnastics, of course.

IN THE LOCKER ROOM

OUR FANTASIES AND REALITY

It should be no surprise that the feature on Outsports highlighting photographs of beautiful athletes, half naked or otherwise, is called "Locker Room." Sports locker rooms have long been the hallowed ground where athletes with beautiful, fit bodies get naked together, shower together, snap towels on each other's asses, and parade around to show off their wares.

For anyone, gay or straight, there's little denying the sexual tension of a locker room. The porn industry, for one, has taken advantage of it—and probably heightened it—for years. Locker room–inspired gay porn titles

San Francisco 49ers running back Garrison Hearst, 2002

Aww, hell no! I don't want any faggots on my team. I know this might not be what people want to hear, but that's a punk. I don't want any faggots in this locker room.

such as *Strokes*, *Swim Meat*, and *Balls between Their Legs* leave little to the imagination and play up the notion that the locker room is a sexually charged atmosphere where anything goes.

It's not just the gay porn industry that has taken advantage of sexuality in the locker room. Straight porn features jocks hooking up with cheerleaders in the same places two baseball teammates in a gay porn movie might go at it. It might involve a more intricate "story line" (heavy on the quotes) to place said cheerleader in said locker room. But once she's there, well, the mind reels.

Straight athletes don't help the issue, either. Locker room talk often ranges anywhere from sex to hot women to more sex to girlfriends to even more sex. Sure, there are tips and tricks shared, some heartfelt hugs and memories passed around. But when you get a bunch of guys together, have them run around for a couple of hours, then strip them down and have them shower, shave, and get dressed together, what else is going to be on their testosterone-filled brains than sex and lots of it?

The locker room, for its part, isn't exactly a sexually charged phenomenon on an island of prudish sport. From men patting one another on the ass after a good play to piling on top of one another in tight pants, sports are chock-full of opportunities to release some sexual tension. It's no wonder some of the respondents in Mike Bryant's study said they gravitated toward sport for the male-to-male contact. Although a large majority of athletes would never call themselves gay, many of them also do have some desire to be physically close to their teammates, some of whom become their best friends and some of whom become their lovers.

There seem to be three main reasons for sexual contact in the locker room. Any given person's actions could be a combination of any of these, but these seem to be the big ones.

The first is just simple horseplay. Guys with little inhibition just messing around with one another. Pretty innocent. These guys most likely either don't put a lot of stock in the stigmata that society places on gay sex, or they see being gay and grabbing somebody's balls as two very different things. It's actually a pretty liberated way of thinking.

The second is the despicable tradition in American sports of hazing: a group of veterans doing embarrassing things to demean younger players. This reason isn't just cognizant of society's stigma on gay sex; it is dependent upon it.

Chris Korman, a graduate from the Columbia Graduate School of Journalism, said he has heard of and watched plenty of curious contact in the locker room. From guys peeing on one another in the shower to rubbing their penises on one another, and even the guys with large penises getting them hard to show their teammates, Korman has been privy to some interesting stories.

He thinks older players establishing the pecking order is the biggest reason this stuff happens in locker rooms. He could be right. Especially in high school, veterans in leadership positions on the team really don't understand what leadership is. If anything, they follow the lead of their coach. Most coaches at the high school level are teachers. In the classroom, they are generally fair and instructional. For some reason, when they walk into the locker room and put on their coaching hat, they become authoritarian. It would certainly be logical that the impressionable kids they're coaching would do the same.

What's interesting, however, is that they would choose to do things like rub their penises on the younger boys to show them who's boss. There are a million ways to show your dominance over someone that don't involve two boys getting naked in a shower.

The third place locker room contact comes from is genuine sexual interest. Whether someone is openly gay, repressed in their sexuality, just experimenting, or secretly longing to be physical with someone of the same sex, there are few better opportunities than the locker room.

What Happens in the Locker Room . . .

There's a bit of a secret code, a set of guidelines, that governs the locker rooms from high school to the pros. It begins with a mantra from the city of sin, Las Vegas: "What happens in the locker room stays in the locker room." Anything goes when you're walking around naked with other men. Drop some soap? Don't be surprised if one of your teammates "jokingly" comes up behind you and starts pressing his goods into your butt cheeks. You get a boner? You'll get teased about it, but there are no worries. As long as the stories about what happens in the locker room stay in the locker room, everybody's cool with a little play on some sexual tension.

The code is predicated on a key assumption: no one can have reason to believe you mean it. The assumption in a team locker room is that no one actually means it when they comment on how hot somebody's ass is

Former Cincinnati Bengals wide receiver–turned–TV analyst Chris Collinsworth wrote a very gay-friendly article on NFL. com, the league's official Web site, after Esera Tuaolo came out. "I relate the issue of women in the locker room to that of an openly gay player in the NFL," Collinsworth wrote. "Do I have the right to deny someone his or her right to do a job because it makes me uncomfortable? No. Could I have made adjustments as to when I showered to allow her to do her job as a reporter? Yes. Would NFL players be uncomfortable with an openly gay player in the locker room? Sure. Could they adjust to make it work? Yes. Would they? I'm not sure. . . . The NFL will have an openly gay player active on a roster. I don't know when it will be, but it's becoming more apparent that the day will come. And when it does, I want to believe that NFL players won't act like cavemen."

Both of these examples are potential previews to how an openly gay athlete could be received in the locker room. If you follow the Penn State example, an openly gay athlete simply wouldn't be received at all—they'd be removed from the team before they ever were allowed to be in the locker room with their teammates.

If you follow the Lisa Olson example, if they were even al-looking or when they slap someone's bare butt in the shower. If that assumption isn't there, the locker room levity breaks down, and suddenly the possibility that it may be serious rears its head.

There can a monumental difference in the tone of a locker room that caters to gay men versus a gym that is dominated by straight men. In the latter, there is often a light tone filled with chatter. Guys are talking to one another, sometimes naked, shooting the shit. It's more of a social atmosphere than anything else.

In gym locker rooms dominated by gay men, the tone is much more serious. There's less chatter, less socializing, more guards put up. The heightened sexual tension is visible in everyone's movement. Men walk straight ahead, not looking down to see what the other guy's got. In a gay locker room, checking somebody out becomes leering, whereas in a straight locker room it's simply comparing hardware.

lowed to remain on the team, they would be ridiculed and harassed. Seems like a scene from a high school gym class, where a student or athlete who is perceived to be gay has his locker filled with shaving cream, gets his head dunked in the toilet, or there is actually some violence toward him. Although you may be thinking that it is far-fetched, consider that locker room "pranks" are a reality in locker rooms at all levels. And if you think the violence is beyond reason, you should also know that it is not abnormal for teammates, after a heated game or when their testosterone is pumping after a rough practice, to attack each other in the locker room.

But at the end of the day, what is most likely to happen is exactly what Andrew Goldstein, the openly gay goaltender in Major League Lacrosse, has experienced. Goldstein said that while with the Long Island Lizards in 2006, he never had any problem from the players. A spokesperson for the Lizards said the front office had never had any complaints from the coaches or players. They both said that the people involved with the team are professionals and that all that mattered was how Goldstein could contribute to the team, not whether or not he had sex with women or men. This is an encouraging thought.

Goldstein has played lacrosse at the collegiate and professional levels, (here with the Long Island Lizards) and he's never had a problem in the locker room.

Photo by Cyd Zeigler Jr.

Women in the Locker Room: A Preview to More

It's not just a gay man that can break the light locker room tone in a men's locker room; the presence of a woman can do the same thing. Female sportswriter Lisa Olson was confronted by a gang of oversexed perverts when she entered the New England Patriots locker room in 1990. Several members of the team surrounded her, flashed their goods, and made some harassing comments. Olson sued the Patriots and the players and settled out of court for a reported quarter million dollars.

Although this over-the-top behavior may be the exception to the rule, the chilling effect of a woman in a locker room of men acting like frat boys is real. When Penn State head football coach Joe Paterno was told that female reporters had to have the same access to his team's locker room that the male reporters had, instead of opening the locker room to women, he closed it to men; he'd rather have no reporters there than have female reporters with his ass-slapping players.

Locker Rooms Give Gays Superhuman Strength

When assumed-to-be-straight athletes are asked about having a gay teammate, the number-one issue they talk about is the locker room. It's a fear that an openly gay man on the team entering the locker room might suddenly lose control, tie his teammates to the benches, and have sex with them against their will. This gay man might somehow summon the powers of Wonder Woman, overpower fifty other football players, and force them to succumb to his every sexual whim.

Of course, that's as ludicrous as the fear itself.

What's interesting is that this forced sex is much more likely to come from a gay person who's deeply in the closet, a repressed person who finds no outlet for his sexual exploration other than someone who's openly gay. Openly gay people find other people with whom to release their sexual urgings, just like (gasp) straight people. Strangely, it's the openly gay person whom many athletes feel threatening.

This is simply an irrational fear. The more likely contact is a slap on the ass, a full nelson in the full monty, or someone simply being ogled for a half second longer than normal. None of these are any more invasive if done by a gay person or a straight person, except in the mind of the person being touched or ogled.

In a sense, many straight men can now accept a female reporter before they can accept a gay male teammate. With a woman, in their eyes, they remain the more powerful aggressor. But with another male teammate of equal strength and sex drive, the tables, they're afraid, could be turned.

Jeremy Shockey on *The Howard Stern Show*, 2002

No, I mean, if I knew there was a gay guy on my college football team, I probably wouldn't, you know, stand for it. . . . You know, I think, you know, they're going to be in the shower with us and stuff, so I don't think that's gonna work. That's not gonna work, you know?

Plus, they're "supposed" to be sexually attracted to a woman; what if there was a gay man in the room and they liked it? That's a scarier thought for many straight athletes than almost anything else.

Out former professional and college athletes to the man have said that they would not have done something in the locker room that might have made their teammates feel uncomfortable. If anything, they would go out of their way to stay well clear of any touching or peeking that might be perceived by a teammate as remotely threatening.

What's really going on underneath that big, masculine armor is the subconscious fear that maybe, just maybe, they might like having a gay guy in the locker room. "I don't want him looking at me" is the typical response from athletes who don't want to get naked with a gay man. Clearly, there is no rational fear of that gay man suddenly getting an uncontrollable erection and chasing this irresistible athlete around the locker room until he succumbs to him—especially with a team of twenty to fifty presumably straight men standing around observing.

On the contrary, if there's a guy in the locker room not staring at any of his naked teammates or keeping to himself, chances are he's the gay one, whereas the guy staring at everyone else's dick, grabbing asses, and making soap jokes in the shower is straight.

With no rational threat of being sexually attacked or touched by this mythical gay teammate, all that's left is the straight athlete and his own thoughts. Most athletes are accustomed to being worshiped and admired. Being admired, even naked, is nothing new to them. Outsports has talked to straight athletes who admit to checking out other guys to see how they measure up, not only "down there" but also in their muscular build. And these athletes have told Outsports that a straight man looking at his teammates or other naked men at the gym is not the exception but the rule.

Whether it's a gay man or a straight man admiring the body of a naked athlete, all that is different is what is going on in that naked athlete's head. He's not going to be touched, not going to be raped, and the gay athlete won't make any different comments than the straight athlete. Just as with the Patriots and Olson, the only difference is what is going on in the mind of that athlete whose libido was heightened when the woman was looking at him, and who's afraid that his libido might also be heightened when a gay man is looking at him. In other words, he's not afraid of what the gay man might do, but what he might do.

"Thou doth protest too much" certainly seems applicable here, just as it has with the debate over female reporters in the locker room. "Straight" male athletes have complained for years about the possibility of both (they've been even more vocal about women in the locker rooms, but, admittedly, that may be because the issue has been talked about for a lot longer).

It's been about thirty years since women began to invade men's locker rooms. In 1977, Melissa Ludtke of *Sports Illustrated* sued the New York

Not every gay man is ready to get off in a locker room. Long-time Outsports reader Munson Man doesn't find them "at all erotic. They are usually too warm and smelly and my goal is to shower and change as quickly as possible. That's not to say I don't take note of hunky guys, but any fantasy usually involves having them follow me home."

"Under no circumstances is sex appropriate in a locker room," Outsports discussion board member Enigma said. "A locker room is not just a place where you change and shower before and after games. It's a place where you can escape from the stresses of the world and just concentrate on one thing . . . going out there and getting the 'W.' It's a place where team-mates bond, friendships are developed and more importantly a group of players transform into a family. You shouldn't ruin that place by having sex . . . keep it in your pants and wait till you get home. Show some respect for your fellow teammates."

Athletes understand the team dynamic, and they under-stand how the locker room builds that. Few athletes, gay or straight, would want to undermine that hallowed part of a team experience.

Still, there is a segment of gay society that thinks it's their God-given right to have sex in a locker room. When Cyd wrote an article for the *New York Blade* in late 2004 criticizing David Barton Gym in New York City for tacitly encouraging sexual be-havior in the locker rooms, he was met with hate mail from many gay people who felt that no one could or should tell them that they can't have sex whenever and wherever they want. But those people are the fringe of gay culture; a majority thinks it's not okay and wouldn't do it.

Yankees for equal access to the locker room to do her job. A judge agreed. Olson's incident with the Patriots helped divide public opinion on the subject, with some sympathizing with her and others saying she deserved what she got.

Openly homophobic former Green Bay Packer Reggie White wrote an infamous column for the *Wall Street Journal* claiming that he had "seen a lot of female reporters and camerawomen ogling guys in the locker room." White urged athletes and their wives to go to court to prevent female reporters from being allowed in the locker room to ogle naked men, saying that it violated the sanctity of their marriages. Apparently, many of them saw women looking at them naked as a violation of their marriages but believed that having sex with women while on the road was fine.

Today, the issue of women in the locker room seems to have died and become accepted. Of course, that may be because another locker room invader is lurking among them.

Outsports Readers: "No Sex in the Locker Room"

The truth of the matter is, despite how erotic both men and women, gay and straight, find the locker room, most gay sports fans and athletes don't think it's appropriate to have sex in a locker room. What? You mean gay men might actually be able to control their sudden urges to have sex with every naked man that moves? Believe it or not, it's true!

When Outsports readers were asked if it was okay to have sex in a public locker room (like a gym), only 14 percent said yes, with another 27 percent saying "sometimes." That number does increase when you're talking about private locker rooms (like that of a sports team). Almost twice as many, 26 percent, say it's okay to have sex in a private locker room, with another 35 percent saying it sometimes is. That "sometimes" could be hours after the game, once the team has gone home and even the janitors have no chance of walking in and stumbling across two people having more fun than might have been appropriate when there was a cheering section.

When asked, "Have you ever had sex in a locker room?" 74 percent of Outsports readers said they had not.

OUTSPORTS
Flashback
#5

DECEMBER 5, 2006

Kevin Nash: Wrestling's Gay-Friendly Champion

Cyd Zeigler Jr.

For some reason, it is surprising to talk to a professional wrestler who is completely gay-friendly. The stereotype of overmasculinized men throwing each other around the ring and bashing each other with fold-up chairs doesn't inspire images of thoughtful, compassionate intellectuals. But for Kevin Nash, a.k.a. "Big Sexy," one of the most popular wrestlers over the past fifteen years, his gay-friendly attitude comes from education and a love of his family.

As a wrestler, the seven-foot Nash has held the WWF Championship, WWF Intercontinental Championship, and WWF Tagteam Championship with the then World Wrestling Federation. In the late nineties, he was part of the New World Order, with Scott Hall and Hulk Hogan, which helped World Championship Wrestling swipe much of the WWF's ratings thunder. Now with Total Nonstop Action Wrestling, Nash is presently recovering from shoulder surgery, spending a lot of time at his home in Florida with his wife and son.

Outsports talked with Nash about gay characters in wrestling, gay wrestlers, and "Big Sexy's" gay family members.

OUTSPORTS: Professional wrestling has a pretty long history of including gay-acting characters. Why do you think characters like Gorgeous George and Adrian Adonis and Goldust and Lenny and Lodi have been so popular?

KEVIN NASH: I think the flamboyancy, because most of those characters are kind of flamboyant characters. I think that wrestling as a whole is such an escapism for a lot of people that it takes it to another level, to escape even further.

OUTSPORTS: When Lenny and Lodi started acting effeminately, GLAAD stepped in and threatened Turner, and Turner pulled the characters. One of the things they said was that characters like Lenny and Lodi are somehow bad for gay people. What do you think of that?

NASH: To me, it's such an exaggeration. It would be one thing if it was a docudrama, and we were trying to depict something that was real life. But it's such a tongue-in-cheek industry as it is. I was one of the writers when that Lenny and Lodi thing was going on. And the story line was going to be that eventually, because they were both orphans, eventually they were going to find out that they were brothers. That was where the story line was going. Everyone thought these guys were lovers, because they kept making reference to this closeness that they felt. And I was really offended because Turner succumbed to GLAAD. We were going to do an end-around on everybody. It would have been like, "Who said they were gay? We aren't depicting these guys as gay. We're depicting different scenarios. You're the ones who said they were gay."

OUTSPORTS: So you were trying to turn the stereotype on its head?

NASH: We were trying to. And then they didn't let us do it. Our standards and practices guy, I'm quite sure he was gay. He sat in our booking meetings. We ran everything by him, and he knew where the story line was going, and he didn't have a problem with it. Bob Mould was also in our creative room at the time. And he's gay, and he was one of the writers.

OUTSPORTS: Do you think that kind of thing had a chilling effect on creating gay characters?

NASH: I think so. All of those home improvement shows have the macho guy, the chick, and the gay guy. Every one of them. I was watching one the other night, and the gay guy said, "What's wrong, you don't think I can operate a power tool because I'm . . . short?" It's okay for him to make a joke of everything, but if the other big macho guy would have said something like that, everyone would have been up in arms. It's such a gray line where you can go to in society. And GLAAD's strong. It's one thing if they go in and slap you on the wrist. They came in and said, "We're going to contact your advertisers." It's hard enough to get advertising on wrestling.

OUTSPORTS: So you had gay people aware of what was going on?

NASH: Absolutely. And I think because there were gay people in the creative meetings, we were very aware of where we could go. I just wondered if there was a gay NASCAR driver, how that guy would get over. If wrestling is "good ol' boy," there's only one thing more "good ol' boy" than wrestling, and that's NASCAR. You can't tell me one of those guys isn't gay.

OUTSPORTS: Chris Kanyon has made claims that he was let go by the WWE [World Wrestling Entertainment] because he was gay. And I've heard guys like Ric Flair say it was because Chris wasn't a good enough wrestler. Do you have any insight into that?

NASH: I don't know what happened up there. Kanyon is very talented. His persona was never really strong, but as far as fundamentally doing the wrestling, there's really nobody any better. But he just never had that look. He had good size. The bad thing about Chris was that he was best when his face was covered over, when he was Mortus. One of the top creative guys for Vince, Pat Patterson, has been openly gay for years. So I don't think him being gay had much to do with him being released. They probably just didn't like him.

OUTSPORTS: So there are people in professional wrestling who are openly gay or are at least known to be gay?

NASH: Yes.

OUTSPORTS: Does it matter to you if one of the guys you're wrestling around with on a mat is gay?

NASH: It doesn't to me.

OUTSPORTS: Do you have any gay friends or family members?

NASH: Oh, yeah. I lost a first cousin to AIDS. I've got members of my family who are gay.

OUTSPORTS: When we talk to athletes in team sports about having gay teammates, we keep hearing they don't want to shower with them. Do you share showers with other wrestlers?

NASH: Yeah, but it's kind of different because you shower as the event goes on. The first match of the night would go out and wrestle, and then they come in and shower. It's kind of a shower-in-shifts thing. When you finish your segment, you go in and shower. It's not like there are fifty-five guys in football, but there are five or six guys in there.

OUTSPORTS: Does it matter to you if a gay guy is looking at you naked?

NASH: No, as long as he's looking and approving.

OUTSPORTS: You seem very educated and gay-friendly on these issues. Where does that come from?

NASH: Number one is just that, education. I've got gay friends. I've been around gay people my whole life. Intolerance is just ignorance. That's all it is. God forbid if some gay people move into your neighborhood: curb appeal will be nice, and the property value will double. God forbid. [Homophobia] is just prejudice like anything else.

OUTSPORTS: How do you think you'd react if one of your longtime wrestling colleagues, for example, Scott Hall, came out to you?

NASH: That's an ongoing angle that I think Scott and I could do is if, after all these years, people find out that Hall and Nash are actually gay. The Disco Inferno. It'd be the biggest thing. For all these macho guys to find out Nash and Hall are gay.

OUTSPORTS: Some of these guys who play gay characters are gay. How does that play off, with Kevin Nash the person being straight, but Kevin Nash the character being gay?

NASH: When Goldust did it, I think a lot of guys got creeped out about it. The part I played in *The Longest Yard*, where I took some estrogen and became a little more feminine, I've had friends go, "Dude, how can you do that?" And I say, "Well, I read the script and it was funny." I was doing a comedy, and I read the script, and none of the guys wanted to play that part.

OUTSPORTS: Why is that?

NASH: It's just the homophobia. That's the way I look at it.

OUTSPORTS: Thanks for taking the time, and thanks for having such a great attitude about gay issues.

NASH: Like I said, when you have family who are "alternative lifestyle," it's not that big of a deal. It's just part of our family. It's no big deal.

TRANNIES ON A TEE

Although gay issues in sports have long been society's focal point when talking about sexuality and sports, there is a potentially more volatile issue that has attracted more and more attention—and a surprising amount of acceptance—in recent years: transsexuals in sports. Outsports was created as a place to talk about gay issues in sports. Even to us, in late 1999 and early 2000, the growing debate of transgender athletes, and in particular their role in women's sports, was an issue worth only an occasional mention as a freakish point of interest or a sidebar. Outsports has long focused more on the social hurdles and barriers in sports that keep gay men quietly in the closet or out of sports completely. But they pale in comparison to the ignorant rules and misunderstanding that all transgender athletes face at some point.

The Birth of the Dilemma

Men's superiority in athletics has been well documented. In track and field, the men's world record for the 100-meter sprint is more than six-tenths of a second faster than the women's; the men's 10K record is more than three minutes faster than that of the women; the men's high jump record is more than a foot higher than the women's. Men consistently run faster, throw farther, jump higher, drive golf balls farther, serve tennis balls faster, and kick footballs deeper than women.

That's certainly not to say that some women can't beat some men in sports. In the famous 1973 "Battle of the Sexes," Billie Jean King beat the pants off fifty-five-year-old Bobby Riggs in straight sets. Although world records may distance male and female athletes, those female world record holders could still wipe the track with most men.

The one area where women seem to consistently compete with and sometimes beat other elite male athletes is ultramarathons, which are races longer than 26.2 miles. The most common distances are 50 and 100 miles. Some women have been winning the occasional ultramarathon outright, and many have been garnering top-five finishes, pointing to the idea that women may actually match men in long-term endurance. However, because men outperform women on a consistent basis in athletic competitions of various levels, men and women have long competed separately.

What does all this talk about the dominance of men over women have to do with a chapter about transsexuals? Everything. It's the conversation that has dominated discussions about how male-to-female transsexuals should compete in athletic competitions.

There has long been a fear that an athlete who was once a man would have an unfair competitive advantage when competing with other women. A female-to-male transsexual likely wouldn't raise an eyebrow on a competition committee because that athlete would not be coming from a perceived advantage (though, interestingly, that person would likely be taking hormones that, outside of medical purposes, could put their eligibility into question). But male-to-female athletes, having produced testosterone for so much of their lives, have not only raised eyebrows but been met with rules, regulations, and protests preventing them from competing as women.

Renee Richards Fights to Play Tennis

Renee Richards famously challenged the old establishment that prevented male-to-female transsexuals from competing in women's tennis tournaments. Born Richard Raskin, he began taking hormone treatments in the late 1960s and received sex-reassignment surgery in 1975. Soon after, as Renee, she began playing women's tournaments until her former identity was discovered, and she was barred from women's tennis. She successfully challenged the ban in court and went on to play in her first U.S. Open in 1977. It was a watershed moment for transgender athletes, but the battle for admittance to competitions has only slightly quieted and is likely decades from going away.

At the heart of Richards's battle was a chromosome test utilized by the Olympics. The usefulness of chromosome tests was strongly disputed even when the Olympics instituted them in 1967. That year, Polish sprinter Ewa Klobukowska, who had won a gold and a bronze at the 1964 Tokyo Olympics, was determined to be XXY and was banned from competition.

Important Gender-Bending Athletes throughout History

Mianne Bagger. Australian golfer who is believed to be the first trans golfer to compete in a professional women's tournament.

Michelle Dumaresq. Canadian professional downhill mountain biker since 2001. After three races, the International Cyclists Union suspended Dumaresq's license and suggested that she compete as a male. Eventually, they reinstated her as a female. Dumaresq has won national championships since then and is one of the premier female downhill bikers in the world.

Ewa Klobukowska. Female Polish sprinter who, in 1967, was ruled ineligible to compete because her sex chromosomes were XXY. She later gave birth to a child.

Renee Richards. Tennis player who challenged the United States Tennis Association's criterion that female players have XX sex chromosomes. Believed to be first trans tennis player to compete on the women's tour.

Nong Tum. Thai kickboxer who was the inspiration for the film Beautiful Boxer. Before sex-reassignment surgery, Nong Tum created a stir at the age of sixteen when, wearing makeup, he beat a more masculine-looking man in a match. In 1999, she underwent sex-reassignment surgery.

Stanislawa Walasiewicz. Polish-born sprinter, later known as Stella Walsh, was the fastest woman in the world in the 1930s. She won the 100-meter dash in world-record time at the 1932 Olympics and finished second in Berlin four years later. She was killed accidentally in 1980, an innocent bystander to an armed robbery in Cleveland, Ohio. An autopsy found that she had testicles, and some reports say that she also had female genitalia. Her birth certificate, which lists her as female, further confuses one of the great sports gender mysteries.

When Klobukowska later gave birth to a baby girl, it fueled the arguments that the chromosome-based gender rules, which permitted only XX females to compete as a female and XY males to compete as a male, were misguided.

Because Richards still had the chromosomes of a man, despite hormone injections and sex-reassignment surgery, U.S. Tennis and other groups said she wouldn't be allowed to compete against women. However, after castration and many years of injections, the physical benefits of testosterone had dissipated, and the New York Supreme Court found that the physical advantages she once enjoyed while a man had been negated.

This was a huge victory for transgender athletes. It wasn't simply because a court had forced U.S. Tennis to allow Richards to play; it was because the court suddenly changed the rules by which gender was to be determined. Although other sports and sports organizations took years if not decades to catch up to the ruling, gone was the chromosome test that permitted only someone born as a female to compete in tennis as a female; a new understanding had taken a foothold in sports.

Despite some of tennis's old-establishment threats that allowing Richards to play would open the floodgates and throngs of transsexuals would want to play women's tennis, the issue lay essentially dormant for the next twenty years. Lower-level male tennis players didn't start lining up for sex-reassignment surgery so they could dominate the women's tour. While our society finally began to openly discuss gay rights and gay issues, in addition to AIDS, the issue of transsexuals in sports sat on the back burner until the late 1990s.

Golf at the Forefront

It may come as a bit of a surprise to some that the sport of golf has helped lead the way for transsexual equality since the late '90s. Viewed as a country club sport controlled by the conservative elite, its image is dominated by rich white men who won't even let women be members at Augusta National, the site of the Masters. Many golf-centric country clubs have also prevented same-sex partners from taking advantage of the same privileges that straight couples receive. Even the dominance of nonwhite golfers Tiger Woods and Vijay Singh has done little to change golf's image. However, beneath the surface is an evolving, forward-thinking sport that has in recent years begun to earn itself a bit of a reprieve from the good ol' boys' image most associated with Augusta National and other white-male-dominated clubs.

Mianne Bagger was born a boy in Copenhagen in 1966. As a boy, she started golfing at the age of eight, and, as her family moved their residence to England and ultimately Australia, she golfed more and more; in the midnineties, she began thinking of entering amateur competitions.

In the meantime, Bagger had begun transitioning from male to female, and in 1995, she had sex-reassignment surgery. When she started appearing in amateur women's tournaments in 1998, many people were aghast and began throwing up the same arguments that Renee Richards had faced twenty years earlier: that her being born biologically a male gave her an unfair advantage. But the Australian Women's Golf Association (AWGA), an amateur golf union, had no birth restrictions on membership, so Bagger was allowed to play. She won her first South-Australian Championship in 1999 and then won back-to-back championships in 2001 and 2002.

In 2003, she hit a brick wall when she attempted to join the Australian Ladies Professional Golf Association (ALPGA). Bagger was refused admittance to the association because, unlike the AWGA, the ALPGA did have a policy that members had to have been born women.

A Hormonal Double Standard?

As the sports world strengthens its opposition to the injection of steroids and testosterone by athletes, many athletic governing bodies are adopting written policies that not only make hormone injections acceptable but actually make it a condition for competing (in the case of male-to-female transsexuals taking estrogen).

Some detractors find the written acceptance of hormone injections in sport to be a double standard. This argument, of course, is poppycock. Society has long made, justifiably so, many allowances for special cases. Athletes who use steroids for medicinal purposes, for example, be it HIV or asthma patients, can be granted special waivers from the rules that other able-bodied athletes must stick to. To say that acceptance and inclusion of transgender athletes somehow undermine the athletic establishment's war on performance-enhancing drugs is an uneducated way of framing what is meant to be a way of building stronger athletic competition and making sports more accessible to everyone.

Statement of the 2003 Stockholm Consensus on Sex Reassignment in Sports

Although it took seven months for formal adoption by the IOC, with some adjustments and additions, the Stockholm Consensus may well be regarded as one of the most important decisions ever handed down regarding transgender athletes. On October 28, 2003, an ad-hoc committee convened by the IOC Medical Commission met in Stockholm to discuss and issue recommendations on the participation of individuals who have undergone sex reassignment (male-to-female and converse) in sport.

This group was composed of Professors Arne Ljungqvist and Martin Ritzen of Sweden, Odile Cohen-Haguenauer and Marc Fellous of France, and Myron Genel and Joe Leigh Simpson of the United States and Dr. Patrick Schamasch of France. They confirmed the previous recommendation that any "individuals undergoing sex reassignment of male to female before puberty should be regarded as girls and women" (female). This applies as well for female-to-male reassignment; those individuals should be regarded as boys and men (male). They further recommended that individuals undergoing sex reassignment

Is Gender Binary?

In the question "Is gender binary?" lies the great misunderstanding that transsexuals face both in- and outside of sports. Many transsexuals feel that they were actually born the gender opposite their outward sexual appearance but that their bodies weren't on the same page as their gender. So if you tell some male-to-female transsexuals—and Bagger was making this argument in 2003—that they had to be born female to compete, their argument is that they were, but their bodies just didn't realize it.

In a culture that sees sexuality as a stable binary entity—you're either male or female—this idea of people being both or neither or changing between the two has caused more problems than it has solved. When Cyd was organizing a gay day with the New York Mets in 2004, one of the issues the team was concerned about was which bathrooms potential transgender spectators would use. They didn't want any trouble, and they from male to female after puberty (and the converse) be eligible for participation in female or male competitions, respectively, under the following conditions:

- surgical anatomical changes have been completed, including external genitalia changes and gonadectomy
- legal recognition of their assigned sex has been conferred by the appropriate official authorities
- hormonal therapy appropriate for the assigned sex has been administered in a verifiable manner and for a sufficient length of time to minimize gender-related advantages in sport competitions

In the opinion of the group, eligibility should begin no sooner than two years after gonadectomy. It is understood that a confidential case-by-case evaluation will occur. In the event that the gender of a competing athlete is questioned, the medical delegate (or equivalent) of the relevant sporting body shall have the authority to take all appropriate measures for the determination of the gender of a competitor.

were mildly concerned that if a trannie walked into a bathroom—be it a men's room or women's room—some of their "less enlightened" fans might not take kindly to it. Luckily, Shea Stadium, where the Mets play, is in New York City proper, and transsexuals have the legal right to use the bathroom that best reflects their gender identity—that gender which they put forward in society—whether they have had reassignment surgery or not. Federal courts have also found the same right to access in the case of employment.

The International Olympic Committee Changes the Rules

In late 2003 an International Olympic Committee (IOC) ruling was the biggest victory for transgender athletes since Renee Richards's legal win. A group was convened in Stockholm, Sweden, in October by the IOC Medical Commission to issue recommendations on the participation of transgender athletes in the Olympics. The committee laid out a set of criteria and recommended that if a transgender athlete had fulfilled the criteria, whether they were male-to-female or female-to-male, they should be allowed to participate as reflected by their new gender identity. The recommendations, known as the Stockholm Consensus, were adopted by the IOC with some modifications in May 2004.

Although the ruling pertained solely to the Olympics, there was a ripple effect throughout sports. The IOC decision drove the ALPGA to rewrite its policy that had kept Mianne Bagger from competing the previous year. And in 2004, Bagger became what is believed to be the first male-to-female transsexual to compete in a women's professional golf tournament. That same year, she played her first professional season on the Swedish Telia Tour, and in 2005 she was accepted on the Ladies European Tour.

Taking the lead of their sisters across the Pond, the United States Golf Association (USGA) opened its women's playing field to male-to-female

Perception Can Be Everything

In February 2006, MSNBC.com ran a two-page story by Elizabeth Chuck about transgender athletes, including cyclist Kristen Worley and golfer Mianne Bagger. The story quoted Jill Pilgrim, general counsel and director of business affairs for USA Track and Field, who was part of a team that researched, among other things, the advantages of transgender athletes. "When a male-to-female transsexual undergoes hormone therapy," Pilgrim told MSNBC.com, "they are reducing their testosterone levels and taking female hormones. They lose muscle mass, which is the advantage testosterone gives you." Still, when MSNBC.com asked readers about the advantages of transgender athletes, the result was overwhelming:

QUESTION: Despite research findings, do you think transsexual athletes have an advantage? (14,517 respondents)

23 percent—No, and other female athletes shouldn't feel threatened.

77 percent—Yes, by size alone, they have an edge.

transsexuals in March 2005 when it shed the old Olympic-style chromosome test. The USGA's new policy welcomes anyone who has, among other things, had sex-reassignment surgery and has been taking estrogen for at least two years.

Why has the stodgy old sport of golf been ahead of the pack in welcoming transsexual athletes? It has to do with the sport itself. Although women can't join Augusta National and many other golf clubs, female golfers have begun competing against men in some professional tournaments, and they've even started beating some of the male competitors. Though no woman has won, or even come close to winning, a PGA Tour event, they are competing, and it's not inconceivable that one day a woman will give the entire field of a men's event a run for its money. And even though the average man can certainly outdrive the average woman from a tee and hit a seven-iron longer, golf is not a sport that is dominated by necessarily the strongest or the fastest. Because most of the scoring in golf happens within a hundred yards of the hole—a distance at which strength takes

Even if slight advantages did still exist, that would reflect the diversity of humanity. Certain people are born stronger, taller, or with a higher aptitude for information. Should these people not be allowed to compete in sports because they have an advantage over other athletes? Should Michael Jordan not have been allowed to play basketball because of his natural talent, or should Tiger Woods not be allowed to play golf because he had a father that pushed him toward golf before he could ride a bike? Hardly.

In fact, the testosterone levels a male-to-female transgender athlete has can be well below that with which elite female athletes are born. But this is more about perception than anything else. As gay men and lesbians fight for equality and access to sports, transgender rights will continue to experience a ride, albeit several years behind, on the coattails of that movement. As more athletes like Mianne Bagger and Renee Richards participate, more sports governing bodies will be forced to deal with the medical realities, and the power of misperceptions will go the way of the designated hitter in the National League.

Molly Lenore—Transgender Athlete Still Dealing with Ignorance

This binary perspective of gender can sometimes have unforeseen consequences, even in the world of gay sports. The Gay Games in Chicago in 2006 featured sex-separated divisions for flag football; whereas other sports had an "open" and a "women's" division, organizers had decided that football would be "men" and "women." Molly Lenore, a transgender athlete and member of the New York Gay Football League (NYGFL), decided to play with the mostly male team that was composed of players from the league, since no women's team was organized by league players.

Lenore brought more experience to the team than virtually anyone else and had enjoyed being a man and playing men's sports. "For me I was never tortured," Lenore said. "It was more of an evolution." Although her fierce competitive attitude on the field hasn't changed, she has noticed that the sex-reassignment surgery and estrogen have made her a little slower, taken away some of her strength, and added more weight retention.

She initially registered for the Gay Games as a female. And because of that initial registration, the Gay Games organizers told her she could not play in the men's division. In softball, she was allowed to play in the "open" division, but she was barred

a back seat to concentration, practice, and finesse—women can quickly make up what they lost on the first shot of the hole. It's the same reason so many golfers in their late thirties and forties are able to compete with players in their twenties and early thirties, and why Jack Nicklaus was able to win his sixth Masters at the age of forty-six.

Golf is the perfect sport for men and women to compete against one another, because the playing field is about as even as it can be in sports. Likewise, it's the one sport in which a player who was once male would have the least physical advantage over female competitors.

Golf has also been coaxed along by transgender golfers such as Bagger. Without her, the ALPGA certainly would have had no reason to revisit its policy. Although the IOC decision was a major impetus for the change, it was Bagger's pushing of buttons for years in Australia and her request to from playing with her league mates in the men's football division because she initially registered as female. Other trans athletes had no problems playing in divisions that reflected their new gender identity.

This was an odd precedent. Here was a trans athlete being prevented from playing the sports of her gender identity at birth, which is how sports organizations for decades had been forcing trans athletes to compete. High-level athletic organizations allow women to play in men's divisions, as the perceived physical advantages are not there. For example, the NCAA has allowed women to play men's football and ice hockey. What was so strange was a gay sporting event being even more conservative than their counterparts at the NCAA. One collegiate sports administrator who heard the story said to Outsports simply, "You've got to be kidding me."

Ultimately, after weeks of requests from Lenore and her team, and Outsports interceding on her behalf, Gay Games organizers saw the problem with their classification of the two divisions for flag football, and Lenore was allowed to play. But the incident reflected the depth of the misunderstanding so many people have about transsexual athletes.

be a part of the tour in 2003 that forced the ALPGA to take the IOC decision seriously and alter its policy to reflect it.

Other major sports entities are now reexamining their transgender policies. The NCAA has been working for some time on a new policy that will open the door for transgender athletes to compete in their new self-identified gender. It was just in 2000 that the NCAA added sexual orientation to its nondiscrimination policy; that they seem ready to take this next step, less than a decade later, reflects the fast-changing landscape of sexuality and sports.

Molly Lenore (top) and teammate Manny Urquiza pose with their silver medals in football at Gay Games VII.

Photo by Cyd Zeigler Jr.

Is There an "Unfair" Advantage?

Although doors have been opened for transgender athletes, at the core of the issue remains misunderstanding about the physical advantages male-to-female transsexuals have over other females. Despite the IOC and other organizations determining that, given certain medical conditions, the physical advantages of years of testosterone are negated, the idea that women who were once men have an unfair advantage continues.

To be sure, without those medical conditions and procedures, there is an advantage. Few, if any, people would advocate that a pre-op male-to-female should be allowed to compete in women's divisions of competitions. The estrogen injections are also key. No one in sports is advocating that Phil Mickelson should be able to put on a dress, claim to be a woman, and head for the women's tees of the LPGA. RuPaul has a ways to go before he can put on some track shoes and race against Marion Jones (not that he'd have a chance in hell, even if she were wearing the high heels). "It's hard to generalize because [physical changes] differ dramatically from individual to individual," said Pauline Park, cochair of the New York Association for Gender Rights Advocacy. "But if someone is living as a post-op, male-to-female transsexual woman, who has significantly enhanced her levels of estrogen, then what advantages there are will be significantly diminished if not, over time, eliminated." Present medical consensus is that in post-op male-to-female transsexuals, muscle mass decreases by about 30 percent and testosterone levels can often actually be below those physically female at birth.

THE GOOD GUYS AND THE BAD GUYS

I t's tough being gay in the sports world for reasons articulated throughout this book. It doesn't make it any easier when players, coaches, and media professionals make homophobic comments. These days, such remarks get greater scrutiny, and some making those comments have been forced to apologize.

Our list of the good guys and bad guys in sports tends to be top-heavy with the latter for good reason. Anyone making a comment perceived to be antigay is going to get more scrutiny than someone who might be tolerant and supportive but doesn't hold a press conference to say it. When Outsports reported that Jeremy Shockey appeared on *The Howard Stern Show* and made antigay remarks, the media was glued to it for forty-eight hours; when Outsports reported that Seattle Seahawk Shaun Alexander appeared on the same show and made gay-friendly remarks, no one noticed.

There are many, many others in sports who have made either positive or negative comments about gay people. This is a sampling of some of the worst of the worst and the best of the best.

The Bad Guys

Just because someone makes one homophobic remark doesn't make him a bigot for life, so their comments are put in some sort of context. However, with some of the repeat offenders, the context is the fact that they have made public antigay comments and not learned.

John Rocker, Major League Baseball

Rocker is the patron saint of antigay remarks. Here's what he said in his infamous interview with *Sports Illustrated*, for which he was suspended from baseball: "Imagine having to take the 7 train to [Shea Stadium in New York] looking like you're [in] Beirut next to some kid with purple hair, next to some queer with AIDS, right next to some dude who got out of jail for the fourth time, right next to some 20-year-old mom with four kids. It's depressing."

Coach Rene Portland, Penn State Women's Basketball

The bottom line is this: if Penn State women's basketball coach Rene Portland had said she did not want Jewish or black players on her team, she would have been fired within a week. It has been twenty years, though, since Portland said she did not want lesbians on her team, and she is still gainfully employed by the university (which has a nondiscrimination policy that includes sexual orientation). In April 2006, action was finally taken against her when the university ruled that Portland created a "hostile, intimidating and offensive environment" based on the perceived sexual orientation of a former player. Portland continues to insist she did nothing wrong.

Portland, head coach of the Lady Nittany Lions for twenty-seven seasons, was required to pay a fine of ten thousand dollars, a written reprimand was put in her personnel file, she was required to participate in a professional development experience devoted to diversity, and she has also been informed that further violations will result in termination with cause. A federal discrimination lawsuit against Portland and Penn State was settled out of court in 2007. Terms of the settlement were confidential.

The player in question, Jennifer Harris, was upset by Penn State's decision. Harris is now at James Madison University, where she was eligible to play her junior and senior seasons. "I am disappointed by this result," Harris said. "Penn State did not take the allegations seriously and does not appear interested in solving the underlying problem."

Helen Carroll, who runs the homophobia in Sports project

He was forced to undergo sensitivity training and in 2006 described what a "farce" he thought the training was. "The guy told me when I got there I had to show up to make it look good for people, so after about 15 minutes I left and walked right out of the room and it satisfied the powers that be," Rocker told the *Chicago Tribune*.

A second incident involved Rocker in August 2002. He was having brunch at Bread Winners Café in Dallas with his girlfriend. Bread Winners is, according to 102.1 FM KDGE openly gay morning talk show host Jagger, known for being "very gay-friendly." According to witnesses

for the National Center for Lesbian Rights and is a former basketball coach, had a mixed reaction. "It is a positive for the university to absolutely say Rene Portland did discriminate and create a hostile environment for Jennifer Harris," Carroll said. "The second part is how to remedy that. . . . We're saying it can't be solved if Rene Portland says there is no problem and it's the university that's mistaken." Carroll questioned how effective diversity training can be for Portland when she insists she did nothing wrong, and she called the remedies, including the size of the fine, a slap on the wrist.

In 2005, Harris, with the help of the NCLR, sued Portland and the university. The complaint said that "despite Harris' outstanding performance as a player during her two-year career at Penn State from 2003 to 2005, Coach Portland repeatedly questioned Harris about her sexual orientation, repeatedly threatened to kick Harris off the team if she found out Harris was a lesbian, and eventually told other players not to associate with Harris because she believed that Harris was gay. In 2005, Coach Portland abruptly told Harris to find somewhere else to play." Portland contended Harris was kicked off the team based on her performance. Harris has said she is not a lesbian.

Even after the fine and reprimand, Portland was unrepentant: "With respect to the administrative decision's conclusions relating to claims involving alleged sexual orientation, I believe the process that was used to reach these conclusions was flawed." Portland was back coaching the Lady Nittany Lions for the 2006–2007 season, but at season's end, resigned.

quoted by Jagger, when Rocker got up to leave, after sitting next to two men at another table, he said, "Fucking fruitcakes." He then left the restaurant to retrieve his car.

Rocker apparently then yelled at a transgendered woman, who happened to be exiting the restaurant, from his car. When the woman yelled back, Rocker got out of his car and got into a screaming match with the woman for what witnesses told Jagger was five to ten minutes. Allegedly included in his comments were the statements "You're nothing but a fucking freak" and "I hope you get AIDS and die."

Rocker issued a written apology, according to the Associated Press, as he gave his version of events. "It seemed as if they were trying to bait me with suggestive comments," Rocker said in the statement. He said he finished his meal and got up to leave. Then, he said, the unidentified patrons followed him out of the restaurant, located in a predominantly gay neighborhood, and made an obscene gesture, the Associated Press reported. "At that point, I admit I was angry and said some things I probably should not have said, but I wanted to make it clear their attentions were unwelcome," he said.

Rocker remained in baseball after the '99 incident, but his career went in the toilet afterward, and he was out of Major League Baseball within five years. Coincidence or not, karma was at work.

Jason Williams, NBA

As a guard for the NBA's Sacramento Kings in 2001, Williams said this to an Asian fan during a game: "Are you a fag? Are you gay? Do you remember the Vietnam War? I'll kill y'all just like that." He apologized the next day "to the Asian community or any other community." Guess the "other community" means gays. Williams's career was not hurt by the incident, and in June 2006 he was a member of the Miami Heat when they won the NBA title.

Goran Ivanisevic, Tennis

After winning Wimbledon in 2001, Ivanisevic gave an interview in which he said, "Then I hit, huge. And that ball was on the line, was not even close. And that guy [the umpire], he looks like a faggot a little bit, you know. This hair all over him. He calls it [out] and I couldn't believe he did it." He should know that most stereotypical gays like smooth, not hairy. He also issued what he must have thought was an apology, saying, "I have nothing against those people. Just that's the thing I say."

Tim Hardaway, ex-NBA player

"I hate gay people, so I let it be known. I don't like gay people and I don't like to be around gay people. I am homophobic. I don't like it. It shouldn't be in the world or in the United States. So yeah, I don't like it."

Hardaway made big news as he uttered these words on a Miami radio station in February 2007 when asked about the coming out story on former NBA player John Amaechi. He later tried to backtrack in a TV interview, saying: "I shouldn't have said that I hate gay people or anything like that. I should have just said I don't condone him being in the locker room."

Hardaway, who played for the NBA's Miami Heat. then made a bizarre comparison to the way he talks about gays to the way he discusses food. "When I was growing up. . . . .we say we hate broccoli, we say we hate potato chips . . . It's just a form of how we talk."

With each subsequent interview, Hardaway made things worse. On ESPN.com, while saying he didn't have a "hate bone" in his body, he added: "You know, we were brought up to not even condone or associate yourself with a gay person. If you knew of a gay person, disassociate yourself with them. . . . When I see gay people holding hands or kissing in the streets, I just don't think that's right."

The reaction was swift. Columnists ripped Hardaway (TIM HARDAWAY IS AN IDIOT was one headline), while the NBA dropped Hardaway from official functions at its 2007 All-Star Game. "We removed him from representing us because we didn't think his comments were consistent with having anything to do with us," NBA commissioner David Stern said

Hardaway also lost his job as coach of a team in the Continental Basketball Association. "As it relates to the CBA, we do not discriminate against individuals based on sexual orientation," league commissioner Ricardo Richardson said.

Hardaway said his life in the week after uttering "I hate gay people" was "hell. Pure hell." He deserved it.

Ivanisevic must use *faggot* as his slur of choice, since he said something similar two weeks before the 2001 Wimbledon, and said this in California three months earlier to the question, "In breaking a racquet, is it mostly in the wrist?" "Hey, sometimes I watch the TV, and then I see the guys when they throw the racquets. They throw it like a faggot, you know. They throw it not to throw it. When you throw the racquet, you throw the racquet. I mean, you break. Sometimes doesn't break, thanks God. But you throw the racquet. You don't throw it and it's going like this. You have to smack the racquet, you know, or you have to get anger."

Julian Tavarez, Major League Baseball

The Chicago Cubs pitcher put his foot in his mouth after a 2001 game in San Francisco. "Why should I care about the fans? They're a bunch of assholes and faggots here," he said. Tavarez apologized the next day: "I want to apologize to the City of San Francisco and say how sorry I am for what I said. I'm a very emotional man and I don't always mean what I say. Sometimes my emotions get the best of me. I am very sorry, very sorry."

Todd Jones, Major League Baseball

Todd Jones, a relief pitcher for the Colorado Rockies, had some choice words in 2002 for the *Denver Post* after a reporter asked the pitcher about the Broadway play *Take Me Out*, in which a professional baseball player comes out of the closet. "I wouldn't want a gay guy being around me," Jones told the *Post*. "It's got nothing to do with me being scared. That's the problem: All these people say he's got all these rights. Yeah, he's got rights or whatever, but he shouldn't walk around proud. It's like he's rubbing it in our face. 'See me, Hear me roar.' We're not trying to be close-minded, but then again, why be confrontational when you don't really have to be?" He went on to say that "if [the team] thinks for one minute he's disrupting the clubhouse—if he doesn't hit fifty homers or win twenty games—they're not going to put up with that."

The Colorado Rockies issued a statement regarding Jones's comments: "The unfortunate comments made by pitcher Todd Jones and published in the *Denver Post* in no way reflect the views, opinions, or attitudes of the Colorado Rockies Baseball Club." Team president Keli McGregor said in the statement: "As an organization and as a part of this community, we are committed to providing an environment for our employees and fans that is free of discrimination and prejudice, regardless of race, color, sex, religion, national orientation, age, disability, or status as a veteran." However, Major League Baseball never punished Jones for his remarks.

Garrison Hearst, NFL

When Esera Tuaolo came out in 2002 to a flood of media attention, San Francisco 49ers running back Garrison Hearst promptly focused the spotlight on himself. "Aww, hell no! I don't want any faggots on my team," he told reporters. "I know this might not be what people want to hear, but that's a punk. I don't want any faggots in this locker room."

Hearst was swept up in a media storm and issued an apology that came across as one of the most genuine an athlete has offered after an antigay remark. "First of all, I want to apologize for the comments that I made, and to the gay community," Hearst said at the team's headquarters in Santa Clara before a packed media house. "I didn't realize it would be so harmful. I want to direct it to my teammates for causing a disturbance among the team before this game. Being an African American, I know that discrimination is wrong, and I was wrong for saying what I said about anybody—any race, any religion. I want to apologize to the San Francisco 49ers organization, the city of San Francisco for the comments that I made, and to my teammates for bringing this distraction upon us. I hope that everyone can accept my apology. Thank you."

The 49ers did not fine or punish Hearst in any way. "It's money out of a paycheck. That doesn't teach us anything," then coach Steve Mariucci said. "The lesson is much more important than any sort of fine. Garrison certainly learned something. I think our team is going to learn something, and I did, too."

Jeremy Shockey, NFL

The New York Giants tight end has gays on the brain. In 2002, in an interview with shock jock Howard Stern, he made this infamous comment: "I mean, if I knew there was a gay guy on my college football team, I probably wouldn't, you know, stand for it. . . . You know, I think, you know, they're going to be in the shower with us and stuff, so I don't think that's gonna work. That's not gonna work, you know?"

Shockey tried to worm his way out of it, telling the *New York Daily News* the day after Outsports broke the story: "It's a show just for comedy. I guess I do regret saying it. I didn't think anyone was going to make a big deal out of it. I'm not prejudiced against anybody's beliefs or what they do in their off time. I do regret saying something like that. Whatever I did to offend people, I apologize. I'm not prejudiced in any way."

A year later, Shockey called Dallas Cowboys coach Bill Parcells a "homo." "I apologize for everything I said that offended people," he said in a classic nonapology apology.

Matt Millen, NFL

The president of the Detroit Lions became a national story in late 2003 after he called a former Lions player a faggot. "You faggot! Yeah, you heard me. You faggot!" Millen was heard shouting at Johnnie Morton, a Kansas City wide receiver who played for the Lions for eight years until leaving following the 2001 season. The exchange, which took place after a game between the Lions and the Chiefs, was reported by *Kansas City Star* columnist Jason Whitlock. There has been bad blood between Millen and Morton since the receiver's release from Detroit. Morton told Whitlock that he felt Millen "tossed me aside like I didn't mean anything."

Following the game, won by Kansas City, 45–17, Millen and Morton passed each other outside the Chiefs locker room. "What happened was I was just walking by," Morton said. "I wasn't going to say anything to him. I walked past him and he said, 'Hey, Johnnie.' I ignored him. And then he said, 'Nice talking to you.' And I said, 'Kiss my ass.'" It was then that Millen used the *F* word twice with Morton, though the receiver said he did not hear it at the time. When told the contents of Millen's remarks, Morton responded: "I apologize for what I said, but I never expected anything like that. What he said is demeaning and bigoted. Jeremy Shockey got in trouble for saying it about a coach [Bill Parcells], and now we have a president of a team making statements like that. It's totally unacceptable. I have gay friends, and I don't even joke around with them like that."

That night, Millen issued this statement to the *Kansas City Star:* "After the game, I was passing the Chiefs' locker room when I stopped to congratulate some of their players. I was talking with Vonnie Holliday, Trent Green, Tony Gonzalez, and one of the coaches, Joe Vitt. I wished all those guys the best and good luck in the playoffs. I then saw Johnnie, and I tried to wish him the best and congratulate him as well. When I called out to him, he just kept walking and then made a derogatory remark toward me, which really upset me. Unfortunately, I retaliated with a derogatory term directed toward Johnnie. I apologize if I offended anyone. It certainly was not meant to do anything other than express my frustration and disappointment."

Millen continued his attempt at damage control a day later, calling a press conference in which he described the incident and again apologized. "I reacted inappropriately and said something I shouldn't have," Millen said. "And I apologize to anybody who I offended with that remark." Millen, however, took no questions.

His performance in trying to explain himself fell flat. *Detroit Free Press* columnist Michael Rosenberg listed four questions he wanted to ask Millen:

1. When you called Johnnie Morton a "faggot," were you implying that he is gay? In your mind, is that an insult?
2. How would you feel about an NFL executive who called a player, in anger, the *N* word? Would that be an "inappropriate" comment, or would it be worse? And if you think that's worse, why?
3. You also said that Morton said something "inappropriate" when he told you to "kiss my ass." Is his comment the equivalent, in your mind, of what you said?
4. You are the president and chief executive officer of an organization with almost two hundred employees. Supposing that at least one of them is gay, would you say that you have created a fair work environment?

Millen survived the incident and was still the Lions' president after a dreadful 3–13 2006 season.

Terrell Owens, NFL

"Like my boy tells me: If it looks like a rat and smells like a rat, by golly, it is a rat," the wide receiver said in 2004 while implying former teammate Jeff Garcia is gay. Terrell Owens should be the last guy inferring that someone is gay. He fits several gay stereotypes: He's single and flamboyant and totally obsessed with his body. He loves parading around during practice clad in form-hugging Lycra warm-up clothes even in the coldest of weather. He also did the gayest thing ever seen on a football field when he shook pom-poms after scoring a touchdown in 2002.

Ken Hutcherson, NFL

A former Seattle Seahawks linebacker, Hutcherson is an influential evangelical minister in Seattle, and stopping gay rights, same-sex marriage in particular, is his primary agenda. He calls same-sex marriage "the greatest danger to America." In 2004, he held a "Mayday for Marriage" rally that drew twenty thousand in Seattle. Months later, he led a similar rally in Washington, D.C., that drew one hundred thousand.

In April 2005, Hutcherson met privately with Microsoft officials and threatened a boycott of its products if it did not rescind its support for a gay-rights measure before the Washington Senate. Coincidence or not, Microsoft, which had supported the measure, decided to stay neutral, and the bill lost by one vote. "If I got God on my side, what's a Microsoft? What's a Microsoft? It's nothing," Hutcherson told the *New York Times*. Hutcherson said Christians who disagreed with him on gay issues were "evangelly-fish" because they lacked a "spiritual backbone," the *Seattle Post-Intelligencer* reported.

Some of Hutcherson's other quotes on gays:

"I kick 'em out," he said if he discovers a parishioner is gay. "I do it three or four times a year. You bring up their names during the church service, and if they won't repent, won't turn away from sin, you have to kick 'em out."

"Christ talks about marriage between a man and a woman, and Christ would have expelled homosexuals."

Gays "can stop choosing to do what they do, and they can hide it anytime they want. They can hide their homosexuality. Could I take a 'don't ask don't tell' policy as an African American? I could try even to pretend I was Puerto Rican, but I'm still going to get blasted for my skin color."

"When [supporters of the gay-rights bill] stepped out and tried to make their policy my policy and other companies' policy and the state's policy, they stepped into a den of snakes, and I was the main cobra."

His actions speak for themselves. Hutcherson is not a man of God, but a man of hate. Microsoft reversed itself and in January 2006 supported an antidiscrimination bill that passed in Washington State.

Ozzie Guillen, Major League Baseball

Perhaps no antigay slurs got more attention than those uttered by Chicago White Sox manager Ozzie Guillen in 2005 and 2006. Guillen's club won the World Series in 2005, which made everything he uttered newsworthy.

In August 2005, Guillen, known for shooting from the hip, had just finished an interview at Yankee Stadium with a pack of reporters when he saw a longtime friend and called out: "Hey, everybody, this guy's a homosexual! He's a child molester!" Reporters said the man seemed to not take offense, and then both men hugged. Two days later, Guillen explained himself to Rick Morrissey of the *Chicago Tribune:* "I have no problem with [homosexuals]. I don't deal with that. To me, everybody's the same. We're human beings created by God. Everybody has their own opinion and their own right to do what they want to do. You have the right to feel the way you want to feel. Nobody can take that away from you."

In addition, according to Dave Buscema, a columnist with the *Times-Herald Record* in Middleton, NY, Guillen had "just about an hour before, around a group of female Japanese reporters . . . called infielder Tadahito Iguchi 'queer,' jokingly saying he should want to go out with one of them."

We would like to think Guillen meant no offense, and he did say he needs to be careful with his words. But equating gay people with child molesters is one of the biggest slurs gay people, in particular gay men, have faced, and Guillen was at least guilty of gross insensitivity. His comment about Iguchi being "queer" adds to the sense that Guillen thinks making fun of gay people is humorous and acceptable.

Almost a year later, on June 20, 2006, Guillen struck again. In speaking to reporters before a game, Guillen said this about *Chicago Sun-Times* columnist Jay Mariotti, with whom he has a feud: "What a piece of [deleted] he is, [deleted] fag."

"Obviously, from an organizational perspective, I don't think in that case that Ozzie was trying to disparage a group," Scott Reifert, the Sox's vice president of communications, told the *Chicago Sun-Times.* "That said, it certainly is a poor word choice. It's insensitive. It's not something we would condone, not something the White Sox would stand for.'"

Greg Couch, *Sun-Times* columnist, ripped into Guillen and said he needs to be suspended. Guillen's explanation to Couch was that, in his home country of Venezuela, that word is a reference not to a person's sexuality but to his courage. He said he was saying that Mariotti is "not man enough to meet me and talk about [things before writing]." He also said that he has gay friends, goes to WNBA games, went to the Madonna concert, and planned to attend the Gay Games in Chicago. "I called that of this man [Mariotti]," he said. "I'm not trying to hurt anybody [else]."

Couch wasn't buying Guillen's justification: "Guillen is not dumb. Let's not insult him. He knows what he's saying, and he certainly knows that it's not acceptable. He has been in this country for a quarter of a century. This offseason, I went to his swearing-in as a U.S. citizen. He was wrong. And he needs to apologize. And he needs to be suspended. Are you listening, Bud Selig?"

ESPN's *Outside the Lines* produced specials in 1998 and 2001 that helped launch a national discussion in sports about gay people. Here is what some people in sports told ESPN in those specials:

DEBBIE BLACK, WNBA: I don't care who's out there cheering for us. I'm just glad that there is someone supporting us.

REGGIE WHITE, NFL: The homosexuals are trying to compare their plight with the plight of black people. Homosexuality is a decision. It is not a race.

TERENCE MATHIS, NFL: You may have three or four gay guys on your team and not even know it.

CRIS CARTER, NFL: I think there would be situations that would occur on the field that would be tough for a person who's homosexual.

AL MACINNIS, NHL: You realize that 10 percent of the population is gay, and out of seven or eight hundred hockey players, you have to assume that there's probably some out there.

JOHNNY ROLAND, NFL: I would assume if that person was of that persuasion, I'm not so sure the quality of his toughness.

DANA STUBBLEFIELD, NFL: You're living with these guys six months out of the year, so you have to get used to what they do, used to what they say, the whole nine. But when you figure out a guy is gay, it's—you just get a real "uh" feeling of being around him.

DANNY KANELL, NFL: Every Sunday he'd probably have to play ten times harder than anybody else because everybody would be geared up to taking it out on him.

LEIGH STEINBERG, SPORTS AGENT: I think it would have a devastating effect in terms of the marketability of any athlete to come out and talk about gayness.

A day later, Guillen sort of apologized: "I shouldn't have mentioned the name that was mentioned. A lot of people's feelings were hurt, and I didn't mean it that way," Guillen explained. "I apologize, but I wasn't talking about those people." "Those people"? How lovely.

Claiming a cultural exemption doesn't wash. Guillen used homophobic language, then tried to cop out with the old "some of my best friends are gay" crap heard from bigots all the time. If he was at the Gay Games, no one Outsports spoke to saw him, and his Madonna Defense was especially lame. Words matter, and Guillen should be held accountable. Winning a World Series shouldn't provide cover.

Baseball commissioner Bud Selig ordered Guillen to attend sensitivity training, the same type of training Rocker labeled a farce.

Joey Porter, NFL

Upset at what Pittsburgh Steelers linebacker Joey Porter thought was a cheap shot by Cleveland Browns tight end Kellen Winslow against a Steelers teammate in a 2006 game, the brash linebacker said, "He's a fag. He tried to dap me up before the game. He's soft though. I don't pay attention to him. . . . [The hit on the teammate] was late. That's what fags do. He's soft. He wanna be tough but he's really soft. He tried to give me a handshake before the game. He's not my friend, he don't know me. What you trying to shake my hand for? He talk too much and he hadn't done nothing. He threw a cheap shot. He's weak. He's for real weak. He's soft. He might want to play receiver because he don't want to play tight end. He's not gonna block nobody."

Porter issued a nonapology, saying, "I apologize to anybody I offended on it. I didn't mean to offend nobody but Kellen Winslow. Pretty much, that's it about that." In trying to justify his use of language, Porter said it was a common word in his upbringing. "I guess how we used that word freely, me growing up using it, I didn't think nothing of it like that," Porter said.

A week later the NFL fined Porter ten thousand dollars for what was termed "vulgar, inexcusable statements." It is believed to be the first time the league has fined a player for making homophobic comments.

Good Guys

Bob Lipsyte, columnist

No one in the mainstream media has done more to champion the cause of gays in sports than Lipsyte, for years an influential *New York Times* columnist and author of young adult novels.

Twice in seven months at the turn of the century, Lipsyte authored articles on gays in sports for the *Times*. Not only was the subject matter unusual at the time, but so was the placement of the articles—front page.

Not front page of Sports, but front page of the entire paper on a Sunday, the choicest real estate in journalism.

The first article ran September 6, 1999, and was about Billy Bean. "All-America Billy Bean burst into his 20's consumed by two driving dreams: to play center field in the major leagues and to deny his homosexuality. Eventually he would have to choose between his personal and professional lives," the article began.

The second article ran April 30, 2000, and focused on Corey Johnson. "When Corey Johnson told teammates on the Masconomet High School football team last spring that he was gay, the two other starting linebackers responded characteristically," Lipsyte wrote.

Big, steady Dave Merrill quietly absorbed the almost physical shock, then began worrying if the revelation would divide the team. Merrill said he decided to take it on as a challenge, a test of the captaincy the two shared and a test of his own character. Jim Whelan, the artist, said he looked into Johnson's eyes and saw a need for instant support. He broke the silence by saying, "More than being teammates we're your friends and we know you're the same person."

Their reactions were critical in the risky, uncharted, carefully planned campaign to bring out of his increasingly claustrophobic closet an American icon, the hard-hitting football hero. The campaign involved Johnson's parents, teachers and coaches, as well as a gay educational agency, all encouraged by the administration of a school with a long history of diversity training.

Lipsyte's articles had an impact beyond the *Times*, a paper that often sets the agenda in American newsrooms. The profiles became launching pads for others in the media to address the issue of gays in sports. Lipsyte was instrumental in helping to get the ball rolling.

Paul Tagliabue, NFL Commissioner

The NFL commissioner from 1989 to 2006 has an openly gay son, Andrew. In 2005, Tagliabue and his wife, Chandler, were honored by the New York chapter of Parents, Families, and Friends of Lesbians and Gays with the PFLAG 2005 Stay Close Individual Leadership Award. Tagliabue had given a sizable donation to PFLAG for their Stay Close campaign.

In a 2006 profile on HBO, Tagliabue was asked by Bob Costas about gays in the NFL.

COSTAS: You're very supportive [of gay rights] and always have been. Some people might say, "Boy, it's ironic, because if Andrew was a football player, he'd probably have a hard time in an NFL locker room."

TAGLIABUE: Well, he might and he might not. You know, I think that's an area where attitudes are changing throughout society, including in sports. We've had some players, [New York Giants] Michael Strahan and others, who have been pretty strong advocates to respect the rights of gay and lesbian Americans. There is some irony there, but for [my wife and me], it's a personal issue and we've got a great son and we think that we need to stand by him just the way he stood by us and our values.

Now that Tagliabue is retired from the NFL, perhaps he can take the lead in getting domestic-partner rights for players and be an evangelist in spreading the word that it's okay to be gay and the only thing that should matter is how you play. During Tagliabue's reign, Tuaolo addressed the league office on sexual orientation as part of a diversity seminar. Tuaolo also spoke at the 2006 NFL rookies symposium and received a positive reception.

Michael Strahan, NFL

Strahan, a linebacker with the New York Giants, has been a supporter of the Gay Men's Health Crisis (GMHC), an AIDS advocacy group in New York, along with the Tisch family, which owns the Giants and for whom the building that houses GMHC is named. In 2006, during a bitter divorce, Strahan's wife accused him of having sex with a man. He denied the charge, and she later withdrew it. "If this were true, it would hit the fan from the get go," Strahan told a radio interviewer. "I have plenty of friends that are bi or homosexual. It's fine with me. This is New York City. If you can't accept people for being people, then you have no business being here. I don't frown on anybody for that lifestyle; it's not my lifestyle. And you know, I just laugh. All that matters is that I'm gonna take care of my kids."

Kiki Vandeweghe, NBA

Former Denver Nuggets general manager Kiki Vandeweghe offered some hope about the acceptance for an openly gay NBA player.

"It's not like 30 years ago, it just isn't," he told the *Denver Post* in 2006. "It just wouldn't factor into what the guy does on the court. If he can play basketball, he can play basketball; that's the end of the story."

Bobby Valentine, Major League Baseball

Bobby Valentine did not mince words during a TV appearance in 2002 discussing whether baseball could accept an openly gay player. "I think most clubhouses could handle it," he said. "They're mature people who understand all the situations we live with in our society, and this is obviously one of them. It's just time to catch up and I think it can be done seamlessly if it's the right person or people. We're in 2002. Let's get rid of

Reaction to Amaechi Overwhelmingly Positive

While Hardaway's reaction to Amaechi coming out in February 2007 was vile, a vast majority of reaction from sports figures was positive and supportive.

Shaquille O'Neal, NBA player, to the Palm Beach Post: "I was always taught as a youngster to never judge people, so I never judge people and to each their own. If he was my teammate and people ridiculed him and jumped on him, I would probably have to protect him."

Tracy McGrady, NBA player and former Amaechi teammate, to ESPN.com: "You could be the most flaming (guy) on earth and answer to a boyfriend and kiss him after the game as long as you don't try it with me. I just want to win. And that's how I am. To each his own, be yourself, and be proud of it. Everything else is just a bunch of crap."

Mark Cuban, Dallas Mavericks owner, to the Fort Worth Star-Telegram: "When you do something that the whole world thinks is difficult and you stand up and just be who you are and take on that difficulty factor, you're an American hero no matter what. That's what the American spirit's all about, going against the grain and standing up for who you are, even if it's not a popular position."

Eddie Curry, NBA player, to *Newsday*: "If one of my teammates came out and said that, I'd be supportive of him because the whispers and let's be real about this. . . . There will be some distractions and we'll have to get through with them."

It's authority figures such as a manager or coach who would go a long way in making a coming out go well. Such a player can only hope he has someone as understanding and forceful on the issue as Valentine.

Brad Ausmus, Major League Baseball

A longtime star with the Detroit Tigers, San Diego Padres, and Houston Astros, Brad Ausmus at one time was roommates with Billy Bean, and Bean still considers him a close friend. Ausmus told *20/20* in 2000: "If Billy Bean is happy being gay then I'm happy for him. I don't pretend to understand homosexuality. I don't pretend to understand why a man

those are my teammates. Those are the guys I went to war with night in and night out. Regardless of what he does off the court, we battle together."

Peter Magowan, San Francisco Giants owner, to the *Sacramento Bee*: "It would not bother me if one of my players came out of the closet. He would get my support."

Doc Rivers, former coach of Amaechi, to the *Associated Press*: "John Amaechi, when I was coaching him, was a great kid. He did as much charity work as anybody in our city, and he's still doing it. That's what I wish we focused on. Unfortunately, we're talking about his sexual orientation, which I couldn't care a flying flip about."

Isiah Thomas, New York Knicks coach, to the Newark *Star-Ledger* and *Newsday*: "If [there was an openly gay player] in my locker room, we won't have a problem with it. I can't speak for somebody else's locker room, but if it's in mine, we won't have a problem. I'll make damn sure there's no problem."

Dwayne Wade, NBA player, to the *Palm Beach Post*: "Anybody who knows me knows I'm a guy who loves his teammates and if anything ever comes up like that, I don't look at that. I look at what guys can do for you on the court. And in the locker room you have great relationships with guys. I don't have any negative views."

loves a man. It doesn't make sense to me, but I don't understand quantum physics either."

Adam Rich, a longtime Outsports reader, offered his own Ausmus anecdote: "Years ago, the Padres offered cap night and had players at various gates to hand out the caps as fans entered. My partner and I followed a family with young girls through the gate where Brad Ausmus was handing out caps. He hugged the little girls as he handed them the caps and so we asked if we could also have hugs. Laughing, he did it. The guy in back of us told him we were gay; Ausmus replied, 'Yeah, they're fans too.' It's only too bad we didn't bring the camera that day, but obviously he didn't have a problem with gay fans."

Byron Chamberlain, NFL

Chamberlain was a teammate of Esera Tuaolo and issued one of the more gay-positive comments after Tuaolo came out in 2002. "It really doesn't concern me, because I'm definitely not homophobic," Chamberlain told the *St. Paul Pioneer-Press*. "I know that there are homosexuals in every occupation, and with the number of homosexuals out there, I wouldn't doubt there are some in athletics. The odds are, with the number of guys I've played with, I've probably been in the locker room with some. We as a culture have to be open-minded to different things and different situations, and that goes for sexuality, religion and different cultures. Because you come in a locker room like this, there are people who are totally different from me, probably grew up in a totally different environment from me. But it just comes down to being open-minded and being understanding of other people."

Joe Valentine, Major League Baseball

Valentine, at the time of his comments a pitcher for the Cincinnati Reds, in 2005 disclosed that he was raised by two lesbians. "It's no different than having a mother and father," Valentine, twenty-five, told *Newsday*. "These are the two women who raised me, and they are wonderful people. It's just not a big deal to me. Why should it be?"

It shouldn't be a big deal, and for Valentine it wasn't. After the story appeared, Valentine's unique upbringing has been met with a shrug and an assumed acceptance. "I haven't heard much," Valentine told the *Florida Sun-Sentinel* three weeks after the *Newsday* article appeared. "I thought it was going to be a little bit bigger deal, but I wasn't doing it because I wanted it to be a big deal. It was something I tried to do for my parents and for the gay community. They're a huge part of the population. I've gotten good feedback [from teammates]," Valentine added. "A lot of guys noticed and read it. They said, 'That's pretty cool. That's a pretty awesome thing.' That's really it." The lack of publicity was pretty remarkable given the still unsettled relationship between sports and homosexuality. Valentine was very aware of this when he told *Newsday:* "I'm a blue-state guy in a red-state sport. But that won't stop me from being proud of who I am."

Sean Salisbury, NFL and ESPN commentator

Salisbury wrote a column about the NFL's "macho culture" following the coming out of Tuaolo, his former teammate. If only every other athlete could have this same self-confidence and perspective:

I'm happy for my former Vikings teammate. It sounds like Esera Tuaolo has lifted a burden from himself. I can't imagine how it must have felt to carry that around. His preference and beliefs are different from mine, but being different doesn't make someone evil. You hear the gay rumor a million times about various players, and it's usually wrong. My reaction when I hear it is, So what?

There are people in the league who have that homophobic attitude, saying, "I could never play with anyone who's gay." It's the macho culture: In football, you're never supposed to cry, you're not supposed to be sensitive, you can't be friends with someone who's gay.

My advice: Get over it. You've probably been playing with someone who's gay. If you think there aren't other gay players, you're crazy. And it takes a lot more of a man to do what Esera has done than it does to threaten someone for being different.

OUTSPORTS

Flashback
#4

Dᴇᴄᴇᴍʙᴇʀ 17, 2003

Apology Not Accepted: Let's Stop the Trend of "Nonapology Apologies"

Jim Buzinski

"I apologize if I offended anyone" (Matt Millen, Detroit Lions president, December 15, 2003). With those words, Millen tried to extricate himself from a mess he created by calling former Lions receiver Johnnie Morton a "faggot." Sorry, Matt (a fellow Penn State alum), but apology not accepted.

It's not that I don't believe in the power of redemption or of an apology made from the heart. What I object to are the words Millen used: "I apologize *if* I offended anyone." Not very sincere and uttered more out of obligation that contrition. It's more like a "nonapology apology."

This new trend in public apologies—in which the offending party apologizes only if they offended anyone—has become rampant, and it's time for it to stop. New York–based writer Joseph Dobrain summed up perfectly why the "nonapology apology" is wrong. In a 1999 business article, he wrote: "One thing many people say, which you should *never* say, is, 'If I offended you, I apologize.' That is the worst sort of fake apology: It's like stealing someone's wallet, and saying, 'I'm sorry if you felt you were inconvenienced.' When you say 'If I offended you, I apologize,' you're implying that the other person is to blame for being so over-sensitive as to be offended, or so selfish as to demand an apology. You're making it clear that you're not sorry for anything *you* did; you just resent the other person's reaction."

In doing just a little research, I was able to come up with numerous recent examples of the "nonapology apology" in the world of sports and beyond, with some being more creative than others

Jeremy Shockey. Shockey has had to apologize twice in the past few years for antigay comments, and you would think he'd get better at it. "Whatever I did to offend people, I apologize," Shockey said after antigay comments on *The Howard Stern Show.* In 2003, Shockey was forced to confront his statements calling Dallas Cowboys coach Bill Parcells a homo. "I apologize for everything I said that offended people," Shockey said.

Arnold Schwarzenegger, California governor. The actor-turned-politician was faced with more than a dozen women who accused him of sexually assaulting them. He denied some allegations, but said others might be true, then tried to end the matter by saying, "If anyone was offended, I apologize, because that was not my intention." Is this a new legal defense? "I'm sorry, your honor. My intention was to molest her while she was sleeping, but she woke up, and I apologize if I disturbed her sleep."

Pierre Boivin, president of the Montreal Canadiens. He apologized after Montreal fans booed the U.S. national anthem this year, causing a stir. "We apologize to anyone who may have been offended by this incident," Boivin said.

Joyce Aboussie, key aide to Democratic presidential candidate Dick Gephardt. Aboussie threatened political retaliation against union leaders who supported Howard Dean. Aboussie issued a qualified apology, saying she was sorry "if anyone felt threatened" by her words.

Trent Lott, U.S. senator. Lott waxed nostalgic about the segregationist policies of Strom Thurmond, a controversy that cost Lott his leadership position. "I apologize to anyone who was offended by my statement," Lott said in his defense.

Patrick Kerney, Atlanta Falcons defensive lineman. Kerney went on an Atlanta radio show December 1, 2003, and said how he was bummed to learn it was World AIDS Day, adding sarcastically that "people who get cancer—it's usually their fault," whereas "AIDS—it's just bad luck."

Kerney then issued a statement through the team, saying (you guessed it), "Whatever I did to offend people, I apologize." Kerney and Shockey must have the same apology writer.

Insincerity is the common thread running through all these examples, and I'm certain these people wouldn't have uttered their "apologies" if no one had complained. This is not the same as realizing you said something wrong and then taking the initiative in trying to make it right.

A "nonapology apology" also puts the onus on those upset. "Why are all of you so freaking sensitive and politically correct?" they seem to be asking. It's something we hear at Outsports all the time when we report on antigay slurs. We have to defend our anger, and that's just wrong; we're not the ones at fault. We've had apologists saying Shockey was only joking, Kerney is really a good guy, and Millen was simply responding to Morton telling him to "kiss my ass."

What's a proper apology? Surprisingly, Garrison Hearst of the San Francisco 49ers offered a good one after saying in 2002 that he didn't want any "faggots" as teammates. I was initially skeptical of Hearst's apology, but it looks better under closer scrutiny.

"First of all, I want to apologize for the comments that I made, and to the gay community," Hearst said. "I didn't realize it would be so harmful. I want to direct it to my teammates for causing a disturbance among the team before this game. Being an African American, I know that discrimination is wrong, and I was wrong for saying what I said about anybody—any race, any religion. I want to apologize to the San Francisco 49ers organization, the city of San Francisco for the comments that I made, and to my teammates for bringing this distraction upon us. I hope that everyone can accept my apology. Thank you."

Hearst did not include the lame "if I offended anyone" dodge, seemed to have learned something ("I didn't realize . . ."), and was able to see a linkage between discrimination he's suffered as a black man and what gay people have to deal with. David Kopay, a former 49er and the first former NFL player to come out, told me he accepted what Hearst said and thought he was sincere.

Apologies are ultimately about learning, about why our words hurt, about putting ourselves in someone else's shoes, about why something uttered in one setting is wrong in another. They are also about healing, about having people with different backgrounds, upbringings, or points of views understand each other a little better. The "nonapology apology" accomplishes none of this. I am unapologetic when I say it's time to get rid of it.

WHEN YOU'RE READY TO COME OUT

The question Outsports gets asked the most by the mainstream media is when an active male professional athlete will come out. It will happen someday, though no one is holding his or her breath. The pressures of simply being a professional athlete, especially male, are enormous, and adding sexuality to that list makes it hard to conceive of someone holding a press conference to declare he is gay. "It's going to have to be a situation where someone is painted into a corner," Howard Bragman, a Hollywood publicist who specializes in helping celebrities come out, told the *San Diego Union Tribune*. "Heroes are people that find creative ways to get out of tough situations."

Bragman is probably right. There are several reasons athletes stay closeted, and understanding them is important to the debate.

The Coming-Out Process

Coming out is not a one-day process; a person doesn't get up one day and decide to tell everyone at once: family, friends, coworkers, neighbors, the postman. It happens gradually and can often take years. This has been neglected by the mainstream media when discussing closeted athletes.

Jim's experience is not atypical. He met his first boyfriend, Bill, when he was eighteen years old, was fairly comfortable with his orientation, but didn't come out to his parents for five more years, even though they knew Bill very well and treated him as part of the family. He came out professionally to one or two people at a time until 1990, when he sold T-shirts to raise money to send his flag-football team to Gay Games III. Since then, he has been totally out.

Because most pro athletes are in their twenties, they can't be expected to be any more advanced about dealing with their sexual orientation than the public at large; they might even be less so since life as a pro athlete can be an all-consuming job and distractions of any kind are not welcome. Why give management one more reason to cut you?

It's hard to imagine an athlete deciding to come out without first having tested the waters with family, friends, and a supportive teammate or person in management. Given the relatively short careers of most pros, it might be easier on the psyche to just deal with it after retirement.

Fear

Being the first is scary, especially when you're unsure what kind of support is out there. When Esera Tuaolo came out, former teammates were asked what their reaction would have been had they known he was gay. "He would have been eaten alive, and he would have been hated for it," former Packers receiver Sterling Sharpe told HBO. "Had he come out on a Monday, with Wednesday, Thursday, Friday practices, he'd have never gotten to the other team." When asked why teammates would have had a problem with Tuaolo being gay, Sharpe replied: "Birds of a feather flock together. . . . Now, I got to answer questions that I'm normally not answering. Question my heart, question my ability. Do not question my machoism, so to speak, my sexuality."

Adding to the fear is the often-sophomoric attitude found in most locker rooms, especially when it comes to matters of sex. A player considering coming out would have to weigh the potential reaction of his team. It must have been hard to be a gay Green Bay Packer during the time when Reggie White was spouting his hateful, homophobic diatribes to anyone who would listen.

The combination of the religious holy rollers (heavily represented in sports) and the ignorant who fear taking a shower with an openly gay teammate has to be a powerful incentive to stay closeted. "Obviously, right now if you go around the corner, there are twenty guys in the shower, and there are only fifteen shower heads," Seattle Seahawks quarterback Matt Hasselbeck said. "It's a little uncomfortable right now for heterosexuals. . . . It's a tough one." Hasselbeck did add, "If someone is professional about their job and is choosing to have the same focus you're focused on—winning football games—[then] great."

Although one can guess the reaction from teammates, there's really no way to know how bad it would be, or if it would be bad at all. Every time the issue of homosexuality in sports comes up, some players say it would be a problem on their team, and others say it wouldn't matter. A majority of players in pro baseball, football, basketball, and hockey would welcome an openly gay teammate, a *Sports Illustrated* survey in 2006 found, with the largest majority in the National Hockey League, with 79 percent saying they'd have no problem; baseball was second with 61 percent, followed by the NBA at 60 percent and the NFL at 57 percent.

The Public and the Media

The public and the media would be less of a concern to a gay player. Society has changed and is much more accepting of gays and lesbians. In reaction to its package of stories on gays in sports, ESPN.com reported that "of the 874 letters received, 75 percent said they would support a gay athlete, 22 percent said they would not and 3 percent did not offer an opinion." Other surveys on the same issue have found similar numbers.

Of course, there would be hecklers flapping their gums at an out jock, but athletes deal with verbal fan abuse all the time. It comes with the territory. But there would also be a countervailing reaction to any fan who got too abusive; he'd likely be roundly booed by other fans, and maybe coldcocked by the gay guy sitting next to him.

Ron Sirak, executive editor of *Golf Digest,* in a column following the coming out of golf pro Rosie Jones in 2004

The fact is, many of the greatest players in the history of the LPGA were and are lesbian. And the equal fact is that who those players are is no one's right to know unless the player decides she wants to discuss it publicly. I have always felt that players who are lesbian could enhance their endorsement situation by being open about it. It is my feeling that companies don't want to enter into a business relationship and then get hit with a surprise. Times have changed enough that marketing an openly gay athlete should not be a problem—millions of Americans welcome gay people into their living rooms every week in the form of popular TV shows.

The media, in all likelihood, would be very supportive. The mainstream media have increasingly covered gays in sports over the past six years, and the reaction within the media to reported stories has been almost universally tolerant and supportive. If the reaction was otherwise, the media is finding as the culture changes, the public won't like it. Ron Sirak, executive editor of *Golf Digest*, wrote a representative column on the subject when golf pro Rosie Jones came out in 2004.

Money

Despite being the premier women's tennis player of her generation, Martina Navratilova was asked to endorse very few products. She's certain it was because she was an out lesbian. Times have changed, and Navratilova now endorses products. When Sheryl Swoopes came out it was partly because of her new deal as a spokeswoman for Olivia Cruises, a lesbian tour company, and Nike kept its deal with Swoopes after she came out.

Is Madison Avenue ready for an openly gay male jock to endorse a product? It would likely work with certain companies. Speedo had an endorsement deal with Olympic diver David Pichler. Former athletes Bruce Hayes, Navratilova, and Corey Johnson all had endorsement deals. But most advertisers hate controversy and might feel they're stepping into a quagmire if they take on such an athlete. Outsports knows of at least one instance when a gold medal winner was talked out of coming out by his agent for fear of losing endorsements. This athlete has never come out despite now being retired.

Athletes have such short careers that the get-as-much-while-you-can mentality is strong. There is an interesting twist to this, however. Billy Bean and others say that only an established superstar would have the

While she has been active in helping gay-rights groups, Sheryl Swoopes hasn't drawn a lot of media attention since she came out in October 2005. And that's just the way her team would prefer it.

Photo by Ross Forman

clout to come out and still stay at the top of his or her sport. At the same time, the lion's share of endorsements goes to these superstars. One could argue that fear of losing endorsements would not be a compelling reason for a nonsuperstar to stay closeted. On the other hand, any advertiser that

Brendan Lemon

It isn't just the money that's involved, it's the pressure. The stress of the top of the heap in pro football, for example, is huge. What they go through during the season day-to-day, week-to-week, without all that other stuff is hard enough. When you add possibly coming out, I totally understand why somebody doesn't want to make that part of their public persona. It's physically and mentally punishing to be at the top of a sport. And I think that's not something that is acknowledged enough by any sports fan.

dropped a high-profile jock who just came out would unleash a firestorm of criticism.

As homosexuality becomes more accepted, especially by younger people, the day may come when a high-profile jock decides he no longer wants to live a lie. Here's a look at how athletes, agents, writers, and coaches see the likely scenarios.

Be a Star

It would likely be easier for a superstar to come out, given the value to his team. "I'm sure it would depend on who the player was. If he hits .340, it probably would be easier than if he hits .220," said Larry Bowa, at the time the manager of the Philadelphia Phillies. Billy Bean agrees. "The superstar would have the solace that he's not going to be sent to the minor leagues the next day."

Others have doubts. "It would take someone capable of realizing the situation he's in—that he's going to be a nobody—and that any media is good media," said sociologist Eric Anderson.

In recent years, some researchers who have studied the issue of gays in sport suggest a more likely scenario is an athlete reaching the pros after they have already come out in high school or college. By the time the athlete turns pro, this thinking goes, his homosexuality will be old news.

Since coming out, Esera Tualohos found a lot of new friends in the gay sports community.
By Jim Buzinski

Time It Right

A baseball player coming out while his team is in the World Series would not be smart. He'd be better off waiting until the off-season when his announcement could get a flurry of attention and die down prior to the start of the next season. This was Swoopes's strategy, and it worked brilliantly. She came out in October 2005, and by the time the 2006 season started in May, virtually no one was talking about her sexuality.

Prepare

Letting key teammates and management know ahead of time would be crucial to lining up support. No one wants to be blindsided. Having a coach such as former New York Mets manager Bobby Valentine would make it easier, since Valentine has said baseball should embrace an openly gay player. However, playing for the likes of an Ozzie Guillen, the Chicago White Sox manager who was fined for using *faggott*, would make someone think twice. Having some friends within the team who know and are supportive would help ward against a coach, manager, or other player who may be homophobic.

Handling the Media

Calling a press conference would be a no-no. Too much, too soon. Pick a friendly media source and steer the story to your best advantage. Afterward, be prepared for a flurry of interviews and attention and be able to deal with it. Don't just issue a statement and jet off to Tahiti.

Howard Bragman has been key in helping four athletes come out: Esera Tuaolo in 2002, after he retired from the NFL; pro golfer Rosie Jones in 2004; Sheryl Swoopes in 2005; and John Amaechi in 2007. Bragman treated each like a campaign, lining up big shots in the media with exclusives (HBO, ABC's *Good Morning America*, the *New York Times*, ESPN), managing interviews, and extensively prepping his subjects on what to expect. Not surprisingly, all three came out to overwhelmingly positive coverage.

Be strong. There is still a lot of homophobia out there, though it stays more hidden. Supportive friends, family, and teammates will be crucial.

OUTSPORTS
Flashback
#3

FEBRUARY 28, 2007

John Amaechi Talks with Outsports

Cyd Zeigler Jr.

Former NBA player John Amaechi, who came out in early February 2007, sat with Cyd Zeigler in New York in mid-February for Amaechi's most comprehensive interview with a gay publication anywhere.

OUTSPORTS: Tell me a little bit about the last couple of weeks.

JOHN AMAECHI: It's been chaotic, hectic. Rushed. I've had so many interviews, I can't even remember what I've done. I've started getting to the point when I talk to people, I can't remember if I've said something to them already, or if it was the person before them. But it has been good. I know there are conversations in the last weeks that we would not have had a week prior. And that's a good thing. But I haven't really gotten to the point where I'm enjoying it much. It's too hectic for me. There are times when it's a little embarrassing because I go places and people know who I am. And there are some very touching things that are happening. I arrived in San Francisco and the room that ESPN had booked me was apparently not a very nice one, so they upgraded me. They put me in the penthouse. They took care of me like I was part of their gay mafia. I went down for breakfast the next morning and the night manager was still on. He came in while I was eating breakfast and said he didn't want to bother me but he wanted to tell me what it meant to him. He started fighting back the tears and then he ran off. It's incredibly emotionally laden stuff.

OUTSPORTS: I was just watching your interview with Bill Maher on HBO, and I wondered what, of all the interviews you've done in the last couple of weeks, was your favorite.

AMAECHI: I think my favorites are the ones that get adversarial. I did an interview with [Steve Malberg, the guest host of the John Gibson Radio Show on Fox News Radio]. He was a bigot of the highest order. He just kept cutting me off. I think it went very well because he ended his conversation with his contention that he shouldn't be assaulted with gay stuff when he watches the NBA with his 7-year-old son. His contention was that it is inappropriate for his son to know there are gay people at that age. He asked me if I thought it was appropriate that children knew about this. I said age-appropriate information is appropriate. And he said, "You think young children should be exposed to gays?" It really revealed him as a bigot. At the end he said he'd rather his son see Janet Jackson's nipple at the Super Bowl than know there were gay people in the NBA.

OUTSPORTS: You were gay in the NBA, and you were British in the NBA. But you're also very bright, very astute. Which of those things— being gay, British and intellectually different from the rest of the players—made you feel most different.

AMAECHI: I don't think that there's one part. I know that when people looked at me, the thing that made me really different was the way the words came out of my mouth. That's what made me different to reporters and fans, and even in the locker room. However, I think it's the interplay of all of those things that gave me the aura of differentness all together. None of them were as identifiable on their own as they were together.

OUTSPORTS: Which one made you feel the most different?

AMAECHI: Both the fact that I looked at basketball in a very different way [and that I was gay]. It was absolutely my ultimate goal to play in the NBA. But at the same time, I always looked at it as what I was doing before I did something more important. So that made me feel very different. And the gay thing was obviously very different. That was a separator. That meant I didn't do stuff with other players. That meant that I would be [hit on] by women when I went out. And so I just avoided those environments and stayed in my house a lot, which did create some separation.

OUTSPORTS: You talk about women. Did you sleep with women or try to be seen with women to put up a good front?

AMAECHI: Nope. I didn't have mythical girlfriends. I had friends who were girls. But no, it never even crossed my mind, actually. I always felt to go through all of that subterfuge was beneath me.

OUTSPORTS: You say in the book that you were hoping that a reporter would ask you a question about your sexuality. If you wanted someone to ask, why didn't you just tell them?

AMAECHI: I spent a lot of time being indignant in the latter stages of my career in the NBA. [I was] thinking about what I want to do next, the important stuff, while doing this job that's very difficult to do, and having no social life. I just started to get indignant. But I realized, on a team whose owner wouldn't [in 2006] show *Brokeback Mountain* in his theaters, would it really help my situation to come out? Would it even personally be better for me, in Salt Lake City, to be out? No, I didn't think so. I thought that would be even worse. And as far as daring people to out me, when people talked to me for interviews, the questions they wanted to ask about [my personal life], I would answer in a way that had subtext much more clearly present than ever before. In a way, it's easier to get outed. All of the fallout, all of the crap that you have to handle with dignity, it's not your fault. Whereas this way, I get emails from people telling me that I am a media whore, and telling me that I'm getting J.K. Rowling-like advances from the book, which if I were, I would tell people.

OUTSPORTS: You said you were indignant near the end of your career. Were you a pain in the ass when you were with the Utah Jazz?

AMAECHI: In what way?

OUTSPORTS: Did you give them reasons to be pains in the ass to you?

AMAECHI: I responded in equal magnitude to what they did to me. When I heard at the early part of my second season there that I hate white people and I'm anti-American, I was done then. I'm not going to engage in this ridiculous kind of war. I'm not going to battle when people have those opinions. I'm a dual-citizen. My mother's white. It's monumentally insulting to suggest these things. But if you have those opinions of me, and then I hear from the ballboys that you call me a fag every five seconds when I'm not around, then I have problems with that. So yes, did I become obstinate and British in the very worst of ways? Yes, yes I did. I would follow every instruction to the letter, and nothing more and nothing less.

OUTSPORTS: In your trips to gay clubs as you started to get more daring while you were in the NBA, did you ever see other players in those clubs?

AMAECHI: Yes. Players, officials.

OUTSPORTS: Did you talk to them?

AMAECHI: Some of them.

OUTSPORTS: And what were those conversations like?

AMAECHI: Very odd. I have become friends with a couple people, and those are people I don't think I would have become friends with otherwise. And it was probably six or eight or 10 months of seeing them around and ignoring them completely, and them ignoring me completely, before they were bold enough to come up to me and say, "hello, perhaps we should have a chat." And now we're kind of fast friends.

OUTSPORTS: About how many people associated with the NBA, either active or retired, do you know are gay or bisexual?

AMAECHI: Quite a few. It's less than 20, but more than 10, that I know of.

OUTSPORTS: Are there more that you strongly suspect or have heard?

AMAECHI: Maybe it's my own lack of curiosity, but I don't speculate that much. I don't know any of the rosters of any of the teams now. I just don't watch sports. And there are probably people whom I've met or seen, and I just don't know because I don't know who they are. Certainly I've been introduced to a lot of baseball and NFL officials and players whom I never would know, because I don't know who they are. So I'm sure there are more than I know. I just don't pay attention to that.

OUTSPORTS: Of all the reactions to you coming out, which reaction were you most surprised by?

AMAECHI: To be honest, I haven't been. I've been surprised by the volume of positive responses, people who take the time to write me an email. But I knew that it would touch a nerve with people to the point where it would be very impactful positively. And I was definitely anticipating the negative.

OUTSPORTS: A lot of gay people like to claim that athletes can't be gay because they like sports, kind of this reverse discrimination. Have you found a lot of that?

AMAECHI: I like sports less than most people. I like some of the tangential stories, which is why I read your web site, because I always find the stories interesting. But it would take a considerable amount of money to get me to watch a game. Unless it's tennis. And Rafael Nadal on clay. The reason people might think I'm not gay is because I'm big and black and, unless I've had four or five gins, reasonably butch.

OUTSPORTS: How do you like your gin?

AMAECHI: Hendrick's with slim lime and diet tonic. Not that I like diet tonic, but I just have to cut down on the calories.

OUTSPORTS: Have you found that some guys hit on you because you used to be in the NBA?

AMAECHI: No. In the past, I've found people were wildly and universally uninterested in me. I don't really tweak the melons of many men. I have a ladies' face, a face that ladies like. But I'm not complaining.

OUTSPORTS: People keep telling me how horribly homophobic sports are, and I've started to take issue with it because, over and over again, when I talk to athletes who have come out, I hear positive stories. The positive stories outweigh the negative stories 10 or 20 to one. And one of the things I hear you say is how there is all of this homophobia, and that it is a big problem. Am I wrong?

AMAECHI: No. What I'm saying is that people want to suggest that it's just sports, and what I'm saying is that's nonsense, and that it actually is everywhere. The fact is, the vast majority of people are not out in any job anywhere. We're talking about everyone up to CEOs on Wall Street. This isn't about sports, sports is just a convenient foil for this particular conversation. There's no doubt there's homophobia in sports, but it's only because there's no doubt there's homophobia.

OUTSPORTS: So, when David Stern says this isn't an NBA issue. . .

AMAECHI: Oh, that's just nonsense. It's an NBA issue. As a participant in society, it's everybody's issue. Organizations have a responsibility to be progressive. Corporations in general are leagues ahead of society in terms of the way they regard equality issues when it comes to the GLBT community. And sports organizations need to be a part of that, even if they have to drag along their constituent pieces. And not by having "gay days," which I'm sure are fun, but by actually making it so that you cannot be fired for being gay within your organization.

OUTSPORTS: One of the things I've been asked a lot is something along the lines of, Will John's mission to help kids be hurt by his coming out?

AMAECHI: I've been asked that question a lot. It's so blatantly homophobic to suggest that. What it actually means is, "gays molest children,

John's a gay, John molests children." That's what it means. I understand that's not what they're saying, but it is what it means. There's no
point in messing around with the subtext. [That thinking says] gays
are less trustworthy, less responsible, less good with children, and
possibly damaging to children. John is a gay, therefore John will be
all those other things. It's syllogism. The question is rooted deeply in
homophobia, an unfounded fear that gays will be damaging to children. The problem with the question is there is no logical answer to it,
because the fears that surround it are illogical, so I can't defeat them.
I can give you a persuasive argument about my track record, I can
give you a persuasive argument about my training and my experience
working with children. There are a lot of children who will give you
recommendations [for me]. But the bottom line is, because the argument is illogical, none of that information is valid for people who hold
these beliefs. And that's why I think the question is dangerous and
why I always challenge it. If people pull their children out, it won't
be based on anything in my track record, it will just be based on an
unfounded fear. It will be based on bigotry.

OUTSPORTS: Is there anything you haven't said about Tim Hardaway's
comments that you've been thinking?

AMAECHI: I feel a little sad for him. I respected him as a player. And I feel
a little sad for him that his empire is crumbling, while I understand
that he deserves it.

OUTSPORTS: That his legacy is being tarnished?

AMAECHI: Yes. I think that's mostly because legacy is very important to
me. I recognize that it's not as important to other people, but when it
crumbles, all of a sudden it becomes more important.

OUTSPORTS: If you could give a young closeted athlete any advice on
coming out, and how to get that across to their teammates if they're
thinking about doing that, what would it be?

AMAECHI: I think they need to find an ally. Someone with whom they
can get a real and tangible connection, someone who can share their
burdens, someone with whom they can discuss their strategy. But
essentially it has to start with one. Unless you are a very influential
senior member of a team, the idea of having a team meeting and just
walking in and announcing it would be quite difficult. Sometimes you
want to come out and you just don't care how, and it could be more
damaging to you if you just let it slip out one day. Make sure that you
control your coming out process. It's a personal process for you. You
control it. Don't let people tell you how fast to do it or how slow to do

The Personal Side of John Amaechi

Do you have a partner or boyfriend?

No.

Do you want one . . . ?

Yes.

What kind of man are you most attracted to, or what is your type?

I don't know. I've dated all different types of people. I find the idea of types a bit odd.

Why?

Because look at me. If that exists, if it must be that there are types, how many people am I the type of?

Describe your circle of friends.

It's eclectic. I have one side of them in Phoenix that, when we get together, looks like the cast of *Noah's Arc*. I have other friends in Salt Lake City who do not look like the cast of *Noah's Arc*, obviously. And Houston, a very eclectic bunch. We all bring different things to the table. I'm the awkward obstinate one who stands in the corner in bars, and they tend to be more outgoing. I don't really have [a circle of friends] in England oddly, because I've been in America most of my life. I'm developing a group of people whom I know quite well, but I don't think we're at the same stage as my friends in Salt Lake or Houston or Phoenix. Simply because we haven't been through the wars, really.

Are most of your close friends gay?

Yes.

Tell me about your home.

I have a home in Phoenix which I'm selling because I'm never in Phoenix. But I'm going to spend more time in America, and it will probably be in New York, I would imagine. In London I have a flat, it's about [2,000 square feet]. It's very, very expensive to live in London. I live on the top floor that has a 360 view of London, which is rare. It's quite nice.

Do you have any roommates?

No. I'm nearly impossible to live with, which is why I'm single.

Do you have any pets?

I'm never in my house for more than two days in a row.

What are your favorite things?

Debate has to be up there, but it's not number one. Nutella. Actually, anything sweet with carbohydrates. Music. I can't survive without it. I don't know. No one has ever asked me that before.

What's your favorite sport?

Tennis? It's the only one I watch on purpose.

Favorite movie?

You see, it's really horrible. Have you seen *Beautiful Thing*? It's not really a good choice I think, but you see, it's formative, it's the thing that made me come out to myself.

Favorite Madeline Kahn movie?

I love *Blazing Saddles*. But *Clue* would be it.

Are you a dancing queen?

No, I am a wall flower.

What album do you listen to most often?

I don't. I have nearly 4,000 CDs, and I rip them onto and off of my iPod on a regular basis. And I just scroll up and down and click and listen to whatever comes up.

What's your favorite restaurant in the U.S.?

I have an addiction to Outback Steakhouse, which is problematic. It's for the starter you get, the cheese fries. It's insanity.

How often do you hear Don Ameche jokes?

Bizarrely often. If there was an antonym to me, it would be a short white straight guy, surely. It's Don Ameche, a dead old short white straight guy. There's nothing similar, not even close, but it happens all the time.

What size shoe do you wear?

15.

Do you prefer boxers, briefs, or boxer-briefs?

Boxer-briefs.

Ginger or Maryann?

I know what you're referring to, but I've never seen that show. I know it's Americana but I don't know it.

I'm going to say a name and you give me the first word that jumps into your head:

David Stern—Brilliant.

Shaquille O'Neal—Large.

David Beckham—Galaxy.

Borat—Crass.

George Bush—Ignorant.

Tony Blair—Follower.

Elton John—Glitzy.

Madonna—I love her. That's so sad. Pop.

Howard Bragman—The queen of L.A. I know that's not one word.

John Amaechi—Convoluted.

Finally, if you were a tree, what kind of tree would you be?

My simple answer would be an oak, but I don't think that's right. I think sycamore. There is an analogy there. Some plants produce seeds that just drop. Some plants produce seeds that have to be eaten and shit out. And some plants produce seeds that fly. And sycamores produce seeds that fly, like helicopters.

it. Find someone with whom you have a real connection and make a concerted plan.

OUTSPORTS: Whom did you seek out for advice when you were planning to do this?

AMAECHI: I'm not really an advice-seeker. The bottom line is, I'm a loner. And although I have a number of really close friends who have always been really supportive, especially during this time, I have a plan, "the plan" that's in my head, that directs me how to behave. I knew I needed it to be carefully planned.

OS: So "The Plan" is still in effect.

AMAECHI: Yes. I think I'm lucky in that it always will be.

OUTSPORTS'S GUIDE TO THROWING A GAY SUPER BOWL PARTY

At Outsports, as with the rest of America, the NFL is the biggest game in town. Despite the stereotypical idea that tennis and swimming and maybe gymnastics are the most popular sports among gay men, the fact is that homos are just like the straights: football is king, and the NFL is the biggest player in the game.

The climax of every NFL season is the Super Bowl, and it's the biggest annual party in America. Although there are certainly more grills cooking on Independence Day and more roast beast on Christmas, no event has more Americans sharing the same experience than the Super Bowl. That experience, as is well documented by its TV ratings and the media buzz it generates annually, is the biggest sporting event of the year—an NFL football game between what are supposed to be the two best teams in the league.

Every year, tens of thousands of Super Bowl parties are hosted across the country. Some bar owners have said that the Super Bowl is actually not a great day for business because it's become ingrained in American culture to make some seven-layer dip, grab some tortilla chips, and head to a buddy's house to watch the game.

As with most any other opportunity to get together, drink alcohol, and have a good time, gays host their fair share of Super Bowl parties, too.

The Allure of a Super Bowl Party

If you're going to host a Super Bowl party, you've got to understand why people go to these events. There are four main reasons.

To hang out with friends. Gay Super Bowl parties aren't much different

Two gay men who eventually came out of the closet have played in the Super Bowl. Roy Simmons was an offensive lineman for the Washington Redskins in Super Bowl XVIII in 1984; his team lost to the Oakland Raiders, 38–9. Esera Tuaolo was a nose tackle for the Atlanta Falcons in Super Bowl XXXIII; his team lost to the Denver Broncos, 34–19. In that game, Tuaolo became the last player to record a tackle on Hall of Fame quarterback John Elway.

from straight parties. Sure, many people at a gay Super Bowl party are likely paying more attention to the guy they're talking to than the game. But if you go to a straight party, it's much the same. Tens of millions of Americans who don't call themselves NFL fans trudge through the cold and snow every first Sunday in February to hang out with friends and enjoy a party; to them—straight, gay, men, women—the event on TV could just as easily be day two of a cricket match in India. As long as everyone's in a good mood and having fun, they're in.

To watch the game. Still, there are plenty of people who do have a big interest in the Super Bowl. Whether one of their hometown teams is playing or they just put down a "nickel" on the favorite team to cover the spread (that is, the number of points the bookies say they should win by), there will be people at every Super Bowl party who are glued to the TV set for every play.

Artist Dylan Edwards lives in Austin and has been designing cartoons for Outsports since 2002.

To see the commercials. There's also a large contingent of people who go to these parties to watch TV, but not the game. For years now, the commercials have been almost as big an attraction for the Super Bowl as the game itself. With more money spent on a single Super Bowl commercial than most of the athletes playing in the game make in a year, the commercials have helped make the Super Bowl even more of a spectacle than just the game itself. Although gays may take a particular interest in many of the commercials, most ads are geared toward a mainstream audience, particularly straight men, who take notice and talk about the commercials after the game as much as any dancing queen in Boys' Town.

To see Janet Jackson's nipple. The halftime show is also a huge draw. Depending on who the performers are, the halftime show could be an even bigger draw at a gay Super Bowl party than the game. When Janet Jackson and Justin Timberlake performed together, anticipation was high in many of the gay publications. When the Rolling Stones performed, not so much. Of course, that infamous Jackson-Timberlake halftime show went down in history as the most memorable halftime show ever, and probably one of the most memorable Super Bowl moments of all time, which made parties at houses with DVRs go wild for a replay as Jackson revealed a nipple.

Although there's not much control a party thrower can have over the excitement of what's on the TV, the key is to remember that what is on the

Super Bowl Commercials

The beginning of Super Bowl commercials as they presently exist was during the first commercial break after halftime during Super Bowl XVIII between the Oakland Raiders and the Washington Redskins on January 22, 1984. That commercial break featured Apple's famous *1984* commercial, featuring a woman running with a hammer through an Orwellian-themed set, and introduced the world to Macintosh.

Since then, more and more money has gone into the production of these Super Bowl commercial spectacles, and the rates for airing the commercials has risen to more than two million dollars for a thirty-second spot.

The most popular series of Super Bowl commercials over the past two decades is likely the Bud Bowl, which aired during Super Bowl XXII, between the Washington Redskins and the Denver Broncos, in 1988. The series of commercials throughout the game pitted Team Budweiser against Team Bud Light, each team represented by bottles as players playing a football game. Team Budweiser won, 20–17. Because the real Super Bowl was a blowout win for the Redskins, it was joked that the only reason people were watching late in the fourth quarter was to find out what happened in the Bud Bowl.

You can see various Super Bowl commercials from 2002 at lfilm.com.

TV is, in fact, the focal point of the party, and everything you plan should take that into consideration. With that said, the social aspect—from chatting with old friends to meeting future ex-lovers—is key, so keep that in mind when drawing up the guest list and setting up the spacing of couches, chairs, and the television itself.

Planning the Party

Though everyone has their way of making a Super Bowl party their own, there are some things that every Super Bowl host should consider. These are our tips and tricks—some things to help you host the most successful party you can.

The food. So many gay parties have no food—or, if they do, it's a bowl of chips and salsa—that it might be hard to believe gays would come looking to eat. But remember, the Super Bowl is from about a quarter past six eastern time to almost ten o'clock; guests are going to be hungry. The amount of energy you put into this can be minimal, or you can go all-out. Some things you should consider offering:

Jim's Chili Recipe

There may be only one guarantee at your party: People will be hungry. You need something of substance to last people the four hours of the game, and Jim's chili recipe is just the thing.

Ingredients

1 large can crushed tomatoes

2 large cans diced tomatoes

16 ounces beer

1 cup diced onion

1 cup diced pepper

1 can kidney beans

1 can garbanzo beans

1 cup mustard

1/3 cup vinegar

1 cup brown sugar

2 Tbsp. chili powder

1 Tbsp. paprika powder

2 pounds lean ground beef

Pepper, salt, and garlic salt to taste

Optional: tomato paste

Preparation: Sauté the diced onions. Put tomatoes, beer, onion, and pepper in large pot. Bring to a slow boil, covered. Stir regularly for up to thirty minutes. Drain the beans and rinse. Add the rest of the ingredients, not including the beef, to the pot. Let simmer uncovered until the tomato base is not overly watery, but not too thick for your liking (it could take hours). You want the sauce to be somewhat thick, but not pasty (add the optional tomato paste to thicken). Sauté the beef until just slightly pink; drain excess fat. Add beef to pot and cook for another two hours.

Early prep: You can make the chili the day before the game. In this case, add the beef one to two hours before serving.

Chicken wings. You can make these or have them delivered. A selection of hot wings, honey mustard wings, and any others are always appreciated. *Extra points:* A combination of wings along with blue cheese dressing, carrot sticks, and celery is a classic.

Chili. It's so easy to make and is always a crowd pleaser. *Extra points:* Create a chili bar with hot peppers, sour cream, grated cheese, and onions.

Chips and salsa. It's the standard for a reason—it's cheap and easy. *Extra points:* Make some guacamole with some avocados and a little bit of the salsa. You can even make your own salsa with some fresh diced tomato, onion, and cilantro. Just make it the night before so the flavors have time to blend.

Hot dogs. You can do full-size hot dogs or little pigs in a blanket. Have at least the standard mustard and ketchup for your guests to dress their dogs. *Extra points:* Create a hot dog bar with all the toppings, including chili, onions, sauerkraut, cheese, pickles, relish, and anything else you think your guests might like.

Sweets. There's no need to go overboard here; chocolate chip cookies (you can even just bake the store-bought dough) are always a favorite. *Extra points:* Homemade cupcakes decorated with the logos of the two teams playing will give dessert that extra touch that will be a topic of conversation.

The drinks. Traditionally, gay men are big fans of anything with vodka or cranberry juice in it. Most gay parties have a healthy selection of vodka and mixers with a smattering of other hard alcohols and some beer.

Super Bowl parties bring out the butch in even the gayest of men. The guys with the longest lisps and least interest in football seem to get into the spirit of this country's most over-the-top display of masculinity. It's no surprise, given all of the advertising dollars poured into football (and the Super Bowl in particular) by beer companies, that most people, gay or straight, trade in their martini shakers and cocktail glasses for a bottle of beer on Super Bowl Sunday. There isn't really a need to provide a wide variety of beers. Most people are perfectly happy to dive into an American light beer, or maybe a Corona, while celebrating the Super Bowl. Plus, chances are good that some of your guests will bring a six-pack with them anyway.

If you do want some variety, try offering some hard cider or hard lemonade. Although wine coolers are officially out, hard cider and lemonade offer a lighter, fruitier taste while maintaining the air of testosterone that Bud Light offers (well, almost).

Super Bowl Ad Generates Snickers

It came as a complete shock to many gay people when some gay activists claimed that a Snickers commercial during Super Bowl XLI told people that they should go get baseball bats and beat up gay people. Yet, that was the reaction of groups like the Human Rights Campaign, the Gay and Lesbian Alliance Against Defamation, and Americablog. The ad featured two gruff auto mechanics working on the engine of a car. One took a Snickers bar out of his pocket and began to eat it. The other mechanic started eating the candy bar from the opposite end until the two, à la the *Lady and the Tramp* spaghetti moment, locked lips in the middle. They each pulled away and one of the mechanics said, "Quick, do something manly." Each of the men ripped off some of his chest hair, screaming in pain.

On the Snickers Website, there were three alternate endings posted. Each ad started the same, with the two men fixing a car, locking lips on a Snickers bar, and pulling away.

Love Boat ending

A third guy walked in and stood between the two men, looking them over. "Is there room for three," the man asked, flipping his longer hair back as though he's Cher, "on this love boat?"

"Motor Oil" ending

After one of the mechanics said, "Quick, do something manly," they all drank motor oil and antifreeze, screaming.

"Wrench" ending

After one of the mechanics said, "Quick, do something manly," one hit another in the stomach with a wrench and a third bashed another in the head with the hood of the car.

All of the endings point to a rather sophisticated message. The two men in the *Love Boat* ending didn't protest or even react to the third man's solicitation. And in the other endings, the two men tried to do something "manly" to make up for their kiss. Instead, they ended up doing things—drinking motor oil and hitting one another with metal objects—that are just harmful and stupid, or they did something—ripping off chest hair—that could be considered "gay."

The sophisticated message seemed to be that the overreaction of "straight" men to homosexual contact is completely irrational, and, in the case of the proposed threesome, maybe that contact is not entirely shunned.

In typical fashion, however, some gay activists totally missed the point and overreacted themselves. John Aravosis at AmericaBlog led with this headline: *Snickers Superbowl [sic] Web site promotes violence against gays and lesbians. Bears & Colts players react in disgust, on camera, to gays.*

HRC's head honcho John Solmonese got in on the act, issuing this statement: "If they have any questions about why the ad isn't funny, we can help put them in touch with any number of GLBT Americans who have suffered hate crimes."

Well, I had about 30 "GLBT Americans" at my party, and they enjoyed the ad. Most of the posts on the Outsports discussion board said the ad wasn't offensive, it was funny. Hell, Rosie O'Donnell and the women on *The View* said they weren't offended; and if they weren't offended, it's hard to believe it was objectively offensive.

The Snickers Website features some of the Super Bowl participants reacting to the commercial. And some, in particular Chicago Bears wide receiver Muhsin Muhammad and Indianapolis Colts linebacker Cato June, weren't overly positive, but they certainly weren't gay-bashing. Some of the featured voices, however, are overtly positive about the commercial.

Colts wide receiver Marvin Harrison took the piece well, laughing along with it and saying, "It's definitely a great piece. I don't know who came up with it, but it's definitely a great piece."

Bears quarterback Rex Grossman had praise for the commercial: "It's up there with some of the best I've ever seen, and there's been some great ones. A lot of people who don't like football will watch the Super Bowl for the commercials and the parties. And those types of people are really going to love this commercial."

The ad was not remotely gay-bashing, as many gay activists claimed. The point of the reaction of the men was so ridiculous that it made the reaction of straight men to homosexual contact the butt of the joke, not the kiss itself.

In the end, the gay activists got what they wanted: Wonderfoods, which owns Snickers, decided to pull the plug on the entire campaign. It's just hard to believe that HRC and GLAAD are now in the business of *removing* images of two men kissing from the most-watched TV program of the year.

The TV. Though most every social party is really about people interacting, they all also have to have a distraction for the crowd, usually music. At a Super Bowl party, it's the TV and the game broadcast that take the places of the stereo and pounding beat of Madonna and Victor Calderone.

The biggest difference, of course, is that what's on the TV is the focal point of the party. Some people will be there explicitly to watch the game and will holler at anyone who dares walk in front of the TV when the ball is in the air. Even the people who claim to have no interest in football will be asking, "What just happened?" by the end of the first quarter and will be pushing for a view of the TV by the end of a close game.

It's key to arrange your chairs in a way that limits the amount of time someone might be walking in front of the TV while maximizing the number of places people can sit with a good view of the game.

Cheat sheet. In case you haven't heard them already, prepare yourself for such comments as, "What inning is it?" "Was that a home run?" and "Where are the pitchers and catchers?" And that's from the people who came to watch the game; people just love to play up the stereotypical gay part of gay Super Bowl parties. Still, there will be plenty of people who won't have a clue on earth about the game. Unless New England Patriots quarterback Tom Brady's involved, chances are they don't know what teams are playing, they don't know any of the players, and they may not even know many of the rules. Part of your job is to help these poor souls not make fools of themselves during or after the game.

Designing and printing small cheat sheets for people will help them understand the game and get a little more excited about it.

Some of the things you can include:

- Pictures of some of the hottest players always helps. If nothing else, some of your partygoers can cheer for the cuter team.

- History of the two teams and how they got to the Super Bowl that given season. It doesn't need to be anything fancy, but little factoids that will impress their coworkers around the water cooler are always appreciated.
- Of the guests at your party, who's cheering for which team. It's a great icebreaker, and people instantly know whom to look for when it's time to high-five.

Fun games. Squares pools have long been a standard at Super Bowl parties. But whatever you choose to do, the key is to keep it simple and random. You want to create a contest in which someone with no knowledge of the game can beat someone who has watched each team's every game that season. A couple of ideas:

Squares pools. The most popular Super Bowl pool is completely random and a lot of fun. On a sheet of paper, a square is divided into one hundred smaller squares. Along the top is written the name of one of the teams playing; along the left is written the name of the other team. Number each one of the rows and each one of the columns zero to nine (randomly, walking down the sidewalk with a Diet Pepsi in his hand. Carson Kressley's head turns, and his jaw drops watching the guy . . . uh . . . can of soda pass by.

Anheuser-Busch, 2003. A guy wearing a clown suit upside down walks into a bar . . . Sounds like the beginning of a joke—whether it was a good joke or a bad joke depends on whom you ask. The clown proceeds to order a bottle of beer and drink the bottle seemingly through the clown costume's butt—to the disgusted looks of various people at the bar. When the clown wants to eat a hot dog, the bartender politely refuses him one.

Diageo, 2003. In a Smirnoff ad, a woman named Alex is on a blind date with a guy named Brad. Alex hits it off with another guy before Brad arrives. When Brad finally shows up, Alex wants nothing to do with him, so the guy she's hit it off with introduces himself to Brad as Alex. Brad takes off faster than Reggie Bush on a kick return.

not sequentially). Cover the numbers so no one can see what numbers correspond to each square. Depending on how many people you're expecting at the party, ask each person to pick a certain number of squares when they walk in; write their name in the squares they pick. When all the squares are selected, reveal the numbers. For Super Bowl XLI, each square would have had a number corresponding to the Indianapolis Colts and a number corresponding to the Chicago Bears. The numbers refer to the last digit of that team's score. So with the final score of Indianapolis 29, Chicago 17, the square that corresponded to Indianapolis (9) and Chicago (7) would win. You can have different prizes for the end of each quarter to give people a better chance of winning something.

Spread pool. Cut up a couple of pieces of paper into thirty-one smaller pieces of paper. On each piece of paper, write a different possible outcome. For example: Indianapolis by 1, Indianapolis by 2, Indianapolis by 3, and so on all the way up to "15 or more." Be sure to include one piece of paper that says "Tie." Pass out the pieces of paper randomly to guests. At the end of each quarter, whoever is holding the most accurate slip of paper wins.

Brief History of the Super Bowl

The first Super Bowl was played on January 15, 1967, and featured a rousing victory for the Green Bay Packers over the Kansas City Chiefs, 35–10. The game was created as part of a merger plan between the National Football League and the American Football League. The term *Super Bowl* was first uttered by Chiefs owner Lamar Hunt, who had been watching his daughter play with a Super Ball; postseason college football games had been called "bowls" for decades. The name was officially adopted for Super Bowl III in 1969. The Dallas Cowboys have appeared in the most Super Bowls (eight, all of them in the 1970s and the 1990s). The winner of the game wins the Lombardi Trophy, named for the Packers head coach who won the first two Super Bowls.

Decorations. This is the one party of the year where the host is almost expected to go as white trash as possible. When you're serving hot dogs and chicken wings, all semblance of being cosmopolitan (even if you're drinking one) is out the door.

Don't be shy about trying to get some big, obnoxious centerpiece for your decorating from some beer company. They've got terrible blow-up beer bottles, life-size cutouts of football players and hot twin babes, ugly piñatas, and anything else you can think of that might be standing in some cheap sports bar in Topeka, Kansas. If you can, get your hands on this stuff and don't let go; guests will appreciate the addition to the decor.

Although design-driven plates and napkins might be frowned upon the rest of the year, not so for the Super Bowl. Party hosts have free rein to offer up the gaudiest paper products and plasticware they can find. Serving platters in the shape of footballs, paper cups with football players on them, and napkins and forks in the colors of the two teams playing are welcomed in the white-trashiest party of the year.

Also, don't shy away from fun little tchotchkes that people can play with during the party or take home afterward. Little stuffed footballs, decks of football trading cards, key chains, picture frames—everyone loves free stuff, and they'll get a kick out of the party favors on Super Bowl Sunday.

OUTSPORTS

Flashback

#2

MARCH 1–2, 2005

Gay Is a Naughty Word to the NFL Shop

Jim Buzinski

To the NFL it's naughty to be GAY but okay to be BIN LADEN. You can be a NAZI but not a LESBIAN. Even a gay man with the last name Gay can't buy a jersey.

This rather bizarre conclusion is reached when trying to order a personalized jersey from the NFL Shop, the online merchandise site run by the league. Anyone trying to buy a jersey with the single word GAY or LESBIAN or GAY PRIDE on the back gets a rejection message that states: "This field should not contain a naughty word."

The wording was changed in the hours since this article first appeared and the NFL contacted. Now when you enter GAY and try to check out you get the following: "The personalization entered cannot be accepted." This wording is no less offensive than *naughty* and doesn't change the issue. Especially when you can buy jerseys with FAG or DYKE or HITLER on them.

Someone running the NFL's web site decided certain terms were "naughty," including a declaration of sexual orientation. But BIN LADEN, TERRORIST, and AL QAEDA are all accepted; just have your credit card handy (personalized jerseys start at $79.99).

This story first appeared in Rex Wockner's column on 365gay.com. It seems that a Louisiana State University (LSU) professor, Leigh Clemons, wanted to buy a jersey with the name of one of her former students. The student happened to be Randall Gay, a defensive back for the Super Bowl champion New England Patriots. Her attempts were initially rejected. "The NFL Shop website said that they weren't allowed to print 'naughty words' on jerseys," Clemons said, according to Wockner. "'I had to call the shop and go through three levels of bureaucracy to get the jersey.' Clemons said site employees lifted the block on the word 'gay' just long enough for her to place her order then immediately reinstated it."

After our article appeared, I received an e-mail from Barry Gay of Raleigh, North Carolina, who sent us the exchange he had with the NFL Shop:

BARRY GAY TO THE NFL: Just wanted to let you know how profoundly offended I am to learn that the NFL thinks my last name is a "naughty" word. When I looked into ordering a personalized jersey online, I entered my last name, which is "Gay," in the appropriate box and was instructed not to use a "naughty" word. To add insult to injury, I just so happen to be gay, so it was all the more hurtful to learn that the NFL believes that God and nature conspired to make me naughty. If nothing else, I have experienced firsthand how frighteningly homophobic—and stupid—the NFL remains even in the 21st century. Thanks for helping me lose all respect for the NFL organization.

PS—While I was trying to complete [the NFL's] name and address field below [to complain], you guys slapped me in the face yet again by alerting me that "You can't use that word or phrase in the last name field" when I entered my last name in that field!!! I actually had to change the spelling (by adding an "e" to the end of Gay) just to get your form to accept my entry. Just where in the world did you manage to find the small-minded idiots who decided for you which words are naughty and which words are nice?

RESPONSE FROM A CUSTOMER SERVICE REPRESENTATIVE: Your last name is not considered "naughty." I realize it is a legitimate last name. However, the NFL reserves all rights to what can and can not be printed on one of its Jersey's [*sic*]. Unfortunately, it is the few that have made this step necessary and have made it bad for the majority of people who do not abuse the opportunity to have an item personalized. In the few cases that may arise with someone abusing certain words or names the NFL does not wish to be associated with any derogatory use of language or words. I am sorry for the inconvenience. Unfortunately there is no way around this issue.

"No way around this issue"? Give me a break. How about creating a better filter? How about concluding there is nothing "naughty" about the word *gay*? This ban is both offensive and silly, it is and unique to the NFL. I went to the online sites for both the NBA and Major League Baseball, and both accepted GAY with no problem.

One would have thought that the LSU professor's complaint would make the NFL web masters realize how stupid it was to ban certain words that were anything but naughty. In addition, there is a player whose last name is Gay, which makes the prohibition doubly absurd. It seems that Randall Gay fans are SOL.

What's even dumber is how ineffective the word-screening program actually is. Add an *s* to most any word, and it is suddenly acceptable (GAYS or COCKS). Or including GAY as part of many compound words is also okay. A reader discovered the list of 1,159 banned words for jerseys. Some of them are doozies (there are 54 variations of *ass* alone), and you wonder who took the time to compile them or had such a vivid imagination.

Note: A day after Outsports ran that article, the NFL changed its policy.

GAY Is Now OK at the NFL Shop

The league reversed itself and will now allow personalized jerseys to have GAY on the back. Dan Masonson, a league spokesman, told Outsports that "there was no message there" to having *gay* on a list of 1,159 banned words. "It should have not been in the [naughty-words] filter," he said.

This decision seems to have less to do with any sexual orientation statement by the league and more to do with the fact that there is a player in the league with the last name Gay, New England Patriots defensive back Randall Gay. (Randall is the first Gay in the NFL since Ben Gay played for the Cleveland Browns in 2001.) For example, Masonson said there was no discussion about removing *lesbian* or other words from the list of banned words and explained the league's thinking: "The idea behind personalized jerseys is for a fan to put his or her name on the back or possibly a nickname." It is not designed for political, social, or other types of statements.

Outsports came up with a variety of seemingly offensive personalized jerseys (see bottom of this page) that were allowed to be purchased, such as HITLER, FAG, DYKE, or TERRORIST. Readers came up with their own, including ANTI GAY. But Masonson said he doubts that such jerseys could actually be purchased. (March 3 update: In the two days since we first published this story, BIN LADEN, BINLADEN, GAY NAZI, and GAYNAZI have been added to the banned list.)

The NFL Shop uses three levels of manual checks to make sure a personalized jersey meets the league's guidelines, Masonson said. He used the example of TERRORIST as a jersey that could make it through the online screening only to be flagged by an NFL Shop employee and rejected.

The league's response was a quick change from just a day earlier when gay man Barry Gay had a request for a jersey with his last name rejected. He received a rather insulting response when he complained. The league owes Barry Gay an apology and should send him a jersey gratis.

I understand the league has the right to control what goes on its officially licensed products and applaud them for removing GAY from the list after realizing the absurdity of, in essence, singling out one of its players. (Although a reader points out that you can't buy a Jets jersey with TONGUE on it, even though there is a Jets player named Reggie Tongue. This shows how dumb their filter is.) But it still rankles to see *lesbian* on a list of banned words and to realize that at some point *gay* was considered off-limits. Masonson did not know the inner workings of how the list was compiled or updated.

In response to my original article, I spoke with a technology consultant who helped the NFL set up its online shop in about 1997. "I did technology strategy at IBM while we were building the custom jersey ordering system for the NFL," said the consultant, who asked that his name not be used. "We tried to tell them that a naughty-word filter was a bad idea because it was impossible to catch everything and you'd keep people from ordering legitimate names (like Gay). We had learned this lesson the hard way in trying to automate profanity filtering in online forums instead of hiring people to screen comments, but the NFL was insistent that they had to have it and it needed to be automated instead of a human approval process. The project manager was showing off the functionality when it was first developed, and I bet him I could get an offensive jersey order through in less than two minutes. I won the bet, and it's the reason SMEGMA is on the list."

The consultant said he understands why the NFL has such a list ("They're very protective of their brand") but thinks there is a better way than simply rejecting an entry outright. He said a better system would be to alert a buyer that a certain jersey name might not meet the NFL's criteria, but give the person a chance to explain via e-mail. This would allow for a person with a legitimate unique name to buy a jersey and save the NFL from "a PR black eye."

FANTASY FOOTBALL

The NFL has a very rich history with Outsports. Just as it is the most popular sports league in America, it is Jim and Cyd's favorite sport. They have spent countless Sundays sitting in Jim's house on warm Los Angeles afternoons watching DirecTV's broadcasts of every single game in a weekend. Whether it is a super matchup or a complete dud of a game, they, like millions of Americans, stay glued to their TV sets if for no other reason than fantasy football.

Fantasy football, for a gay man, can certainly be a loaded term. There's no getting around the fact that young, toned athletes in form-fitting pants are hot, hot, hot—certainly plenty of material for fantasies that are best fulfilled behind closed doors. But for hard-core football fans, fantasy football is an increasingly popular game that gives fans a vested stake in every NFL game. The standard fantasy football league looks something like this:

- A group of ten to fourteen friends gets together and decides to play together in fantasy football.
- The group conducts some kind of draft of NFL players in which each participant selects the NFL players they want on their team. They

Gayfantasyfootball.com

Launched in 2005, Gayfantasyfootball.com is the proud home of several gay fantasy football leagues, including Outsports leagues.

If you're looking for a football player who can fulfill all of your fantasies, you need look no further than quarterback Drew Brees, who has put up some big numbers in San Diego and New Orleans.

Photo by Brent Mullins

can pick from any NFL team, so they could have Titans quarterback Vince Young and Steelers receiver Hines Ward, along with players from several other NFL teams, on their fantasy team.

- Every week, the team of each fantasy participant is matched up against one other fantasy participant's team. A winner of the matchup is determined by how well each team's NFL players do in their games that week. Scoring is determined by various methods, including yards rushed, touchdowns scored, and passing yards.
- At the end of each week, the participants who won tease and embarrass those who lost.

The allure of fantasy football for any fan, gay or straight, is the vested interest in every NFL game that fantasy football gives them. A quintessential example was week thirteen of the 2003 NFL season. The premier game of the week featured a rousing 38–34 victory for the New England Patriots over the Indianapolis Colts. However, many fantasy footballers were glued to the snoozefest comedy of errors between the Houston Texans and the Atlanta Falcons. The game saw both teams switch quarterbacks at halftime—a fantasy football nightmare. There was a lowly 505 yards of total offense in the game. But Texans running back Domanick Davis kept fantasy footballers glued to the set, as his 128 yards and two touchdowns changed the fates of many fantasy matches that week.

Overrating "Fantasized" Fantasy Players

Just as many straight fantasy football participants tend to draft one or two players from their favorite NFL team, many gay fantasy footballers end up taking into consideration how some players look with their helmets, or a whole lot more, removed. And that's fine, except that when these players are drafted a little too high based on their looks, it can become a long season for a pretty fantasy team that can't get a win. If you want to win your fantasy league, remember that no player will get you any points for looks.

Some of the most popular "hot" NFL fantasy players in recent years whom gay men have tended to draft a bit higher than they should be:

Mike Alstott. Despite being overshadowed on the Tampa Bay Buccaneers by various running backs, the fullback has been a popular face with gay men—including fantasy footballers—for years.

Brian Finneran. Though he's been Falcons quarterback Michael Vick's favorite target in recent years, that's like being a gay guy's favorite female stripper. When taking Finneran, gay men end up with a top-two receiver on a team that only throws when it has to.

Trent Green. The Kansas City Chiefs quarterback became a popular fantasy draftee for gay and straight men when then head coach Dick Vermeil took the Chiefs offense to new levels. But even when he was a solid fifth-round pick for straight guys, he was going in the third round in gay drafts. The problem is, the Chiefs score with their running backs, not their quarterback.

Brandon Stokley. When this Colts wide receiver caught passes for more than 1,000 yards and ten touchdowns in 2004, it was finally affirmation for gay men across the country that drafting for looks could pay off. Of course, he came back down to the backup-receiver numbers he'd posted for years.

For anyone interested in the NFL, or interested in getting to know more about it, fantasy football is a lot of fun, and at the end of the season you'll know more about the play of specific players than any of your friends. And if nothing else, you'll be able to tell your boyfriend's father how impressed you were with New Orleans Saints quarterback Drew Brees's 4,400 passing yards. It'll help get you those brownie points from the in-laws you've been trying so hard to impress.

PART III

GETTING IN THE GAME

THE CURSE OF THE HIGH
SCHOOL GYM CLASS

One of the biggest compliments Outsports gets is when gay people say the web site reopened sports for them. So many gay people, especially gay men, abandon sports when they are young because it seems not only has sports abandoned them, but they have been banished from athletics as well.

The stories permeate virtually every corner of society about how gay people are marginalized. There's the restaurant owner in Los Angeles who won't hire gay waiters (shocking, but a true story). There's the lesbian in Missouri who can only get a job as a truck driver. There are the gay actors who are typecast in flamboyant comedic and supporting roles.

Few rebukes, however, seem to sit with gay people as long as those from sports. As kids, many gay people were treated very differently in gym class than they were in the rest of their lives. When it came time to pick teams, they were often the last ones picked, and even when they were picked, it was with a sigh. "Ugh. I guess I have to take Jimmy."

And so it started—the negative relationship with sports that so many gay people have had. Rejection is easy for no one to take. But rejection in gym class, over and over again, in front of all of your peers, can leave a pretty nasty taste in your mouth. It's a taste that can last a lifetime. And even though rejection comes to gay people in all areas of life, it's a lot easier to take a typecast role in the school play when you're surrounded by "drama geeks" than it is to have performance-obsessed young jocks yelling, "Don't shoot the ball!"

This certainly isn't the case with all gay people. The stereotypical lesbian girl is faster, can throw a baseball better, and can shoot a basketball more accurately than the stereotypical gay boy. Plus, there are many young gay boys who aren't so easy to spot. They can perform just as well on the athletic field as any straight boy—maybe even better! These

Outsports.com has offered gay people a supportive environment to enjoy sports since late 1999. The Outsports Discussion Board, one of the most active gay-themed discussion boards on the Internet, is a great place to meet people near you or who just have a similar sports interest.

people—the many stereotypical lesbian girls and nonstereotypical gay boys around the world—have few hang-ups about sports because they have excelled in sports. And when you excel in sports in most any culture, you are liked and revered.

It's Not the Sports Themselves

An important point to recognize is that many gay people have come to dislike sports not because they actually dislike the playing or watching of them but rather because at a very young age sports were used to marginalize and discriminate against them. Gym class and after-school sports were a place where their differences and what they could not contribute became the focal points. Many were even good athletes who were made to feel less-than because they were perceived to be gay. That was certainly Cyd's experience.

In elementary school, he was one of the tallest, fastest kids in his class, and he could jump higher than just about any of them. He had a basketball future, following in the footsteps of his father, who had been a basketball star at the same school just twenty years earlier. He had a junior high and high school future on the horizon full of sports glory and kids arguing over whose team he would be on because they actually wanted him.

Then fourth grade hit, and a nine-year-old girl named Donnella Carter decided to spread the rumor that Cyd was gay. At the time, he had a God's-honest interest in girls; the thought of being close to boys was simply of no interest. Still, that rumor persisted about Cyd for years.

It immediately showed up in gym class. An up-and-coming star athlete through most of elementary school, Cyd started getting picked last for teams. He was shunned from playground sports. He gravitated toward sports where the girls wouldn't harass him: tetherball and the occasional kickball. And he dominated many of those girls, gosh darn it.

Interestingly, as his confidence was attacked by the boys who didn't want to play with him, his performance in sports such as basketball started to diminish. When they played softball in gym class, Cyd couldn't connect the bat with the ball to save his life. In basketball, on the rare occasions he did get the ball passed to him, he often couldn't hit the rim.

That all started to change, though, in junior high school. In seventh grade, Cyd earned his first varsity letter in cross-country; he was the first kid in his class to do so. The snickering didn't stop then, but it certainly quieted. In ninth grade, he earned his third varsity letter, in track and field. By tenth grade, he was nearing school records, leading all scorers at track meets, and won his first of four varsity-team MVP awards. By the time he graduated, he had set two school records that are still standing fifteen years later, and he was named by coaches and teachers his class's sportsman of the year.

By the end, he wasn't a gym-class pariah anymore. Instead of being known as Cyd the fag, he became Cyd the athlete. Not surprisingly, he wasn't picked last in gym class anymore.

If it wasn't for a sports-minded father who *didn't* put pressure on him to play sports, Cyd may have never shed that easily understandable perception that sports were bad. Instead, he stuck with them and made them a part of his identity.

What happened to Cyd before he found track and field is par for the course for many young gay boys: teasing and ostracism lead to a lack of confidence in, and a distaste for, sports. The core of the problem isn't the sports themselves; it's the people in them. It's the kids who understand that excelling in sports is a way to enhance their standing with the other kids, and it's Western culture telling them that to prove themselves as a

You can build a sports community at any age, as these Seattle Frontrunners, who competed in the Outgames in 2006, can attest.

Photo by Cyd Zeigler Jr.

man, they must venture into sports. Those kids subconsciously take that, along with the cultural notion that gays are effeminate and bad, and they beat up gay-acting kids with it.

Although sports are meant to give people something to strive for and are designed to focus on health and mental growth, for many, those gym classes become microcosms of the worst of society, the way all of high school is for many of those kids who are "different," whether it's because they're the first ones with acne, the first with braces, their parents don't have as much money as other parents, or they're the only black kid in a white school.

The Surrounding Culture

The culture that surrounds sports is what dominates people's enjoyment of them. If you score a touchdown and no one sees it, did you really score? If your favorite team wins the Stanley Cup and no one is there to celebrate with you, was it even worth it?

For anyone to enjoy a sport they're playing or watching, they have to surround themselves with a subculture that supports them. It can be a group of buddies who watch Major League Baseball together, a set of co-workers who all take part in an NCAA basketball pool, or a bunch of old high school friends who play football together every Thanksgiving.

In high school, the culture that surrounds most people's experience of sports is driven by the superstars, the high school jocks. Because those jocks often build themselves up by picking on weaker players and easy targets, gay kids or kids perceived to be gay often become the victims of the culture of high school sports.

On the bright side for kids coming through grade school now, high school gym class and high school sports are changing. As more and more teenage athletes come out while they're still excelling in high school sports, in some schools the sports culture that once beat down gay-acting kids is softening a bit. Many coaches are still telling their male athletes not to throw like a girl or run like a sissy, but for many other high school sports programs, that's being left by the wayside for a more inclusive, more team-building approach.

Although many people would consider the wide world of sports to be generally "homophobic," it is the smaller sports culture—the people you interact with every day—that better determines your enjoyment of any given sport. Consequently, the most important key to enjoying sports is building a positive culture around it. If you surround yourself with people who enjoy sports—whether it's playing a sport, watching a team, or playing fantasy football—then you'll enjoy sports more. Luckily, everyone gets to decide how their private sports culture is defined. To be sure, NFL fans have to hear the occasional player spouting off with antigay rhetoric, and rugby players may have to endure the occasional homophobic taunt from straight teams. But, by and large, these isolated incidents won't undermine your enjoyment of sports when you have a close-knit group of gay-positive people with whom to sit in front of the TV and cheer for your favorite team.

Gay men not into sports often find the best, most attractive athletes to be the most intimidating.

Photo by Jim Buzinski

Individual Sports

Building a gay-positive sports culture can be easier said than done for many gay people. Still mentally perceiving sports through their high school–tainted glasses and hearing and reading about reinforced stereo-

types of the homophobic jock, many gay people opt for a sports culture of one, finding their way into individual sports such as track, tennis, wrestling, swimming, golf, and gymnastics.

As opposed to strictly team sports, in these sports, driven generally by individual performance, the final outcome of one athlete's performance does not hinge on the performance of another. Although team scores are sometimes kept for individual sports, one person's ability to "win" does not fall on someone else's ability to catch, throw, or run.

Learning teamwork at a young age certainly can have incredibly positive ramifications later in life. However, for many ostracized young people, the negatives of teamwork can seemingly outweigh the positives. Letting down a teammate, being responsible for other people losing, being the weak link on a team: these things can weigh heavily on the mind of a child or teen-

Outsports reader in 2001.

I am openly gay but have not really stepped into the gay sports arena until this year. I love to play sports, but since high school I have kept the two separate. It's nice to finally bring the two together.

ager. For a gay kid who doesn't perform, who may already be the victim of jokes and criticism, playing on a team can be too much to handle.

Unfortunately for anyone, gay or straight, who doesn't perform well in sports, this thinking is all too common. It's also terribly misled. Teamwork is about the team. It's not about the great athletes winning; it's not about the lesser athletes getting the blame; it's not about the "jocks" carrying the rest of the people she plays with to victory. Teamwork is about acting as one unit and together, the good athletes and the not-so-good athletes, achieving your collective goal. It's easy for kids at a young age to put the focus of their goals on winning; hell, many do it their whole lives.

But when a team puts its focus on teamwork, great things happen. It's a lesson many people don't learn until they enter the workplace, where there are real consequences to failing as a team. There are countless gay people who have excelled at teamwork in the workplace—men and women who have risen to the pinnacle of their professions. Yet these same people wouldn't step foot on a football field for fear of personal failure.

And that is the curse of the high school gym class. Despite all of the lessons learned and accomplishments achieved, after graduating from high school, so many gays simply can't exorcise their psyches from the sophomoric behavior they experienced as kids getting picked last in gym class.

THE RISE OF THE GAY DAYS

One of the things Outsports is most proud of is how the web site and community there have inspired people around the world to take action. There is no greater homage than seeing your vision inspire others and take shape in the results of their hard work.

A very measurable place Outsports's readers and community members have made an impact has been with gay outings to sporting events—better known as "Gay Days." These events, much like the well-known Gay Days in Orlando, bring gay people together for a sporting event, most commonly a baseball game. They sit together at the game, cheer together, and there is often some recognition on the JumboTron or from the announcer that the gays have descended upon the stadium.

Outsports members have created Gay Days at baseball games in no less than three cities: Philadelphia, Toronto, and New York. Outsports members have also created the first NHL Gay Day (at the Philadelphia Flyers) and the first NBA Gay Day (at the Toronto Raptors) that Outsports has seen reported. One Outsports reader has created Gaybaseball-days.com, a comprehensive resource for all things relating to, you guessed it, Gay Days at baseball games.

With so much of the sports machine deftly avoiding gay people and gay issues as they build up sports as the essence of machismo in America, it has been up to gay people themselves to herald their presence and assert themselves where they may otherwise not be particularly wanted. No professional sports team or league has issued an open invitation to its players to come out of the closet, and no one can expect they have any interest in offering an invitation to gay fans to fill their stands, which most sports leagues like to think are jam-packed with families. No, the further presence of gays in sports is something gay people themselves are going to have to force, and they're doing just that with these gay events at pro sporting events.

The Bottom Line

The growing number of Gay Days at sporting events—mostly Major League Baseball games—continues to grab the attention of professional sports. With existing precedents for group outings at their events and the power of the "pink dollar," gay organizers have convinced pro sports teams that they can fill otherwise empty seats if they put together community nights for gay people and start to, despite some of their reticence, openly invite gay people to buy tickets to their games. They have also been able to convince many of the teams to go beyond just setting aside some seats and embrace the events. This has been a source of great annoyance to many, but probably not most, mainstream sports fans who have long bought into the notion of sports as the great bastion of American masculinity.

It has not been easy to convince many of these teams to embrace such events. Sports teams are no more interested in making a social statement about the place of gay people in sports than Terrell Owens is interested in catching another pass from Donovan McNabb. They are businesses that, like all businesses, are interested in one thing: the bottom line. Although the social opportunities and desire to make a statement in the world of sports are the reasons most organizers of these Gay Days put so much time and effort behind their endeavor, it has been the ability of these early pioneers to appeal to sports teams' business interests, not their philanthropic beliefs, that has gotten these early groundbreaking events off the ground.

An organizer's ability to contribute to a team's bottom line in the form of ticket sales will determine how much effort the team will offer to support any endeavor and how closely they'll work with an organizer to get it off the ground; this is no different for a gay event than it is for any other. The buying power of the gay market is well documented, and that extends beyond just the price of admission tickets. The average gay American household income, according to the consumer and marketing research firm Greenfield Online, is approximately fifty-seven thousand dollars, which is about twelve thousand dollars more than the national average. Plus, gay households have, on average, fewer kids, which means the percentage of their income that is expendable is larger. At a ballpark, that can translate into more five-dollar-hot-dog and twenty-five-dollar-T-shirt sales.

No Invitation Needed

Fans of the Houston Astros or Tampa Bay Devil Rays may ask indignantly, "Why doesn't my team have a Gay Day?" The answer is probably very simple: because no one has asked them to.

In June 2006, the *Riverfront Times* in St. Louis did a story about the lack of a Gay Day with the St. Louis Cardinals. Ben Westhoff, the reporter working on the story, called Cyd and asked him why he thought the Cardinals didn't have such an event. The simple answer would have alluded to the homophobia of sports or how the Cardinals were run by rich straight men who didn't care about underserved gays and lesbians. Instead, Cyd asked simply, "Has anyone asked them to?"

Chicago Cubs "Out at the Ball Game" event founder Bill Gubrud

Every year it keeps getting bigger and bigger. Everybody who goes makes a difference. We're community and we're proving that we can pack the ballpark if we want to.

Westhoff called Joe Strohm, the Cardinals' vice president of ticket sales, and sure enough, no one had ever approached them to do it. "We'd be very open to having a new group at the ballpark," Strohm told the *Riverfront Times*. "We would treat any group the same as any other group that comes."

Well why, some may ask, should gay people have to ask the club to organize a Gay Day? Why shouldn't the club just do it on its own? Again, the answer is simple: that's just the way these events work.

When Cyd researched a story in 2004 about why the New York Mets didn't have a Gay Day, he found the same answer Strohm gave: they need someone to do it. Kirk King, who soon became the group-sales rep for the first Mets Gay Day, called "Out at Shea," explained that all of their special community events—from Hispanic Heritage Night to Irish Night—are organized first and foremost by community members: although the Mets group-sales office is happy to facilitate the events, they are created, marketed, and organized by people in those communities.

Though the Mets would love to have a community night for every demographic known to man (remember, these events sell tickets), they, like every other professional sports team, are understaffed and don't have the manpower to pull them all off without a few dedicated community members willing to put in the time. "This is not a matter of the teams doing this on their own," said Larry Felzer, longtime Outsports member and organizer of the Phillies' Gay Community Day. "I don't know of a team being approached to do this that has said no."

One of the rare exceptions to that rule was the Toronto Blue Jays, though the way they came to "organize" the event was rather suspicious. Mark Kari, founder of Gaybaseballdays.com, approached the Blue Jays in 2003 about having a Gay Day at a Blue Jays game the next season. They loved the idea so much they hired the brother of someone in their front office to run the event for them and removed Kari from the process almost entirely. Luckily, the idea of a baseball team taking an idea like this, cutting out the community organizer, and running with it on its own is a rarity. On the positive side, it showed that these events are viable and that pro baseball teams have the interest and inclination to not just have them in their ballpark but to be active partners in hosting them.

Dave St. Peter, senior vice president of business affairs, Minnesota Twins, to ESPN in 2001

This isn't about gay and lesbian; it's about baseball fans. And we're in the business of promoting our game, and that means that we need to be proactive and progressive, and making our games as accessible to as many different people as possible.

If you're interested in creating such an event and you go to the New York Yankees or the Dallas Cowboys and tell them you want a block of seats for a Gay Day, chances are they'll turn you down because they already sell out their games. If you approach the Boston Red Sox and want to have an event during their annual series against the Yankees, guess what? They're going to tell you, "Fat chance." But if you think about the event from team executive's perspective, identify games that might be hard for them to sell out, and present them with a plan to fill some of those seats with five hundred flag-waving gay people, then team executives will be more likely to talk to you.

A Brief History of Gay Days

The success of Gay Days at sporting events has varied a great deal. Events at Chicago Cubs and Philadelphia Phillies games have each attracted more than a thousand people. On the flip side, a 2003 event at a Texas Rangers

Outsports contributor and longtime Angels fan Jim Allen becomes a Phillies fan for a day at a 2004 Outsports outing at a Philadelphia Phillies game.

Photo by Brent Mullins

game drew at most a couple hundred, and the gay attendees were outnumbered by the protesters who took issue with the Rangers associating themselves with a bunch of sinning homosexuals.

It's not clear how many of these kinds of events there have been or when the first one was. On September 6, 2000, there was an event for the Gay and Lesbian Alliance Against Defamation hosted by the Los Angeles Dodgers during a game against the Pittsburgh Pirates. The event was attended by 450 people and may have been the first event of its kind of that size.

But the wave of Gay Days at baseball games was certainly well under way by the autumn of 2001. On June 23 of that year, the Chicago Cubs hosted "Out at the Ball Game," one of the most-attended gay community nights ever at a sporting event. Later that same summer, the Atlanta Braves agreed to host a gay event at a game against the Houston Astros on August 8 to show support for the city's bid to host the 2006 Gay Games (they eventually lost the bid to Montreal). A month later, on September 14, the Minnesota Twins held a gay community night in conjunction with OutFront Minnesota and the Human Rights Campaign.

In addition to the Rangers, Dodgers, Phillies, Braves, Cubs, Mets, and Twins already mentioned, Gaybaseballdays.com lists six other ball clubs that have hosted such events: the Boston Red Sox, Oakland A's, Pittsburgh Pirates, San Francisco Giants, Toronto Blue Jays, and Washington Nationals. Other clubs have hosted AIDS Awareness Nights, including the Baltimore Orioles, Florida Marlins, and Chicago White Sox.

Why Baseball?

Baseball is the perfect sport to host these gay outings for several reasons. First, there are more baseball games in a given season than in any other sport. A Major League Baseball team has eighty-one home games every year. Compare that to the number of home games teams in the other major sports get: forty-one for each NBA and NHL team and only eight for NFL teams. The fact of the matter is, it's harder for most baseball teams to sell out eighty-one games than it is for a team from another sport to sell out half that or less.

The size of the venue is another big one. Certainly, the NFL has the largest venues of all of the big four sports. But, with so few home games, and being the most popular sport in the country, it's still the toughest ticket in town to find. Compare the other three sports, with more comparable home schedules, and the difference is clear: in Chicago, Wrigley

Larry Felzer invited Cyd Zeigler (right, with Outsports contributor Joe McCombs) to throw out the opening pitch of the 2005 Philadelphia Phillies Gay Community Night. Thanks to two weeks of practicing, Cyd got the ball across home plate.

Field holds forty-one thousand people, and the Bulls' United Center holds twenty-one thousand; in Los Angeles, Dodgers Stadium holds fifty-six thousand, and the Lakers' and Clippers' Staples Center holds fewer than twenty thousand; in Phoenix, the Diamondbacks' Bank One Ballpark holds forty-nine thousand, whereas the Coyotes' Glendale Arena holds eighteen thousand. It's a lot easier to find a block of seats when a team plays in front of fifty thousand seats eighty-one times a year than it is when they play in front of twenty thousand seats forty-one times a year.

Despite the disposable income of gay people, ticket prices are a third determining factor. According to a team marketing report, the average ticket prices in 2005–2006 or 2006 for the major professional sports were:

League	Avg. Price	Highest	Lowest
NFL	$58.95	New England, $90.89	Buffalo, $39.37
NBA	$45.92	Los Angeles Lakers, $79.21	Golden State, $23.82
NHL	$41.19	New Jersey, $54.67	Carolina, $26.15
MLB	$22.21	Boston, $46.46	Kansas City, $13.71

The team with the lowest ticket prices in the NFL, Buffalo, has an average price just $7 lower than the highest MLB average ticket price, in Boston. And in the other three sports, the team with the lowest average ticket price has prices still higher than the average Major League Baseball ticket price.

With all of these factors—number of home games, size of venues, and average ticket prices—it's no big surprise that Major League Baseball has had by far the most number of Gay Days.

Women's Sports: A Whole Different Ball Game

Women's sports are a completely different model. Whereas most men's professional sports probably attract the same percentage of fans as they do in society at large, it will come as a surprise to none that several women's sports seem to attract a huge lesbian crowd.

Attending the Dinah Shore golf tournament is the hajj of lesbian sports, even if it's not technically known as the Dinah Shore anymore; it's now the Kraft Nabisco Championship, and since 1983, it has been one of the four majors on the LPGA Tour. In the past couple of decades, the tournament has attracted a big lesbian crowd and taken on a whole new life.

Who Was Dinah Shore?

Actress Dinah Shore helped create the Colgate/Dinah Shore Winner's Circle Championship in 1972. She wasn't a golfer, but a singer, actress, and TV personality. In the 1940s and '50s she recorded dozens of hit records and hosted a popular TV show, *The Dinah Shore Show*, from 1951 to 1963. It was during her run hosting NBC's *Dinah's Place* that she founded the golf tournament. Many other actors of that era founded golf tournaments that shared their names: from 1968 to 1988, what is now the Buick Open carried Andy Williams's name; the Bob Hope Chrysler Classic has shared the comedian's name since 1965; and the Pebble Beach National Pro-Am had Bing Crosby's name attached to it from 1937 to 1986. Shore died in February 1994 of ovarian cancer; some of her ashes are buried in Cathedral City near her second home in Palm Springs.

"Every spring, more than 15,000 lesbians heed some cosmic force and make a mad dash for Palm Springs, Calif., to attend the wild parties surrounding the LPGA Dinah Shore golf tournament," said Outsports contributor Kaki Flynn, who attended her first Dinah Shore shortly after coming out. "Billed by the organizers as the largest lesbian event in the world, the event started in the '70s as a few flyers handed out at gay bars announcing some fun events around the golf tournament. It's grown into a weekend that now includes Rosie Jones, Joan Jett and other superstars."

Several web sites exist to help lesbians get the most out of their pilgrimage to the Dinah Shore golf tournament. Dinashoreweekend.com is run by Las Vegas and Los Angeles lesbian bar girlbar and is dedicated entirely to the five days of events that now surround the golf tournament. The events include cocktail parties, comedy shows, pool parties, sponsored brunches, and dance parties that happen every night. Thedinah. com is run by Club Skirts and hosted by Planetout. It offers its own series of events, including pool parties, the Dinah Film Festival, and, of course, dance parties. Nothing remotely like this event exists for gay-male sports fans.

If you believe some reports, every night at a WNBA game is Lesbian Night. League executives have been very cognizant of its lesbian fan base before they even had their first tip-off in April 1996. Since then, they've tried to walk a fine line between embracing the lesbian fans they know they need to fill the arenas and not making them the belles of the ball, so as not to distance the league from the straight families they also need to pack the seats.

To be sure, there is a higher percentage of lesbians at a WNBA game than an NBA game or a NASCAR race. In the United States, the WNBA has a virtual monopoly on women's team sports. For fans of women's sports (and if there were ever a target demographic, lesbians represent it), there's one game in town, and that's the one that Sheryl Swoopes is playing (and was before Swoopes came out after the 2005 season).

Although no study exists that can accurately determine the percentage of WNBA fans that are lesbians, by all accounts it is strong. Because of this, there are precious few Gay Days at WNBA games because, relative

Jay Mohr, CNNSI.com, September 14, 2005

As my buddy and I sat courtside with other celebrities like, uh, um, well, I'm sure there was somebody else, we realized what a bizarre collection of souls made up the lower tier of the arena. Little girls and lumberjacks seemed to be the primary ticket holders. The little girls looked at the court in admiration of their heroes, and the lumberjacks looked at the court in a completely different type of admiration. Other than my buddy, I was the only guy in my row, so I was hesitant to stand up and move around. I was afraid of offending the brutes surrounding me. These people were large and in charge, loud and proud, and very capable of beating me to within an inch of my life.

Pat Griffin, Outsports.com, Sept. 21, 2005, in response to Mohr's column

Maybe all of the fans at WNBA games will learn that sitting next to lesbians, talking to them, cheering with them is not really so scary after all.

to the percentage of gay people at your average pro baseball game, every WNBA game is Gay Day.

Larry Felzer's Five Must-Dos in Planning a Gay Day

Each year, Gay Community Night at the Philadelphia Phillies has been one of the largest, if not the largest, event of its kind in the country. Larry

Felzer organized the event from its genesis and has become one of the premier resources in the world on organizing events like this, and he has five things that he has found to be key:

1. Build a coalition. Approach your local ball club representing organizations that are interested in supporting a Gay Day, as opposed to going in as an individual. This does a couple of things. First, it adds some credibility. Any sports team would be wary of authorizing an individual with no relationship to the team to use its name and logo to try to sell tickets. Second, and possibly more important, having several organizations lined up to support the event potentially means more ticket sales for the ball club. And, at the end of the day, they just want you to sell tickets.

   With that said, avoid making the event a fund-raiser for a particular group. Felzer thinks this is a key component of his event's continued success: "If you do that, no matter how good or bad that organization is, there are certain people who don't like that organization, therefore don't want to support it or work for another organization that feels left out because they're not a recipient."

   Felzer, who was originally organizing the event to target only members of Gay and Lesbian Lawyers of Philadelphia (GALLOP), got tons of groups to promote it to their members and constituents because he stopped making it about GALLOP and started promoting it as a larger community event.

2. Study the team's group-sales plan. Virtually every sports team has a group-sales plan for ticket sales and an entire group-ticket-sales department. These plans have very specific benefits for groups, depending on how many tickets they sell. Some offer the opportunity to throw out a game's ceremonial first pitch, some offer free giveaways such as pins or bobble-head dolls, and still others can go as far as meet-and-greets with the players.

   The more tickets you sell for them, the more they'll give you. Don't expect any special benefits because you're a gay group. You should also expect to not be cheated out of benefits because you are a gay group. In Philadelphia, the Phillies allow any group selling more than five hundred tickets to choose someone to throw out a game's opening pitch. Each year Felzer has met that goal, and each year, including 2005 when Cyd was invited to Philadelphia for the honor, he has chosen someone to throw out the opening pitch of the game.

3. Think of the team as your friends. Whether you expect an icy or warm

What's in a Name?

Although the management of every sports team wants to sell out its games, it doesn't necessarily want the term *Gay Days* on flyers with the team's logo. The team may much prefer "Out at the Ball Game" or "Out with the Tigers" or "Gay Community Night." This is okay. The name of the event is not the important thing; what is important is that you're treated fairly, the group is treated equally, and you have a great time.

reception from the team to your idea, go in with the positive attitude of a fan looking to support her team. "It's a lot easier to establish a good working relationship when you're not going in from day one with a confrontational attitude like, 'You have to do this for us, we're entitled to this,'" Felzer said. Felzer does admit that, if things aren't going well with the team, there could come a time when you have to start getting aggressive with them. However, if you start trying to bully them by waving a rainbow flag in their face and threatening to go to the media with complaints, you won't get very far.

When Cyd first approached the New York Mets' group-sales office about having a Gay Community Night in early 2004, he was met with intrigue and some resistance. They had already been approached by another gay man, a longtime Mets fan, about holding the event. The team hemmed and hawed about it, had internal discussion after internal discussion, and finally decided that it would facilitate the event but wouldn't recognize it on the official team calendar. The team had Irish Night, Hispanic Heritage Night, even Pakistani-American Night, but it would not add Gay Community Night to its calendar. In addition, it did not want the word *Gay* in the title of the event, sanctioning only "Out at the Ballpark." Finally, the team would not comment on the event in any way to any press.

Although Cyd kept pushing and pushing for more, the decision he had to make was clear: take what they're giving you, or don't hold the event at all. With a couple of solid contacts in the New York media, he could have made a stink about it, embarrassed the Mets, and created a strained relationship that would have never healed. Instead, he went about promoting and organizing the event. He continued to push the Mets for what he wanted, but never tried to bully them. In the end, the

Mets treated the group of three hundred gay people who turned out for the game exactly as they would have treated any other group of three hundred people: names of some of the attending organizations flashed on the scoreboard, everyone got to sit together, and everyone received a Mr. Met bobble-head pin. The event went off without a hitch, the Mets were six thousand dollars richer for it, and they were contacting Cyd about doing another event the following year.

Sometimes, though, you've got to make a scene to get a ball club to recognize you. In 2002, lesbian fans of the New York Liberty did have to take some drastic actions to get their voices heard. The Liberty management had allegedly refused to recognize gay pride during an annual Liberty home game that coincidentally fell every year during New York's gay pride weekend. They also avoided showing lesbian faces and lesbian couples on the JumboTron in Madison Square Garden during games, instead focusing on kids and straight families. Simply wanting the recognition the team was giving their heterosexual counterparts, a few lesbian fans started a group called Lesbians for Liberty and staged a kiss-in at one of the team's games.

4. Get the word out. If you're interested in a gay-themed event at a ballpark, chances are thousands of other people in your area are, too. Spreading the word as early and quickly as possible will reap huge benefits in the form of higher attendance. Utilize everyone in the community you can get on board. Create flyers to leave in local establishments, send out e-mails to everyone you can think of, get the local sports press and gay press to publicize the event for you, and utilize Outsports.com and Gaybaseballdays.com to help spread the word.

Maybe most important, in your messaging, make sure you're always positive about the event. If you had trouble with the ballpark or ball club in organizing the event, don't spread that around in your marketing of it. Make sure people see the evening as a fun way to spend some time with several hundred of their new friends.

5. Be ready for all kinds of reaction to your event. Some of it can be quite negative. In the days leading up to the Phillies' first Gay Community Night, letters to the editors of local newspapers and callers to sports talk radio were largely questioning whether such an event should take place at what some deemed a "family" event. "I don't want my kid seeing that," some parents said, beating the same old drum that has been rolled out so many times before, as if the gay people in the stands wouldn't be able to control themselves, would run onto the grass naked and start an orgy right there in the outfield.

Two years later, at the Phillies' 2006 Gay Community Night, two protesters showed up in the stands in right field with a banner that read: "Homosexuality is sin. Christ can set you free." Interestingly, the letters and calls to local media outlets the next day largely rebuked the two Christians with the banner, saying the gay people weren't bothering anyone. For the most part, the fans also criticized the Phillies for allowing the men to display the large banner, surrounded by police and security guards. The Phillies claimed that it was the men's First Amendment right to display the banner because the gay people, by simply being together at the ballpark, were making a political statement.

Before the start of the next season, the Phillies and Citizen's Bank Park adopted a new policy that forbade banners such as the one they claimed was protected by the First Amendment just eight months before.

SO YOU WANT TO START
A GAY SPORTS GROUP

Outsports got its very start through a gay sports group: the Los Angeles Motion flag-football team. The group had been in existence, in various capacities, since the late 1980s. Jim took charge of it in 1994 after leading the team to a gold medal in flag football in the Gay Games that year. Cyd joined the group in 1996, just a month after coming out of the closet. Like so many young people coming out of the closet (he was just twenty-three at the time), Cyd was looking for a place to fit in. He had already walked Santa Monica Boulevard late at night, and he had spent evenings in a quiet coffeehouse, the Abbey, and in a couple of dance clubs. Although the atmosphere of the Abbey (which was, at the time, just a quiet little coffeehouse) appealed to him, he recognized that sports were where he had developed so many of his straight friends; why should it be any different with gay men?

He had heard about the gay football group from a friend with whom he played Ultimate (Frisbee), P. J. Henry. Henry had been Cyd's first date, first kiss, first everything. Henry had played with the football group on occasion and thought Cyd would fit right in—word of mouth is a powerful tool.

When Cyd met him at L.A. Gay Pride, Jim was an incredibly friendly face through a sea of shirtless bodies and nonplused stares. Jim was working a booth for the L.A. Sports Alliance, an umbrella gay-sports organization in southern California, promoting the gay football group he had been running for several years.

It was because of that football group that we became friends, started Outsports, and, eventually, wrote this book together. Gay sports groups are an incredible way to meet friends and, inevitably, lovers. Though so much of gay culture and social life revolves around bars, clubs, and parties, those venues simply aren't conducive to meeting and making solid friendships. The best relationships often begin with some kind of shared experience that goes beyond a cocktail and ear-splitting music.

Gay sports organizations offer that shared experience. Going through a season of touchdowns and interceptions, home runs and strikeouts, or blocked shots and steals, athletes, whether on the same team or not, can't help but feel closer to their teammates and opponents for the events they walked and ran through together.

These sports groups also offer the opportunity to meet people with a shared interest. Most gay bars are chock-full of gay men or lesbians with only one common interest: the same sex. Sports groups give their members another point of common interest: the sport itself.

Although a couple of cities in the United States seem to offer a gay league or team in just about any sport you can think of, there are many cities that do not. Even in Los Angeles and New York City, there are sports that presently no gay group in those cities offers. Though joining a mainstream sports league has its pluses, creating a gay sports league can be a transforming experience for not just the people who organize it but the city itself.

Cyd and Jim led the Los Angeles Motion to victories in Gay Super Bowls 1 and 2. The group has been in existence since the late '80s.

It can be a daunting task to start any organization, and the thought of starting a gay sports group can be overwhelming. When batting around the idea with gay friends, whether men or women, the reaction can also be discouraging. They may claim that there's no real interest

in such a group, or they could tell you that it's just too much work.

When Cyd moved to New York, he knew only a handful of people. Still, he longed for playing football with a group of gay guys and building a new set of friends through it. He knew of two people who had separately tried to organize a gay football league in the Big Apple but had both separately failed. They told him that it would be nearly impossible to build a gay football league in the city for a few reasons: (1) too many gay sports groups, from softball to hockey to rugby, had already taken a foothold in New York, and there just weren't enough people to go around; (2) New Yorkers were fickle, and the idea of a regular football league that took up too much of people's time flew in the face of the stereotypical noncommittal gay New Yorker; and (3) football just wasn't a gay sport and wouldn't be able to take hold in a culture dominated by Chelsea boys.

Just four months after Cyd found a group of men committed to the same thing, the New York Gay Football League held its first season in April 2005 with more than 70 players on six teams; by the autumn 2006 season, the league had 220 registered players. How did Cyd and the other founders of the league do it? The way anyone else could do the same thing in their city.

Vision

The most important thing to do is determine what your vision is for your new organization. Without a central vision, you will find it difficult to get people to buy into the project, and, further down the road, you'll have trouble setting priorities and making decisions. From a driving vision, you'll find growth will come faster and the group will be more satisfying for the organizers.

That vision should be a greater, loftier goal than simply presence or growth. It should aim to affect people's lives, change the way people look at themselves, or improve life in the city as a whole in at least one small way.

The vision should also be easily expressible in a couple of sentences, so people can take the vision to others. It doesn't have to be a couple of words, but should be easily repeated. It can and should be something that speaks to the core of what you want to accomplish at a deep level—something deeper than just "playing football."

The vision behind the New York Gay Football League is and has always been the following: "The NYGFL is a place where every person feels welcome, no matter what their sexuality, sex or playing ability. It should be a place where people can make friends, have fun, do their personal best and explore the wonderful world of competitive sports." This direction has proved incredibly important in attracting people to play, especially the many gay men who before joining the league would have never thought of themselves as "football players."

One thing to avoid in a group's stated vision is "changing stereo-

Jeff Kagan's Must-Dos When Starting a Gay Sports Group

Jeff Kagan knows a thing or two about starting a gay sports group: he has cofounded three successful gay sports organizations in New York City—the New York City Gay Hockey Association, the gay-sports umbrella group Out of Bounds, and more recently the New York City Gay Basketball League. He offers his five key steps to following in his footsteps:

1. Plan. Start by putting your ideas down on paper and planning them out. Assemble a small team of people who are interested in working with you on launching this project. Plan it out together.

   Find a home venue (courts, rinks, fields, and so on), approach the venue that is most centrally located (and easily accessed through public transportation), and work with it to meet your needs. Most cities have many public facilities that are available year-round.

   Speak with the leaders of established sports organizations in your area and get their advice. Find out what problems they faced when starting up, and learn what they did to get around them.

2. Promoting your organization comes next. Reach out to the community! Start with Outsports.com and the Internet; they will be your best source for outreach. Set up a web site and create an open line of communication for people to reach you anytime. Put ads on online bulletin boards, blogs, and hook-up sites (you'd be surprised how many people will read about your organization there!). The more visibility your organization has, the faster it will grow. Submit (free) listings to local gay magazines and newspapers. Create postcards and

types." Although this may be one of the outcomes of your organization, it will not serve the founders of the group or its members to make this part of the vision for the organization. It focuses too much on people who aren't members of the organization and puts undo focus on something you can't necessarily change: what other people think. It is likely that, if you're successful, you will in fact shift the way people view gays and lesbians; it may

drop stacks in local bars and at the community center. Think big: contact local press and suggest they do a story on your fledgling group!

3. Communicate. Now that you're out there, you'll start getting hits of interest. People will contact you telling you how happy they are that your league is starting up. Respond to them! Don't take too long. Each e-mail or phone call is a potential new member. Communicate! Keep them in the loop about upcoming events and meetings. Don't let them get away.

4. Meet. Pick a place. Your LGBT Community Center will provide relatively inexpensive meeting rooms. Another popular option is a meeting at a bar. Host a kick-off party! Arrange this with the bar management in advance, and have them help you promote your club in their mailing lists. Most bars have thousands of people on their lists. That's more exposure for your group.

You may also need team or league jerseys or T-shirts. Many bars will gladly sponsor your organization by buying these in return for your team's patronage of the bar after games.

5. Lead. Assemble a "board." Choose strong leaders. Lead by example. Be fair, open, and honest with your group. Set up a rule structure that works for the group and put out fires before they get too big.

If you follow these steps, you should have your group up and running within a few short months, and you'll provide an outlet for people to get in shape, make new friends, and have some fun.

Jeff Kagan got his start in gay sports in hockey, but his ventures into the building of other sports groups has made him one of the biggest names in New York City's gay sports scene.

Photo by Patrick Chin-Hong

be a wonderful by-product of your efforts. However, focusing on that in your vision or mission statement is a mistake.

Your vision will serve as the foundation of your new group. It could be the group's mission statement or part of it. It is meant to provide direction for the founders and the other people who will join in the endeavor, so make it good and make it true.

Coalition of the Willing

Possibly the biggest mistake anyone could make is to try to do it all themselves. If you're truly dedicated to starting a gay sports team or league, then chances are there are many other people who could become equally dedicated. There is a lot of work to be done and a great amount of responsibility in trying to forge something from nothing—whether it's in business or in someone's personal life. Get others to help; you'll find there are people just waiting for something to do and someone to give them direction.

This doesn't mean that you should just throw a group of people together and send them on their merry way. The beginning stages of the group will take several perspectives with one unified vision, but each of those people will also be looking for direction from the person who started the ball rolling.

You should also expect help from local gay businesses and publications. There are a lot of ways these businesses can help, and many of them are eager to do so. Some of the ways you can ask them to donate to the cause:

Cash sponsorship. Whether it's printing flyers, renting a place to play, or getting T-shirts for your players, it costs money to do what you're doing. Offering a business exposure in the form of its name on T-shirts, posters, and flyers, as well as promising to patronize the business, could seal the deal.

Exposure. Most every city and region has at least one gay publication. Contact them and ask for editorial coverage of what you're doing, or at least a free ad. Ask other local businesses to hang a flyer or have handouts for their patrons.

Hosting an event. Of particular interest to some bars and restaurants may be hosting a registration or fund-raising event at their establishment. It will bring in paying customers for them and will be an opportunity to meet new recruits or raise money.

Kind of Group: Team or League, Loose Pickup or Organized?

Probably the most critical decision to be made is what exactly you're building. You may want to decide this direction on your own, but you'd most likely be better served figuring out the direction once you've recruited a core group of several people to help spearhead the group. The advantage of deciding the direction on your own is that you can tell potential group leaders exactly what they're getting into. The advantage of waiting for

Details, details. Although these two items may seem like minor details, they are key components that every group must line up before diving too deeply:

Facilities. Where exactly are you going to practice and play? Some cities have an abundance of athletic facilities, whereas others can't meet the needs of their residents. Locking down where you'll be playing before you begin recruiting is key in not letting down potential members. Our helpful hint: send a box of Mrs. Fields cookies to whoever is in charge of allotting the field space in your city.

Officials. Who's going to officiate your matches? Will you have professional referees? Will players on the field officiate themselves in good faith? Our helpful hint: get players and volunteer refs to be your group's officials; it will help players learn the rules and will allow nonplayers to participate.

the input of others is that it's easier to get them to work hard in a direction that they helped set, rather than one that they were given. Either way, it's time to figure out what you're building. You've got a couple of questions to answer, and these questions will help guide all of your efforts, particularly in the group's infancy:

Are you looking to build a team or a league? You may live in a city where there is already a league for the sport you're looking to participate in. It's not advisable to try to build a second league of the same sport for several reasons. First, people will start to paint you as a divider. The gay community loves to turn on its own, and if you're perceived as a threat to the status quo, you'll catch heat for it. Second, it's simply going to be harder to find people who are willing to join an upstart league, as opposed to one that has been around for several years or, in some cases, decades.

The best reason to consider creating a "rival" league, though, is vision. So many gay sports groups have either lost their vision or never had one. Many are overrun with infighting and drama and have driven people away from their group. There are good reasons to start a second league in a city; make sure you're doing it for the right ones.

If your city has a strong league in the sport you want to play, then you may be looking to start a team to play in that league. Even in this case, your team will still be best served by following the steps laid out here.

If you live in a city without an organized group of your sport, then your decision is more difficult. There are successful models of individual teams and organized leagues in many sports all over the world. Gay rugby in the United States has taken off on the strength of individual teams in various cities building themselves up, practicing by themselves, and competing in national gay tournaments and local mainstream leagues. There are teams in cities as large as New York and Los Angeles and as small as Charlotte, North Carolina, and Portland, Oregon.

Gay softball began like gay rugby, with some teams scattered here and there across the country, and has blossomed into one of the largest gay sports in the country. The North American Gay Amateur Athletic Alliance is the governing body for most of the gay softball leagues in the country. It presently has member leagues in more than thirty cities. Each of those leagues comprises many teams that are divided into divisions based on skill level. It's a well-organized system that has allowed for the sport of gay softball to explode in the past thirty years.

Depending on your vision for the group, you can find incredible success creating either a team or a league; you just have to figure out which one fits you best.

How organized is the play? Whether you want to build a league or a team, you have to decide how organized you want the group's athletic play to be. Some groups consist of pickup games and practices, with teams changing every week. These groups don't have standings and don't have team "records," but they're a fun way to get together with other sport-oriented people to have a good time.

The Los Angeles Motion football group is a successful example of this. Every Saturday at noon, from Labor Day to Easter, a group of ten to twenty men (and the occasional woman) heads to Penmar Park in Venice for a fun game of pickup flag football. Each week people play different positions with different teammates. No records are kept. The games don't "mean" anything. Although the level of play can get very high, and individual games can get heated, it's a relaxed, social atmosphere with a lot of fun teasing and trash talking. And it's a great model for a group with loosely organized play.

The other format is the more traditional, more organized system of play. People organize into teams they play with over the course of a season. There are standings, records, and, generally, an eventual "champion." Your organization may be the umbrella league for many teams, or it might be just one team in this system.

Gay sports groups aren't always just about the sport. There is plenty of primping, posing and gold lame that can go along with it.

Photo by Cyd Zeigler Jr.

You can also build a group that does both of these things. It can have some pickup games and can organize into a structured league during part of the year.

The biggest benefit of the loose system of play is that there is little commitment involved. No one is on a set team, and they can come and go as they please. The biggest downfall of the loose system is the same thing: because there is no commitment, it can be hard to get people to come out to play, especially when the weather turns cold or there's a big game on TV. Depending in part on your schedule and what kind of commitment to playing you're looking to make, you can find success building either kind of group.

Two Parting Shots

Keep the drama at bay. It should be no surprise that gay sports groups are often riddled with drama and tension. This kind of energy cannot only undermine the enjoyment you and other players get out of the league but ultimately destroy everything you've worked hard to build. Everyone has a different reason for joining a group such as the one you're building. For most people, it's all positive. A select few, though, place incredible self-worth on entering organizations and disrupting them. Yes, there are "drama queens" in sports, too.

The key is to identify them immediately and deal with them effectively. This will most likely be the toughest action you have to take. People who cause trouble are also the same ones who create cliques. If you deal with this person by removing them from the group or punishing them in some way, you will incur the wrath of that clique they've surrounded themselves with. As long as you have a thick skin and always do what you believe is for the best of the group, you will be fine. If you let this person push his or her agenda behind the strength of a clique of a few loud voices, you face being pushed out of your own organization and seeing the group fall into undeserving hands.

How do you identify this person? There are a few telltale signs. Lying is possibly the most common. People who create drama love to lie and stretch the truth. When you catch someone doing this, get the truth cleared up and make a strong mental note so you can identify a pattern. Another sign is the creation of a clique. There is a big difference between a circle of friends and a clique. The former focuses on inclusion; the latter focuses on exclusion. When you start to see a clique forming around one of your core leaders, chances are they're at work to grab power and change direction. If you let that person continue to be a leader of the group, you will be at odds with them until you or they step down—and odds are they're going to stick around until you're long gone.

Set manageable goals. When Cyd started the New York Gay Football League, there were two lines of thinking. The first was that it would never get off the ground. New York gay social life just didn't revolve around sports, and certainly not football, the thought process went. The other line of thinking was that, with so many gay people living in Manhattan alone, the league would be turning people away. Hundreds of New Yorkers would flock to this new idea called "gay football." Or so the thinking was.

The core leadership of the league decided very early on that the main goal of the league's first season would be to ensure that everyone had a good time. With that ultimate goal in mind, they decided to focus on recruiting about fifty people to fit onto four teams, while being open to up to eighty people on six teams. The demand was very high, and they did turn away a lot of people in the first season. But they reached their maximum and then focused on making sure those eighty people had a good time.

Part of the manageable goals is forcing managed growth. One of the worst things a gay sports organization can do is get too big too fast. Although there's the constant desire to welcome everyone who wants to be a part of the group, your organization will flourish if you focus on keeping the membership at a level that ensures annual growth and keeps the size of the group well within manageable limits.

"I'M DATING A GUY WHO'S INTO SPORTS . . . HELP!"

There are a lot of issues that can be a bump in the road of a happy relationship. Some couples struggle with who does the laundry. Others have to navigate the choppy waters of unaccepting families. Somewhere between taking out the trash and all-out cheating is a touchy subject that hits the nerves of many gay men and lesbians and has been the cause of who knows how many breakups: sports.

To be sure, sports can be a wedge issue in any relationship, whether the people are straight or gay. Countless sitcoms have played off the dynamic that is often created between the sports-loving husband and the shopping-obsessed wife that straight relationships so often deal with. The story works on TV sitcoms because it's a situation that so many straight couples understand, have gotten into huge fights over, and inevitably can look back at and laugh.

For some reason, many gay couples take the issue very seriously. The battle over whether to watch *Desperate Housewives* or the Bills-Ravens Sunday night game can be as good in a gay household as any WWE match. Part of this comes from the raised expectations of coming out and the two incredibly different perspectives on sports that can come to a head in a relationship.

In one corner is the sports jock. He's played or watched sports all his life, and the revelation that he's gay suddenly means, for him, the joy of having sex while watching a Dolphins game. As he's coming out, the realization that the perfect world—one where sports and sex coexist peacefully—is upon him inspires the same feeling as running back an interception for a touchdown. Inevitably, though, he is met with a gay world seemingly full of Broadway Nancys and circuit queens who have far more interest in Fosse and Junior Vasquez than the slugging percentage of Barry Bonds.

In the other corner is the antijock. He's lived all his life far more interested in painting and pretty dresses than in any sport played with a ball not physically attached to someone. When he comes out, he expects to fall deeply in love with someone who will spend every Monday night watching a Judy Garland marathon on American Movie Classics. Thank heavens gay people don't like sports, he says. Cut to two years later, and he's dating a hot stud who is more interested in the men in tight pants on the gridiron than the men in tight pants on stage.

One of the big mistakes that these couples make is they turn the sports issue into a cause célèbre. Each draws a line in the sand, and there they stand their ground, not budging. What many straight couples have come to accept is that this simply isn't a big issue. If she wants to go shopping on a Saturday afternoon while he watches March Madness, then so be it. Gay couples all too often transfer their problems in the relationship to this one issue, and it becomes the hot-button issue for the couple.

A little understanding for the other side goes a long way. To better understand the other person, you've got to dig into where they're coming from and what history they have with sports. Doing the little things you can will make a big difference.

The biggest difference between straight relationships and gay relationships is that (duh!) gays are attracted to what's like them, whereas straight people are attracted to the opposite sex. That same dynamic sometimes gets transferred over to other areas of the relationship, including hobbies and interests. Whereas straight couples seem generally fine with the wife having her nails done and going shopping while the husband plays poker and watches basketball, so many gay couples are stuck trying to do everything they do together. If one's a circuit boy, the other must be a circuit boy. If one watches hockey, the other must watch hockey. This kind of thing can be good and bad. The good: maybe someone's eyes will be opened to something they truly take to. The bad: someone starts resenting the fact that they have to sit through a St. Louis Cardinals game for three hours.

Just as straight couples do, gay couples should open themselves up to embracing their differences of interest instead of trying to dissolve them.

Whether you're teammates or a "mixed" couple, there's nothing more inspirational than a lock of lips before a big softball game.

Photo by Brent Mullins

"I'm Dating Someone Who Loves Sports. Help!"

There are a couple things to keep in perspective here. First, just because he loves sports doesn't mean he doesn't love you. Just because your boyfriend wants to go to a baseball game instead of spending the evening with you, or just because your girlfriend would rather head to the bowling lanes with her friends instead of being curled up on the couch watching Logo, doesn't mean he or she doesn't love you with all their heart.

Sports can be an incredible outlet for the expression of passion and excitement. To the sports fan, it is intoxicating. But just because he's jumping up and down on the sidelines of a game or yelling at the television when his team takes the field doesn't mean he won't have energy left over for you when the lights go out. Plus, consider the possibility that all of that excitement actually fills him with more energy and more excitement for you!

If she's a big sports fan or athlete, it's likely that it started when she was a child. It's who she is, part of her identity, and what makes her so special to you. To take that away or try to limit it in some way might sound enticing to you, but in the long run that will do a couple of things: (1) taking away or limiting part of her identity will affect her happiness because she's now not able to use sports to fully express herself; and (2) she will start to resent you for trying to take away something that has meaning to her. You like or love her for who she is, and sports are a (potentially big) part of that. Different interests can make a relationship richer, so relish them.

You should ask yourself why you dislike sports so much. Remember, he's not your dad who pressured you to play baseball when you were a kid;

he's not the quarterback who teased you endlessly in gym class. He's the guy you've fallen for, for whatever reason. Don't screw it up because you don't like one of his hobbies; just use the time to do something you like that he's not particularly interested in. That way, everyone wins.

"I'm Dating Someone Who Can't Stand Sports. Help!"

Often, it's the person who loves sports who ends up looking like the "bad guy." It may be because he "spends too much time playing sports" and not enough time (in the other person's eyes) paying attention to his significant other. It may be because much of the gay community shuns sports and the other person is so used to vilifying sports that it carries over here.

Whatever the reason, it's most important for any sports fan dating a non–sports fan to communicate and understand where the other person is coming from. There may be some real sensitivity your partner has to sports. Whether it was being teased or failing at his athletic endeavors, sports can be pretty traumatic for some people when they're young. Talk

You don't have to be wearing the same jersey to find friendship or romance at a gay sports event, as these two Bingham Cup players found out.

Photo by Cyd Zeigler Jr.

to him about it. Ask him about it. Try to figure out with him where his hostility toward your interest in sports is coming from. Chances are it has a lot more to do with his personal past in sports than with your present interest in it.

You also have to make sure she knows you care for her. If you're an NFL fan, it can be hard for someone you're living with to watch you sit in front of the television for twelve hours on Sunday without some decent interaction. Take time out at halftime to give her a hug and a kiss. Tell her the TV's all hers before the games start. Plan some loving sex for after the game. It's possible she simply wants more of your attention and couldn't care less if you were watching football or a *Three Stooges* marathon. As long as you give her some affection, that just might be enough to keep her from throwing her high heels at the television (or you).

A potentially disastrous mistake: pushing your partner too hard to enjoy sports with you. Both Cyd and Jim have been in long-term relationships with men who have little or no interest in sports. Although it's always nice when they want to share your excitement for your favorite team or play catch with you, the worst thing you can do is try to force them to like it. Let them know the door is open: invite them to participate, and share an occasional quip about your sports experience with them. Just don't push too hard; otherwise, you just might lose them.

THE GAY GAMES, OUTGAMES, AND BEYOND

THE GAY GAMES: PAST, PRESENT AND FUTURE

In 1982, San Francisco played host to the first Gay Games. It was a cozy affair, with eleven sports and more than thirteen hundred athletes. The Games drew little attention outside of San Francisco and were considered by many to be a novelty. In the rest of the gay sports world, softball and bowling were about it when it came to playing a team sport (and the latter was just barely one itself).

Fast-forward to 2006. Two international gay sports events were held in Chicago and Montreal, hosting about eighteen thousand athletes in more than thirty sports. The gay sports calendar has exploded with hundreds of events each year in dozens of sports. Softball and bowling are still mainstays, but they're now sharing space with the likes of flag football, snowboarding, and even curling.

The explosion reflects the growing visibility of gays and lesbians in Western society. More people are out, which has fueled demand for leagues and groups that cater to gays (and, increasingly, nonhomophobic straights). Although professional sports may be the last closet for gays, on the recreational level it's a case of, to take a line from one of Outsports's top movies for gay people, "Build it and they will come."

The growth of the Gay Games reflects the surge of interest in sports among gays and lesbians. Founded in 1982 by Dr. Tom Waddell, an Olympic decathlete himself, as a "vehicle for change," the Games rested on a foundation of inclusion and participation. Medals were awarded, but playing the game was what mattered the most.

Waddell had named his competition the "Gay Olympic Games," but the U.S. Olympic Committee successfully sued, forcing Waddell to (on some posters and print material literally) scratch out the word *Olympic* and use *Gay Games* instead. The 1986 Games in San Francisco drew thirty-five hundred people from seventeen countries in seventeen sports. Waddell died of AIDS in 1987, a year after the second Games were held, but his legacy was secure.

The Gay Games Explode

The next decade saw the Games take off. The 1990 event, in Vancouver, hosted seventy-three hundred athletes in twenty-seven sports from thirty-nine countries. The move from San Francisco marked the growing international appeal of the Games. The Canadian city was awash in rainbow flags, and same-sex couples had little compunction about displaying their affection in public. The organizers used the site of the 1986 World Expo for a Gay Games Village, which became the place to go each night. One highlight was the speech by openly gay member of the Canadian Parliament Sven Robinson during the opening ceremonies, a foreshadowing of what would be increased visibility of gays in political life in the 1990s.

Holding the Gay Games in New York in June 1994 seemed a perfect fit. They were occurring near the twenty-fifth anniversary of the Stonewall riots that had ushered in the modern gay movement, and the closing ceremonies were held the day before a giant rally commemorating that event. Hundreds of thousands of gays and lesbians came to New York for the Games and the gay pride march coinciding with the Games.

New York in 1994 was the first Gay Games that attracted widespread media coverage. Two years earlier, Bill Clinton had been elected president

Tom Waddell

The Gay Games are not separatist, they are not exclusive, they are not oriented to victory, and they are not for commercial gain. They are, however, intended to bring a global community together in friendship, to experience participation, to elevate consciousness and self-esteem, and to achieve a form of cultural and intellectual synergy. . . . We are involved in the process of altering opinions whose foundations lie in ignorance. We have the opportunity to take the initiative on critical issues that affect the quality of life and we can serve in a way that makes all people the beneficiary.

and courted gays and lesbians more than any presidential candidate in history. Anna Quindlen, writing in the *New York Times* on June 25, 1994, answered those who wondered why the Gay Games were needed: "[There is] the question of why there's a need for Gay Games in the first place,

These Chicago flag football players won bronze in the women's division.

Photo by Jim Buzinski

which has been asked more than once as events unfolded. It reminds me of the question kids always ask about Mother's Day and Father's Day and why there is no kid's day. Of course, we all know the answer is that every day is kid's day. Every big athletic competition has been essentially the Straight Games. Allegedly the Olympics are open to everyone, and there have been plenty of gay athletes who have competed. But they understood that if they were to get the publicity and the endorsements—and in some countries, stay on the team—it was best to pretend."

The Games in New York attracted eleven thousand athletes, at the time more than competed in any Summer Olympics. Speakers at the opening and closing ceremonies included David Kopay and Martina Navratilova, and Olympic gold medal diver Greg Louganis came out. Noted sports journalist and Waddell biographer Dick Schaap, who was straight, played doubles tennis with James Hormel, a gay man who would later be named ambassador to Luxembourg by President Clinton. "Dick tells a funny story in [the book] 'Gay Olympian' about playing doubles tennis at New York's Gay Games," Susan Kennedy, copresident of the Federation of Gay Games (FGG) in 1994, recalled in a 2001 tribute to Schaap. "He could hit a forehand shot with either hand, and in one game when he had the occasion to suddenly hit left-handed his opponent stopped after the point and called out, 'Are you bi-?' Dick said, 'I thought you'd never ask.'"

Jim's flag-football team won the gold medal in New York, and he was on cloud nine the rest of the week, wearing his gold medal around his neck everywhere except the shower. He remembers being stopped by construction workers and high-fiving them when he told them what the medal stood for. Other medal-winning athletes reported similar experiences: New York seemed like one giant gay lovefest that week.

But there was a disturbing side to all the visibility, one that would rear its ugly head again in 2004 with advancements in gay-marriage rights. "Remembered by most gay and lesbian New Yorkers for the Gay Games and the 25th anniversary of the Stonewall uprising, June 1994 now turns out to have a darker distinction. More antigay attacks were reported in New York City that month than in any other in the 14 years such records have been kept," the *New York Times* reported in March 1995.

The backlash to the Games in some quarters did not stop their growth. In 1998, the Games moved out of North America for the first time, with the winning bid coming from Amsterdam. There were more than thirteen thousand registrants, which included almost twelve thousand athletes and some eleven hundred who participated in the cultural festival. The city, well known for its tolerance and relaxed attitudes, was packed during the nine days of the Games, which were kicked off by the annual floating pride parade down the canals. It was hard not to have a good time.

The Games' Financial Woes

Unknown to most participants, the Amsterdam Games were almost canceled before they began. In early August, the Games' board of directors announced the event had cost overruns of $1 million and fired the executive director. "We won't deny that the financial situation has been very serious," board president Len Rempt told the *Advocate*. The City of Amsterdam stepped in and agreed to pony up $2.5 million to cover debts and avert a canceled event.

Amsterdam's financial woes pointed up a contradiction in the events, which were wildly successful in terms of bringing gay and lesbian athletes together but duds when it came to turning a profit or even breaking even. Weeks after the 1990 Vancouver Games, organizers sent athletes letters requesting money to help pay off debts. The situation following the New York Games was even worse. "Two months after the Games ended in 1994, Karen Merbaum, co-president of the Gay Games IV board, acknowledged that the group had $1 million in outstanding debts, which would be partially offset by income yet to be collected. The board tried to defray some of the debt by fundraising and selling commemorative videos," the *Advocate* reported.

The Games Go Down Under

The story was the same in 2002, when the Games were held in Sydney, Australia. Headlines on Outsports leading up to the event told the tale: "Late Cash-Flow Problem Getting Serious," "Gay Games CEO Resigns," and "Sydney Relying on Dance Parties for Success."

Comments from then executive director of the Federation of Gay Games Bill Wassmer in 2001 suggested that the Games might be moved from Sydney; the resulting controversy saw Wassmer lose his position. Wassmer's concerns about the financial condition of the Games proved prophetic when Sydney's executive director quit ninety-two days before the start of the event.

Sydney was another financial fiasco. In "the aftermath of Sydney, taxpayers could be forced to foot much of the $2.5 million in unpaid bills of the Sydney Gay Games, after the company organizing the games went into voluntary administration," the *Sydney Morning Herald* reported in December 2002, a month after the event. "Lackluster ticket sales to

Aloha from part of the Hawaiian contingent at the 2006 Gay Games.

Photo by Cyd Zeigler Jr.

sporting events, the opening ceremony and the fundraising parties, and the effect of the September 11 attacks on sponsorship and international visitors, were last night blamed for the problems. . . . The company owes money to about 150 creditors, which include the international Gay Games organization, Qantas, state and federal governments, venue operators and many smaller creditors."

The financial struggle in putting together an event with thousands of athletes and dozens of venues can be traced to the lack of an infrastructure in the gay sports movement. The Federation of Gay Games, which awards the event to a new city every four years, is a volunteer organization that has not had a paid executive director for most of its history. Each city, therefore, has to scramble to find sponsors and spend a lot of its time raising money.

This is a situation similar to the Olympics, where cities such as Montreal in 1976 and Athens in 2004 took on great debt to hold the event. The financial cushion with the Olympics, though, is greatly lessened by money earned from broadcast rights (NBC is paying the International Olympic Committee more than $2.2 billion to broadcast the 2010 and 2012 Games). No major network has ever paid to broadcast the Gay Games.

To the athletes in Sydney, though, the financial woes were not noticeable. The Games have become almost too big to fail, relying on the tremendous goodwill and patience of the community of gay and lesbian athletes. It's a group that will forgive a lot as long as a good show is put on. Events came off, with some minor exceptions, on schedule, and the volunteers were uniformly helpful and courteous. For most athletes and visitors, it was a week of bliss, beginning with the opening ceremonies.

The biggest sustained applause among the thirteen thousand athletes waiting to stride into Sydney's Aussie Stadium for the opening ceremonies came when it was announced that India and Pakistan would be marching in together. The small contingent from the two South Asian lands, where blood flows easily from decades of hatred, did what neighbors are supposed to do: they embraced and walked together. If only gays ruled the world.

It was hard not to have a grand time Down Under. The Australians are an utterly charming bunch who went way out to their way to help. "No worries, mate" seems to be the national motto. Sydney itself is very cosmopolitan and lent itself well to such a big event. The city's inner core is quite walkable, and the public transportation is terrific. Add sunny, warm weather, and you had an ideal setting for the Games.

However, most people in Sydney seemed not to know the Games were going on, and this is the major fault of the organizers. Many people

Outsports spoke with either didn't know the Games were under way or had only a dim knowledge of them. One problem was the lack of signs, especially when compared with New York in 1994 and Amsterdam in 1998. There were a handful of large Gay Games banners in the city, but they were all concentrated in one area near Hyde Park, a small part of the sprawling city.

The lack of public awareness of the Games was most noticeable at Olympic Park, site of several major competitions, including tennis, aquatics, volleyball, and track. One would have expected the complex to be festooned with colorful banners and filled with booths selling merchandise and food—kind of a mini Olympic Village. But there was nothing to unify the venues, and it resulted in a dead atmosphere.

The success of each sport was very dependent on the organizing group, and this made for uneven competitions, though almost all went well. The wrestlers and swimmers, for example, raved about their meets, from the choice of venue to the officials. Basketball players were almost uniformly positive about their tournament. Ice hockey players, though, compared the surface they played on to "frozen oatmeal."

This Outgames beach volleyball player leaves little to the imagination.
Photo by Cyd Zeigler Jr.

The lack of media coverage was another notable absence. Of the mainstream press, only Anthony Dennis in the *Sydney Morning Herald* provided daily coverage; the rest seemed not to care. Part of the problem was that the organizers were not very helpful to the media, and reporters simply gave up trying to deal with them. Part also seemed to be that the press still has no clue how to cover the Games: are they competition, or are they entertainment? Part, though, no doubt came from the provincial attitude that their readers didn't want daily doses of pooftahs on parade.

A Rift Develops

Money dominated the selection for the 2006 Games host city. In 2001, Montreal won the right to host Gay Games VII, but a contract was never signed. After the two sides could not agree on a contract, negotiations broke off and the Federation of Gay Games in 2004 awarded the Games to Chicago. Montreal formed a rival organization and announced the first Outgames. The Gay Games were held in mid-July 2006, while the Outgames were two weeks later.

Both events came off with few hitches and were well received, with thousands of athletes competing in more than thirty sports. The aftermath was less successful. Chicago ended 2006 trying to close a $200,000 deficit, but the news was worse in Montreal where the organizing committee declared bankruptcy, leaving $5 million in debts, including $2.2 million to dozens of suppliers.

Although which event was "better" is a totally subjective measurement that can be made only by people who attended both, the consensus was that Montreal had more of a big-event atmosphere, with a lot more signage and an Olympic-style village. In contrast, Chicago was flat in terms of atmosphere, mainly due to the lack of foreign athletes, and seemed too much the American Games.

On the other hand, the athletic competition appeared stronger in Chicago for most sports, owing to the large number of Americans in the top sports. For example, a gay water polo tournament without West Hollywood (as was the case in Montreal) is like a golf tournament without Tiger Woods. Even the winners of the gold medal in men's basketball in Montreal considered that tournament, which included no U.S. teams, a joke. In soccer, the internationally designated championships were in Chicago, with only one elite team going to Montreal. Sadly, the best soccer teams from Germany declared a pox on both and did not attend, so it's not clear a true champion was crowned in either city. And swimming isn't quite the

Cyd Zeigler on the Quadrennial Games Rift

Although it was a great accomplishment for the Chicago organizers to pull off the event they did, the real winner in 2006 was the Outgames. I attended both events, and it was like night and day. The Outgames were fun, energetic, and had a real presence in the city; the Gay Games seemed to reflect the odd tone set by an off-putting, two-hours-too-long opening ceremony.

Although the Gay Games certainly have a leg up in brand awareness, I have spoken to several athletes who say they regretted the choice of Chicago over Montreal. That kind of regret sticks with people. I think the Outgames coming a year before the Gay Games will end up helping them drastically, as people decide they don't want to miss the fun of Copenhagen.

But most important, I have little faith in the Federation of Gay Games' ability to put politics and pettiness aside and get the job done. The sport they are best at is politics, and that will continue to drive good people away from the Gay Games, the same way it drove eventual Outgames organizers away.

To be sure, Montreal's financial woes are a black eye for the Outgames. But these financial problems are the worries of a tiny minority of people. The average basketball player in Atlanta doesn't care about an event losing money; they just want to have a good time. And if the Outgames can show they're a better time, as they were in 2006, then they will be around for a long, long time.

For me, I won't miss the Outgames in 2009; as for the Gay Games, it'll be a wait-and-see.

same without the large influx of elite U.S. swimmers. Of all the key sports, only rowing appeared to be of a clearly higher caliber in Montreal.

Chicago Saves the Gay Games

It's not a stretch to say Chicago saved the Gay Games, the way Los Angeles saved the Olympics in 1984. The 1976 Olympics nearly bankrupted Montreal, and the 1980 Moscow Games were overshadowed by the U.S.

boycott. It took Los Angeles, judged a financial and athletic success, to get the Olympics back on track when many people were questioning their viability.

When Montreal and the Federation of Gay Games could not sign a contract in 2003, the future of the Gay Games was very much in doubt. Organizers, though, were able to put together a financial plan that worked. "Chicago raised more in sponsorships than any previous Gay Games," Gay Games co–vice chair Kevin Boyer said. "Our total cash raised in sponsorships was around $3.5 million. Our overall budget was $9.5 million in cash with another $10 million value in kind donated in services and products." Boyer noted that corporate sponsorships made up 35 percent of the total cash revenue.

That's an impressive achievement that should serve as a model for future gay sporting events. Getting corporate sponsors is vital to their success, especially if little or no government money if forthcoming. However, a big part of Chicago's success with sponsors was the fact that these were the first Gay Games on American soil in twelve years. It is unclear whether U.S.-based companies will be as generous with the 2010 being held in Europe. Despite all Chicago's fund-raising success, the event was still $200,000 in the red as 2006 ended.

From a sports standpoint, Chicago was mostly a hit ("It was arguably one of the best run international soccer competitions in which I have competed," one player said), but the misses were glaring. There was no Gatorade or water at the mountain biking events and no air-conditioning at the basketball venue despite a severe heat alert. Mix-ups in seedings and schedules affected softball and volleyball. The worst, though, by all accounts was track and field. In Sydney in 2002, everyone raved about the track and field. "If your heat was going off at 2:17, it went off at 2:17," one athlete told Outsports in admiration. They were also raving in Chicago, but in the "stark-raving mad" sense. Lars Rains, a New York City cop and veteran track athlete, said it was easily the worst-run track meet he had ever been to. One Swedish track athlete was so disgusted he wrote Outsports an e-mail saying he regretted choosing Chicago over Montreal.

The organizers and volunteers of Chicago deserve a round of applause for rescuing an event that could have descended into oblivion. Asked what advice he would give Cologne, the Gay Games host in 2010, Boyer said, "Think big, but plan conservatively to ensure that dreams do not exceed the ability to perform. Don't be afraid to trim nonessential elements in order to ensure the success of the core program. The Gay Games are ten times larger and more complicated to produce than most people realize.

Former UCLA sprinter Brian Fell (left) brought some star power to Gay Games track & field in 2002 and 2006.

Photo by Cyd Zeigler Jr.

Resist the temptation to agree to many seemingly reasonable but extra demands until you are confident that you can successfully deliver the core experience that people will expect."

The Outgames Take Off in Montreal

From the moment people arrived in Montreal in late July 2006, they were aware the Outgames were happening. Signage was everywhere, and the Athletes Village drew raves. The organizers had been very cooperative with Outsports the two years leading up to the Outgames. They communicated with Outsports constantly, offering updates and buying advertising on the web site. In addition, they were endlessly positive, promising an event like none gay athletes had ever seen (and they delivered).

If there was a major criticism to be made before the Outgames, it was this: people in Montreal seemed invested in the idea that their event was going to be bigger than the Gay Games, and hence by implication better. Extravagant boasts almost always wound up being scaled back. It led to highly inflated projections of how many registrants they were going to have. Before the split, they were hoping for 24,000. Organizers settled on 16,000, though the final total was 12,083 (which included 10,248 athletes and 835 cultural participants), according to the Outgames. They also claimed 500,000 spectators attended events. Based on every media report ("Organizers Claim Success Despite Poor Attendance" was one headline), this was not possible, unless most spectators came disguised as empty seats. Tourism Montreal was a big driver of the Outgames, and no one can spin like a tourism rep. But even gay people need to realize that size does not always matter.

I have heard a few athletes say they support "the Outgames vision," but I haven't seen where it's any different from the Gay Games vision first espoused by Dr. Tom Waddell a quarter century ago. It seems more like a group of well-meaning people who want to reinvent the wheel, thinking they know better. Putting on one successful event hardly a movement makes.

Knowing American vacation habits, it's hard to see that many people being able to afford or desiring two European trips in a twelve-month period when the Outgames are in 2009 and the Gay Games are in 2010 (though Copenhagen and Cologne are both fabulous cities). This is especially true of teams, which have a hard time organizing within the United States, let alone trying to pull off two overseas trips in a short time. As long as the governing bodies of swimming, soccer, and others recognize the Gay Games, this will be the event Americans will choose if they can pick only one.

From my own personal athletic standpoint, playing in the Gay Games' flag-football event was the best tournament I've been associated with. All the players and teams were highly competitive on the field and incredibly friendly off, and we had plenty of liquids and medical staff. I played with the "Dream Team" in terms of attitude, ability, and lack of drama, and winning the gold was icing on the cake. For this reason, Chicago will always have a warm spot in my heart.

Spin or no spin, the event itself was a success for those who attended. The sports events in Montreal were very well organized, there was a festive atmosphere throughout the city, the Athletes Village at Square Viger was special, and the opening ceremonies were the perfect start to an incredible week. Outgames athletes told Outsports in the final days of Montreal that the Outgames were "top-notch," "completely organized," and "extremely well run": "the officials were terrific," "the venues were great," and "the volunteer base was phenomenal."

The Future

The fallout from Montreal's bankruptcy will be hard to predict. The next Outgames are scheduled to be in Copenhagen in 2009, a year ahead of the Gay Games in Cologne, not a week later like in 2006. As of early 2007, it was hard to tell what spillover effect Montreal's money woes would have on plans for Copenhagen. But there is no sign that the split in the quadrennial games has been healed or that there is any interest in doing so. The Federation of Gay Games seems determined to go its own way, and the Gay and Lesbian International Sport Association (GLISA), the competing body set up by the Outgames, is doing its thing.

The Gay Games have an edge in brand awareness. They have been around, every four years, since 1982 and have built a loyal following. Neither deficits nor bankruptcies have deterred gays and lesbians from going to the next Games. People have heard of the Games (even if they call them the Gay Olympics), whereas "Outgames" elicits a puzzled look and an explanation; almost no one has a clue what GLISA is.

In the race for media coverage, there was no contest in 2006: in the United States, the Gay Games got much more than the Outgames. A search of Google News and of the Dow-Jones Factiva database turned up more than twice as many stories and mentions of the Gay Games as the Outgames. The events in Montreal were covered well in local media, but totally ignored in the United States. Even many gay publications and news outlets (Outsports being an exception) gave more coverage to Chicago than Montreal. Traffic on Outsports was also higher for the Gay Games than the Outgames, reflecting a more intense awareness and interest from an audience that is mostly American. Of course, this was largely because the Gay Games were in the United States and the Outgames were not. If the venues were flip-flopped, chances are the amount of American media coverage would have been, too.

This brand awareness for the Gay Games could give a leg up to Cologne, and the fact that the next Gay Games are in Europe will make the event geographically diverse once again. It is hoped that the Cologne organizers will seek out their Chicago counterparts for advice and will not repeat the same financial mistakes made in Amsterdam and Sydney. Also, the Cologne advisers should take a hard look at what sports did not work well in Chicago and focus on making those better. But learning from past errors has never been a strong suit of most Gay Games organizing committees.

The Outgames' biggest hurdle, in addition to the cloud of bankruptcy, will be convincing people how they are different from the Gay Games, and to overcome the bad publicity from the five-million dollar deficit. The events in Montreal, though perhaps better organized and with a better atmosphere, in essence copied the Gay Games: an opening and a closing ceremony, medals, inclusion, and an emphasis on participation. They even copied the International Gay and Lesbian Aquatics' wildly popular Pink Flamingo swimming event and called theirs "Outsplash."

GLISA promises to host "continental games" in Calgary in 2007 and Australia in 2008, sort of mini Outgames of eight to ten sports. That sounds nice, but even if these events come off, they will simply draw Canadians in 2007 and Australians in 2008. With every major gay sport having national and international events yearly, is there really a need for another organization putting on its own event? This will likely lead to "major event" fatigue, and the continental games, at least in North America, will likely not have a long shelf life. As one Australian athlete wrote on Outsports:

> I think the idea of GLISA growing by having games everywhere, every year, will only water down the true blues who support these events. Whilst good in theory, with Eurogames 2009 deleted due to Copenhagen and probably 2010 deleted due to Cologne, this can only be to the detriment of the Eurogames. And as for the Asia Pacific games, well in Oz we can barely get two states together for a national Aussie games, so not sure how it will work trying to encompass our large and underpopulated area. . . . Not all of us (especially women) have the time or money to attend all these games and besides some of

us attend major events in the straight sports world. We need to become one again not this continual watering down."

In an ideal world, the FGG and GLISA would declare a truce and try to coexist, playing on each other's strengths and visions and making the gay sports movement truly universal. In a time when Pat Robertson now believes in global warming, anything is possible. But given the extreme animosity between the two sides, no one should hold his proverbial breath. The ideal vision was stated in Montreal by Markus Bremen, a German athlete who lamented the lack of Americans at the Outgames. He told the *Montreal Gazette:* "I hope the two Games will get together eventually. It would be better to focus our energy and to have the whole world share the same stage."

THE GAY SPORTS CIRCUIT

It was the spring of 2000, and it had been six years since there was an intercity gay football game. Not since the New York Gay Games in 1994 had gay flag-football teams from two different cities squared off against one another. But when the San Francisco 69ers visited the Los Angeles Motion in April 1999, it was the rebirth of gay flag football in the United States. Three years later, Boston joined the mix, and the first Gay Super Bowl was held as a three-team tournament hosted in Los Angeles. And that began what has been a growing addition to the gay sports "circuit."

Gay men and lesbians have looked to Outsports since its inception for information and insight to both create and develop their organizations and events, and those events have expanded in the first few years of this century like no one could have envisioned just ten years ago. There is now, for all intents and purposes, a gay sports circuit that offers an alternative to the party circuit so many gay men have fallen into. A large segment of gay culture revolves around "circuit parties." These parties are largely driven by techno music, rampant sex, and drug use. Although many clubs aim to create a weekly circuitlike atmosphere, the true gay party circuit is a series of one-night or one-weekend events that can attract more than twenty-five thousand gay men. Some of the biggest include the Black and Blue Party in Montreal, the White Party in Palm Springs, and the Black Party in New York City. Not all circuit parties are named after a color, though the exorbitant cost of these parties, from the travel to the entrance fee to the cost of drugs, not to mention the antibiotics many have to take after the parties, can leave some of the participants in the red.

Sports and Circuit Parties Are Similar—Kinda

Although gay sporting events have quite a different focus than the often-illicit activities that dominate circuit parties, the two are similar in many ways. The biggest draw for both is the opportunity to meet new people. Sports have become in most cities in North America, Europe, Australia, and other parts of the world a viable and increasingly popular way to meet people away from the bar and party scenes, of which the circuit parties are the ultimate event.

Whereas someone may meet a couple of dozen, or at most a couple of hundred, other sports-minded gay people at an event for a local gay league, gay sports tournaments offer the opportunity to meet many hundreds, if not thousands, of gay athletes. Certainly, most every athlete goes to these events hoping to compete strongly and see his or her team do well. But given that no one is going to earn any six-figure signing bonuses for his or her performance at a tournament, meeting new friends—and sometimes lovers—is a much longer-lasting, more rewarding outcome, and many gay athletes approach these tournaments hoping to make friends first and take home the gold second.

That isn't to say that the level of competition isn't very high. As more and more athletes come out of the closet, more elite athletes are doing the same and finding their way to some of these events. Swimming events attract Olympic gold medalists, football tournaments bring out former collegiate and professional football players, and former NCAA track stars are now taking their positions in the blocks and racing in gay track events. World records have even been broken at gay swimming events, including a world masters record set by Dan Veatch at the Outgames in Montreal in August 2006.

The social benefits of these tournaments are overwhelming and likely longer lasting than the glory of victory. When Cyd and Jim started the Gay Super Bowl (along with a couple of key people in San Francisco and Boston), it was an opportunity to play football with new people. For years, they had been playing football every week with the Los Angeles Motion football team. Great friendships grew out of those pickup games. But they also recognized the opportunity to meet new people and make new friends through the struggles they experienced together on the field. Plus, playing other cities would bring a change of pace from lining up across from the same people week after week.

Five years after that first multicity tournament, the gay flag-football community has grown to include more than one thousand players in more than a dozen cities. Beyond just the tournaments that are held, when those players now travel to Boston, Washington D.C., San Francisco, San Diego, and many other cities, they have some new friends to call upon to toss the football around.

Maybe not surprising to some, many circuit partygoers talk about their drug-induced experiences at those parties as being life altering. Many of the "circuit boys" feel somehow addicted to the parties, much the way athletes feel addicted to sports. Part of this life-altering experience, to be sure, is because of the presence of so many other men doing what they love: taking drugs, dancing, and having sex. The web site for the documentary about circuit parties, *When Boys Fly*, which features Brandon Del Campo, an openly gay former runner at UCLA, describes the experience of these parties in these simple terms: "There is an intense sense of camaraderie that, tied together with great music, great drugs and great sex, creates a dizzying world of beautiful men living for festivity."

One of the greatest similarities between gay sports events and circuit parties are the bodies. These two Gay Games athletes could fit in at either.

Photo by Cyd Zeigler Jr.

The Drug-Free Elation of Sporting Events

One friend of Outsports, who goes to circuit parties on a regular basis and attends circuitesque parties in Manhattan on a weekly basis, has said the energy and experiences of the men at these parties are changing the shape of New York City. He believes that attendance at these parties answers some higher calling.

Although it's much less drug induced, the feeling that they've experienced something that has changed their lives is at least as prevalent among those who attend national gay sporting events. Part of it comes from the camaraderie that is inherent in sports and needs no drugs to help along. It also comes from the longtime oppression of gay people in the sports world and athletes in the gay community. Many of the athletes have played in countless mainstream tournaments, at the high school, collegiate, or amateur level. They have gone as closeted men and women, or, if they weren't closeted, they found few other gay people with whom to connect. The revelation that these great sporting events can be an extension of their sexuality can be truly life changing.

Maybe the most profound explanation comes from the simple human bonding that shared struggle magically produces. Competing in these tournaments is never easy. It involves hours of travel, hundreds if not thousands of dollars, injuries, ailments, victories and letdowns, and physical exertion that, depending on the tournament, could go on for a day or as long as a week. When a group of people go through all of that together, you'd have to be colder than Lambeau Field in January not to feel some connection with the people around you.

Also like circuit parties, to be sure, the promise of romance is often very strong in the air at gay sports events. When you put hundreds of toned athletes all sharing a common bond in sport together for a few days, romance (or just straight-out lustful sex) will surely blossom. That's certainly nothing specific to gay sports events. The Olympics are notorious for being sex filled. At the Summer Games in Sydney in 2000, an original order by the organizing committee for 70,000 condoms in the Athletes Village went so fast, they had to order 20,000 more. In the 2002 Winter Olympics in Salt Lake City, 250,000 condoms were passed out to the participants—25 condoms per athlete, and they were there only two weeks! It's no surprise that lube and condoms are in high demand at gay sports events, too.

If circuit parties transformed into gay sports events. . .

- The Gay Softball World Series would be the White Party. It's the biggest event of the year and is a must-attend for the parties and hook-up potential.
- The Bingham Cup would be the Black Party. Most of the guys are big, they've never seen a razor they liked, and they're more interested in tackling one another than looking good in a Speedo.
- The West Hollywood Water Polo team would be the circuit boyz. They're hot, they're cocky, they can dance, they're willing to strip, everyone says they hate them but they really want to get into their Speedos, and they know it.
- Percocet would be the new Tylenol PM. After a brutal week or weekend doing your thing on the field, court, or ice, there's only one thing that will help you get to sleep.
- Gatorade would be the new bottled water. The tweakers, high on God-knows-what, have made bottled water the new cocktail of choice at circuit parties. For the athlete, Gatorade is the high-performance cocktail of choice.

The Positive Effects of the Gay Sports Circuit

It's hard to argue that circuit parties have a positive influence on society or gay culture at large. In fact, it's easier to argue that, with the preponderance of drugs and unsafe sex, these parties do damage to our culture both as an example to the mainstream culture of the dark side of being gay and through the spreading of sexually transmitted diseases and drug overdoses that sometimes lead to death.

On the other hand, it's not hard to see the positive effects gay sporting events are having on our culture. At an individual level, these events actively promote health and activity in a gay culture that seems bombarded by messages promoting drugs, alcohol, and one-night stands. Make no mistake: gay sports events are not void of these things, just as professional sporting events have their share of drugs, alcohol, and sex. But the focus of sporting events is the health and welfare of the athletes playing them, and that's a step in the right direction.

Gay sports events also offer the benefit of changing the impression of gay culture in the eyes of straight people. Although the circuit scene isn't wrong or inherently bad, most straight people (heck, even many gay people) have a tough time giving legitimacy to a culture that highlights boys in their underwear dancing for twenty-four hours straight and having a series of unsafe sexual partners under the hypnotic power of crystal meth. It's understandable. If you open up any of a number of popular magazines targeting gay men, such as *Genre*, *Instinct*, or New York's *HX*, you'll see page after page of sex toys and nearly naked men. In the back of some of these magazines, you'll find contact information for male hustlers, sex clubs, and hook-up web sites and chat lines. Every once in a while, you'll see an article about gay sports.

Whether it's right or not, organizations that oppose gay equality hold up these events and magazines as examples of what's wrong with gay culture. And whether it's right or not, the image that straight people have of gay people is damaged because of it. A great example occurred a couple years after the 2002 Gay Games in Sydney. Kraft had signed on as a sponsor of the 2006 Gay Games in Chicago, and the American Family Association (AFA) wasn't happy about it. On its web site, it posted three pictures allegedly from the Games in Sydney. The pictures showed attractive young men with "Gay Games" and "Horny Boy" painted on their chests, in underwear or Speedos, showing their bare asses and being fondled by a drag queen. The AFA web site offered this insight: "The following photos were taken at the last Gay Games events and are shown here for the sole purpose of educating Kraft customers to the types of activities Kraft is supporting." Also: "The photos below were taken at the last Gay Games. This is the type of activity Kraft spokesman Marc Firestone says Kraft recognizes, respects and values." That statement is not entirely accurate. Those pictures were taken at the circuit parties that coincided with the Gay Games. The AFA did not use pictures of gay people playing basketball together, racing against one another, or accepting their medals for a job well done; they chose to highlight nearly naked men partying together for a very strategic reason of their own.

Does this mean people shouldn't party however they choose? Absolutely not. Everyone makes choices in his or her life. Some people choose athletics, other people choose drugs and parties, some choose both. Grown adults are free to make their own choices. However, every choice has a consequence. Again, whether it's right or wrong is irrelevant: images of naked men dancing together and doing drugs have the consequence of marginalizing gay culture.

Sporting events, on the other hand, help showcase how gay people do fit into mainstream culture. Sometimes that is a goal of the event. The Gotham Knights Rugby Club hosted the 2006 Bingham Cup. One of the club's four stated missions is: "Refute negative stereotypes." Other organizations, such as the North American Gay Amateur Athletic Alliance that promotes gay softball in North America, do not make it their mission to challenge stereotypes (nor do they make it their mission to reinforce them), though they certainly do along the way.

The fact is that the stereotype of gay men is that they're a bunch of sex-crazed, drug-taking sissy boys who couldn't tell a basketball from a bowling ball. And, like with all stereotypes, there are some gay men who fit that description. Reinforcing that stereotype, in the context of mainstream culture, only serves to put more distance between straight people and gay people.

Gay sports events, in which gay men and lesbians challenge one another in physical competition, design elaborate schemes and plays to outwit their opponent, and push themselves to the limit of human exertion, can't help but drive people in mainstream culture to question gay stereotypes and consider gay men and lesbians a little bit more like themselves. For the advancement of gay equality, that is a good thing.

When the rift between the Gay Games and Outgames began in 2003, many people wondered which event Outsports would support. It was interesting to see so many strong supporters of the Gay Games point fingers at Outsports and stop just short of calling us "traitors" for running paid advertisements for the Outgames on the web site. It was too bad, because it became painfully clear that many of them had lost what is important about gay sporting events: participation.

A Dozen Stops on the Circuit

Outsports encourages everyone to get involved locally and travel nationally for these great events. Don't fret about whether to attend the softball tournament in Atlanta or Los Angeles on any given weekend—just pick one. The list of events on the gay sports circuit is incredibly long. This is just a sampling of the events every gay man and lesbian gets to choose from:

Softball. The annual Gay Softball World Series is one of the longest-running gay sports tournaments in the world; it has run every year since 1977. It is generally held in August, though Phoenix won the right to hold the 2007 tournament in October. Its location shifts every year, with San Francisco, the original host, having held the event four times, the most of any city. On the men's side, a team from Los Angeles has won the highest division sixteen times; there has been no dominant city in the women's bracket. Held over the course of an entire week, it's the longest gay sports event in North America outside of the quadrennial Gay Games and Outgames. Almost as anticipated as the games is the annual talent competition, which showcases the off-field talents of the participants. With more than 175 teams from all over North America in 2005, it is one of the largest single-sport tournaments on the gay circuit.

Flag football. From 1994 to 1999, there were no known intercity gay flag-football tournaments until a 2000 challenge match between Los Angeles and San Francisco. With the addition of Boston in 2002, that event became the Gay Super Bowl. The event is held every Columbus Day Weekend. Each participating city, of which there are more than a dozen, gets one bid to participate in the tournament. If there is enough space in the tournament, select cities receive a second bid. Unlike other sports, gay football has very few tournaments and intercity games throughout the year other than this championship tournament. Jim has been the Gay Super Bowl–winning quarterback twice, both with Los Angeles; Cyd has won the championship three times, twice with L.A. and once with New York.

Water Polo is one of the fastest growing gay and lesbian sports. Two members of the QUAC team from Salt Lake City at the 2006 Gay Games.

Photo by Jim Buzinski

Rugby. The marquee gay rugby event is the Bingham Cup, which began in 2002 as a gay rugby tournament to honor Mark Bingham, who had a hand in two gay rugby teams: the San Francisco Fog and the Gotham Knights of New York. Bingham was killed on flight United 93 as he attempted to stop four hijackers on September 11, 2001. The event was first held in 2002 in San Francisco and is held every two years. Alice Hoglan, Bingham's mother, has been a staple at the event that honors her son.

Swimming and diving. Held every year, the International Gay and Lesbian Aquatics Championship is the pinnacle of the swimming circuit. The event was first held in 1987 in San Diego, with San Diego taking the first championship (and the city's only competitive swimming championship ever). DC Aquatics has taken the majority of Large Swim Team Championships, whereas West Hollywood Aquatics has dominated the water polo competition.

Rodeo. No doubt the popularity of gay rodeo events took a seismic leap following *Brokeback Mountain.* Long before that movie was even a short story by Annie Proulx, however, gay men and lesbians were getting together throughout the Midwest and West at gay rodeos, the first of which was in Reno, Nevada, in 1976. The gay rodeos have traditional rodeo events such as bull riding and mounted breakaway roping. They also have "camp" events such as "steer decorating," in which two people try to tie a ribbon to a steer's tail; "wild drag race," in which three people aim to coax a steer to walk seventy feet with a drag queen on its back; and "goat dressing," in which two people attempt to put a pair of briefs on a goat. The International Gay Rodeo Association Finals, the biggest of the events, is generally held in October or November.

Wrestling. The oldest sport on the books also offers gay men one of the most unique events on the sports circuit. When Outsports first heard about the annual Hillside summer wrestling event in Pennsylvania, it was very hush-hush. The event is a little more open now, and all interested wrestlers are welcome. It started in 1994 at the Hillside Campground in Gibson, Pennsylvania, about 150 miles northwest of New York City. It is an intimate weekend of generally just more than one hundred men that focuses on good wrestling, good beer, and good friends. If you're a gay wrestler, this is your hajj. The other annual wrestling event of note is the Golden Gate Wrestling Club's Memorial Day Tournament, which attracts some female wrestlers to the male-dominated sport.

Bowling. The International Gay Bowling Organization (IGBO) is a sports circuit in and of itself. In 2006 alone, there were at least forty-five IGBO tournaments in North America. Its two big tournaments are the

Tennis is one of the most popular sports in the gay community, for both watching and playing. The annual gay tennis calendar is fully twelve months out of the year.

Photo by Cyd Zeigler Jr.

IGBO Annual Tournament, generally held over Memorial Day weekend in May, and the IGBO Mid-Year Tournament, generally held in November.

Basketball. The National Gay Basketball Association (NGBA) is a relatively new organization that represents a collection of all of the American-based gay basketball groups. The "pseudo national championship of basketball," according to NGBA vice president Ted Cappas, is the Coady Roundball Classic (formerly the Chicago Hoops Classic) held every April.

Tennis. The Gay and Lesbian Tennis Association (GLTA) is an international group that sanctions more than forty tournaments a year all over the world. It culminates in a unique invitational tournament called the Champions Race, to which only the top eight players in the world, based on GLTA's ranking system, in each division are invited.

Ice hockey. In North America, there are three annual tournaments that dominate the gay hockey calendar. The Friendship Tournament in Toronto and the Coors Cup, which alternates between Los Angeles and Denver, are the two biggest, most competitive tournaments. The Chelsea Challenge, held every June in New York City, offers a different format, with players from different cities playing on the same team.

Soccer. With the United States being one of the few countries in the Western Hemisphere in which soccer isn't considered a major religion, it's no surprise that there is more of an international flavor to the biggest gay soccer tournaments. The largest annual event is the International Gay and Lesbian Football Association Championships, which has been held in the United States, Germany, Denmark, England, the Netherlands, and, in 2007, Argentina.

Volleyball. One of the most popular sports for gay people to play, there are usually twenty or more gay volleyball tournaments annually in North America alone. The North American Gay Volleyball Association has its annual championship tournament in late May.

OUTSPORTS

Flashback
#1

SEPTEMBER 19, 2001

Oliver Sipple and Mark Bingham, Heroes a Quarter Century Apart: Remembering the Man Who Saved a President and the One Who Fought Back against Terror

Jim Buzinski

Their stories have eerie similarities: Two men in their thirties. Both were from San Francisco. Both were athletes. One saved the life of the president; one saved untold lives during a terrorist attack. Both were gay.

I was struck by the commonalities of Oliver "Billy" Sipple and Mark Bingham, and also by the enormous differences in their stories of bravery and the ensuing reactions. These differences speak of different eras for gay people and show we have made much progress, though hurdles still remain.

By now, many people have heard of Bingham. The tall, athletic thirty-one-year-old public relations executive and rugby player is being credited with helping to bring down the hijacked United Flight 93 over western Pennsylvania on September 11. Although we may never know the complete details, he appears to have been among a group of passengers who stormed the cockpit of the plane, causing it to crash into an abandoned strip-mine area instead of continuing on to its target: Washington, D.C.

It was a decision totally in character for Bingham, whom I knew somewhat. The University of California grad was a man who loved mixing it up on the rugby or football field and had run with the bulls at Pamplona. This was also a guy who, according to the *Daily Californian*, "at the Big Game [between Cal and Stanford] in 1992 ran onto the field at halftime and tackled the Stanford tree mascot." Such a man would not hold back as other passengers decided to make a move. Their collective action may have saved countless lives and proved the ultimate sacrifice.

"An Ordinary American Citizen"

Sipple's story is long forgotten, but he too performed a heroic act and saved a life. Just ask Gerald Ford. It was September 22, 1975, and Sipple—a former marine and high school football star—was at Union Square in San Francisco to catch a glimpse of President Ford, who was on a visit to the city.

Sipple, thirty-three, was standing in the crowd next to would-be assassin Sara Jane Moore, who suddenly pulled out a revolver and fired at Ford, standing about thirty-five feet away. She missed. Before she could get off a second shot, Sipple grabbed her arm and prevented her from firing. Moore was arrested, and Sipple, a Vietnam veteran, became a national hero. The intense media attention revealed a secret that Sipple had been hiding from his family: he was gay.

The news came out in Herb Caen's column two days later in the *San Francisco Chronicle*. Sipple was outed by San Francisco supervisor Harvey Milk, who knew Sipple from their political work together. "Harvey's whole attitude was to show people that not everyone who was gay runs around with lipstick, high heels and a dress," Bob Ross, publisher of the *Bay Area Times* told the *Los Angeles Times*. "This was an ordinary American citizen, and he was a gay man."

Sipple was mortified by the disclosure, which soon received wider publicity. According to a short biography on RandomHouse.com: "A despairing Sipple told reporters: 'I want you to know that my mother told me today she can't walk out of her front door because of the press stories.' He insisted: 'My sexual orientation has nothing to do with saving the President's life.' Apparently President Ford thought it did. There was no invitation to the White House for Sipple, not even a commendation.

Milk made a fuss about that. Finally, weeks later, Sipple received a brief note of thanks."

Sipple's life went downhill from there. A high school dropout and dyslexic, Sipple had been living on veteran's disability for psychological and physical problems resulting from his Vietnam service. He was a heavy drinker, and the anxiety caused by the disclosure made him take even more to the bottle. "I have a lot of stress and I take it out on booze," he said. He was disowned by his family, with even his own mother refusing to talk to him. When she died in 1979, his "father made it clear that he was not welcome. He could go to the funeral home or the cemetery, but not when his father was there," the *Los Angeles Times* reported.

In anguish over the pain caused by the revelations, Sipple filed a fifteen million–dollar lawsuit against seven major newspapers who had reported he was gay, alleging invasion of privacy. His lawsuit was dismissed after a five-year battle. Sipple's story is still used as a case study in ethics at journalism schools.

In 1989, Sipple, by now an alcoholic, lived near the Tenderloin area of San Francisco, weighed close to three hundred pounds, and was in poor health. Sometime in mid-January he laid down on his bed, surrounded by bottles of bourbon, and went into a sleep from which he never awoke. His body was not discovered for two more weeks. His funeral was attended by only thirty people. In a letter of condolence sent to Sipple's friends, former President Ford and his wife wrote: "I strongly regretted the problems that developed for him following this incident."

A TV Blackout

Like Sipple, Bingham's homosexuality became widely known in the days following the plane crash. The *Washington Post*, *Los Angeles Times*, and *Sports Illustrated* were among publications that mentioned that Bingham helped to found the San Francisco Fog, a gay rugby club. The *Post* detailed Bingham reconciling his love of rugby with being gay. Tributes to him sprang up on the Internet, and there was no shame or embarrassment in the disclosure, only pride. In fact, a columnist for the *Sydney Morning Herald* in Australia wrote two columns mentioning Bingham. "When I mentioned Bingham in my first piece, all I knew was that he was a rugby player," columnist Peter FitzSimons told Outsports. Finding out about Bingham's sexual orientation prompted a second column. "Why do I include all this in a column now? Dunno, precisely," FitzSimons wrote. "Probably just because, beyond helping to save perhaps thousands of people, it would also be good if Bingham's death could stand towards what the entire world needs right now—the lessening of hate and bigotry, and the maximizing of friendship and understanding."

Bingham's sexual orientation is important, especially in light of the comments by Jerry Falwell and Pat Robertson when they blamed gays, among other groups, as having had some responsibility for bringing the attacks on America. Falwell and Robertson are to Christianity what the Taliban is to Islam. Americans need to know that gay people— which included the pilot of one of the planes—suffered as much as their fellow citizens.

In the days following the hijacking, Bingham's family and friends have spoken with love, pride, and admiration about the type of man Mark was and the legacy he leaves. As for Sipple, his brother George told the *Los Angeles Times* in 1989 that his brother was proud of what he had done, despite the fallout. "He said somebody will pick up a book and see Oliver Sipple saved President Ford's life," George Sipple said.

Congressional leaders have already expressed a desire to award the Freedom Medal to passengers aboard Flight 93, including Bingham. What would Jerry Falwell and Pat Robertson think about that? When our country and its symbols were attacked, Oliver and Mark got busy saving our citizens; Falwell and Robertson got busy assigning blame to our citizens.

To some in this world, the villains are heroes. And heroes are villains. We know the difference. Sipple and Bingham are heroes.

OUTSPORTS LOOKS FORWARD

When Dave Kopay came out in 1975, he expected to be the first of many high-profile athletes to do so. Thirty years later, it has been more of a trickle than a deluge. And while there has been a revolution in sports since 1999, there is still a long way to go.

The most positive signs of changing attitudes lie in demographics—younger people, according to polls, are much more comfortable with gays than their elders. A Pew Forum poll in 2006 found that "young people are twice as likely as their elders to approve of gay marriage: 52 percent of those age 18 to 29 favor it, compared with only 22 percent among those 65 and older." In sports, acceptance is also growing, as witnessed by several polls mentioned here that show a growing tolerance of gays by athletes and fans.

Though a few elite athletes have stormed out of the closet and a few handfuls more of collegiate athletes are making waves as out athletes, it is still a tiny fraction of the number of men and women who are in sports struggling with their sexuality. The progress has been measurable, and that speaks to the strength and courage of every gay, bisexual, and transgender person, whether they are an athlete or a coach or keep sports at arm's length, who lets herself be herself.

That progress is also thanks in large part to the straight athletes and sportswriters who have opened their hearts and minds and been vocal about their acceptance of gays in sports. Blacks could not have won equality without whites. Women could not have won the right to vote without men. Gays in sports will never win equality without the generosity of straight people who are able to see them simply for the touchdown-scoring, draft-analyzing, run-stopping, backhand-smashing, home run–hitting, season preview–writing, team-inspiring, goal-saving people they are.

The big question on the minds of so many has been for years, "When will the first active male pro athlete come out?" Our response would be, "What are you doing to make our culture easier for him to come out in?" We all want a hero, but that hero needs heroes, too. He needs encouragement and support. He needs more open minds in the sports world, from team presidents down to trainers, from newspaper owners to copy editors. He also needs more understanding from gay people. The marginalization of sports in gay institutions has been very real and has had a chilling effect for far too long. That is changing, but that change cannot come fast enough. With more open arms and stronger support from gay people, that day when a pro athlete feels he can come out will come. And on that day, the issue of gays in sports in America will change forever and the Outsports revolution will come full circle

SPORTS GLOSSARY FOR GAYS AND LESBIANS

Gay people have had fun with sports double entendres for years. T-shirt companies have sold thousands of T-shirts promoting the wearer as a "pitcher" or "catcher;" witty gay-magazine editors have fun with headlines involving "tight ends" and "balls." But the obvious ones are only the proverbial tip of the iceberg. Below is the inspiration for every gay T-shirt designer's new summer line.

Ball boy (various). These are the people, usually young kids or teenagers, who run out onto the court or field chasing after errant balls and cleaning the sweat off a court. You see them lined up at either side of a tennis net or sitting crouched beneath a backboard in basketball.

Ball carrier (football and soccer). Quite simply, the person with the ball. No, that does not mean that every man on the field is the ball carrier. This refers to the person in possession of the ball a team is trying to score with. Oh, never mind.

Banana kick (soccer). It's not nearly as painful as it sounds. It refers to the trajectory of a ball when kicked in a particular fashion that gives an arc to its flight. The most famous "banana kicker" is surely David Beckham. The movie *Bend It Like Beckham* got its title from Beck's strange-looking kicks.

Butt-ending (hockey). Even in hockey, this could take on a couple of meanings. But the one that is intended is the major penalty called when a player takes the shaft of his stick and jabs it into an opponent. It's hard to see what's so wrong with that, but it's obviously not a laughing matter for hockey players. Most penalties draw a two-minute suspension that ends if the other team scores. This penalty is one of the few that draws a five-minute penalty, the entire length of which must be served regardless of whether the other team scores—which means the NHL takes butt-ending very seriously.

Catcher (baseball). The player, generally wearing extra protection, who sits behind home plate, gives signals to the pitcher, and grabs the balls that the pitcher throws at him.

Cox or coxswain (crew). The person at the rear of a crew shell or boat who maintains the cadence of the oarsmen by yelling "Stroke!" as they dip their oars into the water. They often either speak to the oarsmen through a megaphone or what is called a cox box. It's beneficial for the boat to have the smallest coxswain possible, and many men's crew teams have a female cox for that reason.

Crease lines (hockey). The red line that creates a semicircle around the goal. There are specific rules regarding when you can shoot and score if a player is in the crease.

Team Names

Bears and Cubs (football and baseball). Both the NFL's Bears and Major League Baseball's Cubs play, not coincidentally, in Chicago. It's not a coincidence because the Bears actually got their name from the Cubs. The Bears are also referred to as the Monsters of the Midway. The mind reels.

Drillers (baseball). The Tulsa Drillers have been a minor league baseball team located in Tulsa, Oklahoma, since 1977. Several years ago, Outsports approached the Drillers about selling their merchandise on Outsports.com. Not surprisingly, they declined. It seems the team has gotten ribbed for years not only because of its name but mainly because of the logo they long used that featured a tall, upright rig spewing "oil," which, for some reason, was often white. They changed the logo at the beginning of the twenty-first century, but they just can't get away from the fact that their nickname is the "Drillers." Other logos have included a "T" with a drop of liquid dripping from the tip or a man, apparently a "driller," shoving a pointy device into a ball. Notable former Drillers include Ruben Sierra, Kevin Brown, and Sammy Sosa, who was also a Cub at one point. No word if they still consider themselves Drillers.

Oilers (football). The NFL team formerly based in Houston that moved to Tennessee and became the Titans.

Double team (various). When two people cover one. Duh!

Dribble (various). The act of a player essentially passing a ball to himself. In basketball, the player is bouncing the ball off the floor; in soccer, he's playing footsies with the ball.

Eligible receiver (football). Believe it or not, not every player at some levels of football are eligible to receive. In the NFL, offensive linemen and the quarterback are not eligible to receive a pass unless they declare themselves eligible to the referee before a given play. Not surprisingly, in the National Gay Football League everyone is an eligible receiver.

Finger spin (cricket). A style of bowling in cricket in which the bowler releases the ball from the front of his hand as the ball rolls over the index finger. It gives the ball a different spin, depending on whether the bowler uses his left or right hand.

Packers (football). The Green Bay Packers are often joked about as the gayest team in sports. "Packers" is just about as close as gay people will ever get to having a professional sports team named for them, as it's doubtful the Green Bay Queers is going to fly anytime soon. The Packers got their name from the Indian Packing Company, and later the Acme Packing Company, both of which concurrently sponsored the team. The team was at one time referred to as "the Big Bay Blues" (they wore blue until the late 1950s), which might be even gayer than "Packers." The Packers are partially owned by gay men and lesbians, since they are currently the only publicly owned major professional sports team in the United States, with around 110,000 stock holders, and it would be safe to bet the proverbial farm that at least .001 percent of them are gay. Interestingly, both David Kopay and Esera Tuaolo, two of the very few former NFL players who have come out of the closet, both played for the Green Bay Packers, albeit almost twenty years apart. Tuaolo was drafted by the Packers in the second round of the NFL Draft in 1991. Although some may wishfully think that some other Packers from the past and present, such as Brett Favre and Mark Chmura, are indeed packers, only Kopay and Tuaolo fit the bill, as far as the public knows.

Foursome (golf). The standard-size group that heads out on the golf course together. Many golf courses won't allow more than four golfers in a group, and in the busy season, most golf clubs mandate four golfers in every group. The first two days of many professional golf tournaments put four golfers to a group as well.

Fuzzy Zoeller (golf). No, this is not a product available at the Pleasure Chest. Fuzzy Zoeller is a professional golfer who won six PGA Tour titles, including the Masters and U.S. Open. He became a professional golfer in 1973 and joined the Champions Tour for senior golfers in 2002.

Gay (various). Every once in a while there is a big-name athlete to hit the scene whose last name is Gay. Ben Gay was an exceptional high school running back in Texas who landed at Baylor; he had trouble staying on the field there, but he eventually ended up with the Cleveland Browns, where he wasted away. He's regarded by some as the greatest unrealized potential in football in decades. Randall Gay was a defensive back on the 2004 New England Patriots championship team, Rudy Gay is in the NBA, and Brian Gay is a professional golfer.

Goalmouth (soccer). Yes, it's entirely possible that you saw a guy in a Gay.com chat room with this very handle. In soccer, though, it's the term that refers to the front opening to each goal. Teams spend the game trying to put the ball into the goalmouth.

Going for it (football). What a football team is doing when they opt to not punt the ball on fourth down. If they don't make it, the other team gets possession of the ball.

Header (soccer). In soccer, a player is not allowed to touch a ball with his hands, so he is left with the rest of his body to move the ball. Although a player generally uses his feet to advance the ball, he also often uses his head—thus, the header.

Loose ball (various). When a ball is not in the possession of a particular team or player and anyone on the field has an equal right to grab or kick the ball.

Man-to-man (various). A style of defense in which each player is matched up with, and must defend against, one other player. Along with zone defense, it is one of the two standard forms of defense.

Pitcher (baseball). The player who stands on the mound and throws balls at the player swinging the bat, the batter. If the batter doesn't connect with the ball, the catcher will catch the ball and throw it back to the pitcher.

Quick release (various). When the player with the ball is able to shoot or throw the ball with little arm motion.

Score (various). Both a noun and a verb, the word can refer to the total number of points a team or player has posted, or it can refer to the action of a player acquiring points for her team.

Scrum (rugby). This term comes from the word *scrimmage*, which is still used in football. It is the exciting restarting of the game, putting the ball back into play, when players on both teams put their arms around one another and try to bowl into the other team.

Shoot (various). When a player throws, kicks, or hits the ball toward a goal hoping to score.

Shooting range (various). Quite simply, how far away from the goal a player can shoot accurately.

Skins game (golf). A golf tournament in which four golfers square off against one another for eighteen holes. The format of the tournament is a progressive jackpot. If one of the foursome beats the other three players outright on a hole, he gets the prize money for that hole. If not, the prize for that hole is rolled over into the next hole, and so on and so on until someone wins a hole by himself. Although skins games take place at all levels of golf, the most popular is a two-day Thanksgiving-weekend tradition that started in 1983 involving four of the world's top golfers. Fred Couples is the king of the skins game, with five wins and three second-place finishes.

Sticky wicket (cricket). When the pitch gets wet and the trajectory of the ball becomes more erratic and unpredictable.

Stroke (various). Depending on the sport, it can refer to any of a number of actions. Generally, a stroke is the swinging of an object to hit a ball—for example, a tennis racquet, a golf club, or a croquet mallet. In crew, it refers to the moving of the oars through the water.

Stroke play (golf). A system of scoring in which swinging your club is counted every time you do it. It is the most popular scoring system on the PGA Tour, used in virtually every tournament, in which a player's "score" is determined by how high above or below par (for instance, plus 5 or minus 3) he is. If players are still tied at the end of the regulation tournament, they have to untie themselves with more stroke play until someone finishes ahead of the other one.

Swing man (basketball). One of the most versatile players on the court, the swing man can play either guard or forward. They're usually some of the toughest players to cover because they have the large size of a forward but the speed, agility, and shooting ability of a guard.

Tag-team (wrestling). Popularized by the men-in-tights-filled professional wrestling, tag-teaming pits two groups of wrestlers against one another. Generally, only one person from each team can be in the ring at a given time, but without fail two wrestlers will get an opponent in their corner and start pounding him together.

Third-man-in (hockey). A gay man clearly did not invent this rule. The term refers to the rule forbidding a player to enter into a melee between two other players. It's meant to discourage fights from escalating, or from two teammates attempting to tag-team another.

Tight end (football). Along with wide receiver, *tight end* is one of the most popular sports terms among gay men, for obvious reasons. Not only is a good tight end a rare and highly prized specimen, but the best ones are incredibly versatile. The tight end is the player lined up at the end of the offensive line. Most tight ends are good at either blocking or receiving; the best ones can do both effectively. For years, the NFL featured mostly blocking tight ends. But the success of players such as Denver's Shannon Sharpe and Kansas City's Tony Gonzalez opened the eyes of NFL owners and coaches to what a receiving tight end can do for a team.

Two-on-one (various). One of the most desired situations in sports such as hockey and basketball, it refers to two players advancing the ball or puck ahead of the rest of the field against one defender who must take on both advancers and try to stop them from scoring. Sounds like the makings of a great porn movie!

Wide receiver (football). Even more than tight end or pitcher and catcher, *wide receiver* is probably the most popular sports term among gay men, as the double entendre couldn't be more black-and-white. The wide receiver is the offensive player nearest the sideline who, as chance would have it, catches the balls. Although the public refers to anyone lined up outside the tight end as a wide receiver, there are specific terms used to describe different receivers: split end, flanker, and slot receiver. Some of the greatest wide receivers of all time include Jerry Rice, Cris Carter, and Steve Largent.